D1053125

Praise for ADOPTION JOURNEYS

"As parents of an adopted daughter from the Philippines, my wife and I know what a glorious gift that adoption can be. But we also know how much frustration and anguish there can be in the process of adoption. With a marvelous mix of stories about some disparate families who have adopted, Carole S. Turner has told the story that the Defords know so well—about parents and children coming together, despite all the pain, all the obstacles. She shows so beautifully how sometimes it is but the hope of love that conquers all."

—FRANK DEFORD, Senior Contributing Writer at *Sports Illustrated,* weekly commentator on National Public Radio's *Morning Edition,* author of several books including *Alex: The Life of a Child,* and Chairman of the Cystic Fibrosis Foundation

"This book is alive with the voices of couples who have chosen to build their families through adoption. It is a valuable asset for those who are themselves considering adopting a child, as it vividly portrays the course of becoming an adoptive parent. I am happy to have this as a resource for my clients who are making the transition from infertility to adoption."

—GERI M. FERBER, Ph.D., Clinical Psychologist at The Center for Fertility and Reproductive Health, Harvard Vanguard Medical Associates

"Carole Turner's well-written, well-documented book provides a collection of soulful insights into the reality of adoption, which will help us all—parents, professionals, extended family and friends—understand what is really meant by adoption. This is a book for all those who care to be sensitive to the intimate nature of adoption."

—FREDERICK MANDELL, M.D., Senior Associate in Medicine at Children's Hospital, Boston, Associate Clinical Professor at Harvard Medical School

"Carole Turner has written a wonderful book for anyone interested in the heartfelt realities of life. She has managed to demythologize and desensationalize adoption at a time when adoption is too often oversensationalized. She takes her reader moment by moving moment through the development of several adoptive families. These "real time" accounts of the adoption process, while creatively asking and answering some of the most important issues in the field, are also therapeutic and restorative. A true gem."

—LINDA M. FORSYTHE, M.D., Child and Adult Psychiatrist
at Massachusetts General Hospital and in private practice,
Instructor at Harvard Medical School, co-founder
of The Interdisciplinary Adoption Study Group

"Turner sensitively explores thought-provoking issues inherent in the evolving field of adoption—the pros and cons of open adoption, the challenges facing people who adopt transracially and transculturally, the additional hurdles for gay couples and single people—through personal accounts from adoptive parents. Presenting the parents in their own words lends an immediacy to the bitter frustrations and elated joys of the process. A realistic, and ultimately positive, look at adoption, offering expanded definitions of parent and family.

—SARAH SAFFIAN, author of *ITHAKA:*
A Daughter's Memoir of Being Found

ADOPTION JOURNEYS

ADOPTION JOURNEYS

Parents Tell Their Stories

CAROLE S. TURNER

McBooks Press, Ithaca, New York

Book and cover design by Paperwork.

Library of Congress Cataloging-in-Publication Data

Turner, Carole S. (Carole Stevenson), 1949-
    Adoption journeys : parents tell their stories / Carole S. Turner.
        p. cm.
    ISBN 0-935526-53-6 (hc.)
    1. Adoption—United States. 2. Adoptive parents—United States.
    3. Interracial adoption—United States. 4. Intercountry adoption-
-United States. I. Title.
    HV875.55.T87 1999
    362.73'4'0973—dc21   99-17949
                                                        CIP

Distributed to the book trade by
Login Trade, 1436 West Randolph Street, Chicago, IL 60607
1-800-626-4330.

Additional copies of this book may be ordered from any bookstore or directly from McBooks Press, 120 West State Street, Ithaca, NY 14850. Please include $3.00 postage and handling with mail orders. New York State residents must add 8% sales tax. All McBooks Press publications can also be ordered by calling toll-free 1-888-BOOKS11 (1-888-266-5711). Please call to request a free catalog.

Visit the McBooks Press website at http://www.McBooks.com.

Printed in the United States of America

9 8 7 6 5 4 3 2 1

For my parents

George and June Stevenson

CONTENTS

What a difference it makes

to come home to a child.

Margaret Fuller

FOREWORD

THERE is not just one reality in life; there are multiple realities.

This is a book of multiple realities.

This is not a book about how you should adopt, nor is it about what is the right thing to do or the wrong thing to do, in adoption.

Carole Turner, an adoptive parent herself, is a careful listener and recorder of the stories of a number of individuals and couples who have entered the world of adoption.

The reader is given the rare opportunity to hear, in a person's own words, what his, her, or their experience of the process, and the early years of adoption has been like.

As a family therapist, and adoption expert, an educator, and trainer of adoption professionals, there are times in the book when I get concerned that some issue is being avoided, or that some situations might be misconstrued, and then I am able to suspend my worries and clinical concerns and just sit back and *listen*.

These are not stories of instruction, they are not to be judged or debated.

They are stories to simply listen to and to hear, with one's mind and one's heart, the true present experience—and I say present because, in the lifelong process of adoption, people's stories, and their minds, change. My hope is that Carole re-interviews these same people in about ten years, and perhaps some of the children as well, so that we can revisit them and learn more about their joys and challenges and their beliefs about themselves, and about adoption.

For now, you must just sit back and open your heart and your mind and hear the words and feelings of a variety of families who have had a variety of experiences with the adoption practice and with their own adoption process.

There is not just one kind of adoption, there are many. There is not just one reality; there are multiple realities of adoption.

DR. JOYCE MAGUIRE PAVAO
Executive Director of the Center for Family Connections
Author of *The Family of Adoption*

ACKNOWLEDGMENTS

TO THE parents who so generously shared their adoption stories with me for this book, I am enormously grateful. It was not an easy task for any of them. Telling their compelling stories meant reliving painful moments as well as joyous ones. Many tears were shed during the interviews. But these wonderful people wiped their tears away and kept on talking— dedicated to the idea that others could be inspired by their experiences.

Dear friends and kindred spirits: Paula DeMore, Patricia Mitchell, Cathy O'Rourke, Romey Poston, Hannelore Reiser, Alain Renaud, Lee Sprague, and Emilie Stuart were unwavering in their belief in me throughout the years I spent on this project. I could not have written this book without their love and friendship.

Dalia Geffen provided superb editing skills and moral support as I wrote the first draft. Wendy Skinner, my editor at McBooks Press, was a delight to work with.

My agent, Carolyn Krupp, is a cool professional with a warm personality—the most perfect combination any author could hope for! Her enthusiasm for my manuscript at the very earliest stage gave me an incredible boost.

Vida Heskestad, L.S.W., read the entire manuscript one chapter at a time as I wrote, and cheered me on. She answered numerous questions and shared invaluable professional insights.

Joyce Maguire Pavao, Ed.D., L.C.S.W., L.M.F.T., advised me on the range of family profiles necessary for a comprehensive sampling of the contemporary adoption experience in America.

Steven L. Nickman, M.D., and Linda M. Forsythe, M.D., gave me the opportunity to present one of these stories to their Interdisciplinary Adoption Study Group at Massachusetts General Hospital in Boston before publication. Their reflections on how these stories could be a useful tool in family therapy greatly encouraged me.

Thank you to Lucy Aptekar, Mary-Brenda Cortel, M.B. Flanders, Amy Fleming, Barbara Grossman, Mary Henderson, Pat Larsen, Louisa Paige, Corrine Rayburn, Michele Renaud, and Pam Trippe for their advice, suggestions, and comments.

Christine Boos, Mary Boyle, Jane Donovan, Faye Gaffney, Carol Jurgens, Carmen Patterson, and Dean and Jean Perry are old and cherished friends who lifted my spirits whenever I called them.

I'm fortunate to be in a reading group with Ginny Bride, Suki DeBragança, Hope McDermott, Judy Reece, and Martha Volpe. The pleasure of our discussions enhances every book we read.

Thank you also to Pamela Dawson who helps me to keep fit, to Richie Meuse who keeps my home in good order, and to four extraordinary young women: Adeline Fabre, Barbara Kirschner, Erin Mitchell, and Yun Wu, who provide loving childcare for my daughter, Emma.

I want to thank my parents, George and June Stevenson, for their love and support. They instilled in me a strong belief in families and helped me understand how to be a good parent. I am lucky to have a sister, Pat, who is also my dear friend. She read each chapter carefully and gave me thoughtful responses and questions to consider.

John Turner provided the enthusiasm, encouragement, and support I needed to take on this project and see it through. The family John and I created came together through birth, step-parenting, and adoption. Our four wonderful children occupy equal space in our hearts. Thank you, Berenice, Joel, Brian, and Emma for being who you are.

INTRODUCTION

ON April 8, 1988, I moved into the house of our good friends Hellmut and Irene Kirchner to look after their three adopted children—four-year-old twin girls and an infant son—while they flew to Chile to adopt another son. On that day, halfway around the world in Thailand, a baby girl was born. That baby is now my daughter.

Until then neither my husband, John, nor I had considered adopting a child. Our marriage (in 1986) was a second one for each of us. John had two grown children and I had given birth to my son in 1976. We had not contemplated more children, so while planning our wedding ceremony, we asked the minister to eliminate the phrase *Be fruitful and multiply* from the service! But then we fell under the spell of the Kirchner's twins, Antonia and Theresia. We enjoyed a close and affectionate relationship with them.

Hellmut and Irene explained the circumstances of their twins' adoption in Thailand and I often found myself pondering the life these girls might otherwise have led. This was when I first became aware of the depth of the adoption experience; I was enchanted to hear about the exceptional moment when their family was created. When we learned that the Kirchners were about to move back to their home in Germany, John and I realized that we would miss the girls, but we couldn't possibly have known how much!

Several months after they moved, my husband turned to me one night and suggested we go to Thailand to adopt a baby girl for our family. I was astonished but thrilled by the idea and instantly agreed. I realized that raising a daughter was something I had missed doing and it would be wonderful for us to parent a child together. We never discussed trying to have a biological child together; our desire was to adopt a little Thai girl.

It took us seventeen months to adopt Emma, who was twenty-one months old by the time she was entrusted to our care. It is difficult to describe the emotions we experienced when Emma was placed in our arms. We were awed by the love and responsibility we embraced in this tiny child. People who have attended hundreds of births admit they still experience a moment of awe when a new life begins. The same experience occurs in adoptions. When arms reach out to embrace a child and enfold it into a new life in a loving family the magic touches every participant and observer.

My position as a parent allows me to proclaim that the love one feels for an adoptive child is equal to the love one feels for a biological child. Many of the parents I interviewed for this book are convinced that they love their adopted children more than they could possibly have loved biological children. They reason that the extraordinary circumstances which led them to that particular child at that particular time in that particular place were simply miraculous and therefore unique in human experience.

When Emma was five years old I wrote down her adoption story in words that she could understand while trying to explain the process as thoroughly as I could. As I wrote, I relived the emotions of the entire experience—the frustrations, anxieties, highs and lows of waiting for the bureaucracies of two governments to process her papers. I also relived the magic. The moment we first saw our beautiful baby girl in the arms of a Thai social worker is forever imprinted in my heart.

After reliving our adoption experience I decided to interview other adoptive parents and to tell their stories. There are no composites in this book; each chapter tells the true story of a family who adopted one child or more. Names, as well as some dates, locations, and other identifying factors, have been altered to ensure privacy.

My purpose in writing this book was to share the adoption experiences of several different families with the hope that their poignant stories will allow the reader to better understand and appreciate the exacting and often complex journeys taken by adoptive parents; that they will increase admiration for adoptive families while dislodging prejudices about adoption; that people who were adopted will better understand the experience adoptive parents go through; and, finally, that those considering adoption will be inspired and encouraged to begin their own journeys.

ADOPTION JOURNEYS

1 / Mark and Allison
An open adoption

"It seemed wise not to have any secrets; secrets breed dysfunction in a family, and I thought, *Perhaps if there are no secrets, there won't be dysfunction. If my child knows from the very beginning about his birth parents, maybe it won't be a big deal. It will be a fact of life, like having freckles.* If there's any kind of adoption that makes sense to me, it's open adoption."

MARK AND ALLISON are a devoted couple who struggled with infertility for seven years. Their infertility took a tremendous toll on them as individuals and as a couple. It forced them to carefully examine their fears, motivations, and expectations about having a family. This introspection led them to conclude that honesty—to each other and to their child—was of primary importance to them. When they began the process to adopt a child they decided that an open adoption was the only kind that made sense for them. Their experience was not easy, yet despite their difficulties, they remain persuasive advocates of open adoption.

Allison was the second daughter born into a suburban family in New York in the early 1950s. An exuberant dark-haired woman, Allison speaks candidly, intensely, and incongruously of a troubled childhood and tragic events in her family.

"My mother was a well-known artist," she began. "When I was about nine months old she had a nervous breakdown, which marked the beginning of her fairly severe mental illness. I was sent to live with my father's mother, and my sister was sent to our other grandmother. When I was three-and-a-half, I went home for about six months, but my mother was unable to handle me and sent me back to Nana's. I went back and forth so many times that to this day I have trouble with transitions and hate to say good-bye to people."

Allison's parents divorced when she was a teenager; she chose to go to boarding school. When Allison was in her senior year of high school, her mother committed suicide. "It was not completely unexpected," said Allison. "She had made several previous attempts. But it was obviously a shock." As a result of this tragedy, Allison spent several years in therapy and delayed starting college.

Mark, by contrast, had a happy childhood with loving parents and an older brother. A confident man with a round, friendly face, Mark sports a trim beard. His career in public relations makes him quite approachable. A failed first marriage left Mark a bit wary; nevertheless, two years after meeting Allison he proposed.

"He asked me to marry him on Christmas Day," remembered Allison. "A diamond ring was at the bottom of my Christmas stocking. He had tears in his eyes and couldn't speak when I opened it. I said, 'Does this mean you want to have children?' He just nodded. I said, 'Can we start trying right away?'

"I was twenty-six years old when we got married. We were living in Philadelphia, and I still had a year-and-a-half of college left to finish a nursing degree. We agreed that I would finish school before trying to get pregnant; then Mark wanted me to work for a year, but I said, 'No, I've wanted to be pregnant for a long time. We've been married almost two years, we own a house, I'm almost thirty, and my clock is ticking.'"

Mark recalled, "When we started trying to get pregnant we had wine in front of a crackling fire—we wanted it to be memorable."

Allison added, "The first month there was great romance and wonder. I was sure I was pregnant and was shocked when my period came. After two or three more months it no longer felt like we were making love; we were trying to make a baby. I began to feel a sense of urgency. After nine months, I saw my first infertility specialist."

Thus began a stressful period of trying to pinpoint the reasons for their infertility and of experimenting with different ways of overcoming it. "We got sucked into the game," said Mark.

First Allison had a laparoscopy, which showed no endometriosis. Then she took a fertility drug, which caused large cysts to grow on one of her ovaries. When medication failed to eliminate the cysts, they had to be surgically removed. Allison said, "I talked to my former doctor about what I was going through, and he tried to urge me to work with somebody else; he didn't think the specialist was someone I should trust. But I was totally focused on this doctor; he had helped a good friend of mine get pregnant, and I wasn't interested in finding anyone else."

After three years Allison quit her job at the hospital and became a visiting nurse because of the more convenient schedule it offered. "I only had to work one weekend a month and no nights," explained Allison. "I really wanted to concentrate on getting pregnant. My new job had a different health care plan, which covered infertility but forced me to switch doctors. My life became a series of two-week cycles: menstruating, waiting to menstruate, waiting to find out if I was pregnant. It was awful, a really miserable time. I was feeling angry, discouraged, hopeless, helpless, furious . . . I couldn't believe this [having a baby] would be denied to me. I thought, *I've been through a crazy mother, a suicide, a mixed-up childhood; I made it through, I got married, I'm happy, and now I can't have a baby?* I was in complete shock."

Mark talked about his side of things. "For me it was a depersonalizing, dehumanizing experience. It wasn't about having a child together; it was all about science—giving samples, very clinical. I felt like a machine who was expected to produce sperm on demand; it was never when I was in the mood. I went through a couple of episodes of sperm donations that were horribly insensitive to me. They put me in a small bathroom, and nurses were standing outside laughing and talking to each other. It was humiliating."

Five years into their quest to conceive, Mark and Allison went on a fishing vacation with friends. Allison had gone in for a pregnancy test on the morning they were leaving; the nurse told her to call about two-thirty for the results.

"By mid-afternoon we were driving through a sleepy little town in New York," said Allison. "I pulled off the road to use a pay phone. For the last hour I had been thinking, *Could it be? Well, maybe this time . . .* I called and was put on hold. Then the nurse came back and said, 'Allison, I have wonderful news for you. You're pregnant!' When I came out of the phone booth I saw Mark standing next to our car. I screamed at the top of my lungs, 'We're pregnant!' I was hysterical! People were looking at me. Back in the car Mark said, 'This can't be!' We kept looking at each other and saying, 'I can't believe it!'"

Mark continued, "I instantly became lightheaded. It was surreal, bizarre. All of a sudden I was transported into a world of fantasy. While Allison went out fishing with our friends, I sat with a book but couldn't concentrate; all I could think about was having a child. This was great! The next morning we crashed. Allison began to bleed and miscarried. It was horrible. I tried to put the best face on it—this wasn't meant to happen, et cetera. I believe that nature selects and that pregnancies end for a reason. That's the intellectual side. But this was emotional. Allison was shattered; I felt protective of her. Our poor friends had to watch the whole thing unfold."

Allison described her emotional state, "I cried all the way home. I was a mess; it was a horrible crash."

"We came out of this experience thinking, *We did it—there's hope! We got pregnant, by God, and we'll do it again,*" said Mark. "But it never happened again, and that's when it became really dehumanizing. I think we continued for two more years. It kept dragging on and gradually felt more and more invasive. Allison's body was like a pincushion. I was giving her shots all the time. We'd take a month off and then come back to try again. It was not good for our relationship. It raises hell with a normal sex life. There was a growing sense of desperation, which started to invade our lives."

Allison added, "I went from being a happy-go-lucky, free-spirited, joyous person to someone who was barely able to present a veneer of her old personality; beneath that veneer was a seething rage because I was unable to have what came so easily to everybody else. I reached the point where I couldn't go to baby showers; I had good friends who got pregnant and I could no longer talk to them. It was too painful. Then I would feel guilty and ashamed for having those feelings.

"Eventually I was able to admit to myself, *I don't want to feel like this anymore. I don't want to become the person I am becoming.* I decided to try one last thing, GIFT [gamete inter-fallopian transfer]. This is a procedure where they fill you with Pergonal and make as many eggs as they can. Then they aspirate the eggs off the ovary and mix them with selected sperm, inject the two parts together back into your fallopian tubes, and leave the rest to nature. I knew this had a better rate of success than in vitro fertilization, and that the success rates after three attempts dropped off dramatically. That's why I decided to do three.

"I told Mark that this was the final procedure I was willing to undertake. He said, 'If it doesn't work, then we'll adopt.' I seized on that idea and thought, *Fine, I'm not sure I'm ready to adopt, but we'll get there if this doesn't work.* The first two attempts failed, and on the third try, as they were putting me under general anesthesia, tears streamed down my face. The anesthesiologist asked, 'What's wrong?' and I said, 'This is it. If this doesn't work, I'm done. I can't do this anymore.'

"When the third attempt failed I went to see my doctor. He started talking about the next attempt, but I said, 'No, there's no *next month.* I'm done. I came to say good-bye and thank you.' He asked me, 'What are you going to do?' I said, 'I don't know, but I can't do this anymore. I can't believe that I'm saying I'm ready to stop, but I can't do it again.' He said, 'Well, you can always come back.' But I said, 'No, I need closure here. I need to end this process because I just can't take it anymore. Physically I can't take it, my marriage can't take it, I'm done.' I felt relieved but terribly sad.

"The ultimate reason why I stopped our infertility treatments was that it was going to consume our marriage. It was going to eat it up and spit it out in a form that would not be acceptable to either of us. It was clear that it had already begun to do very destructive work. I was resentful. It also prevented us from dealing with any other problems in our marriage. All we dealt with was the infertility. There was no room for any other problem. I realized that you can't put other issues on hold forever and ever. We needed to have time to deal with other things, or we wouldn't survive."

"It was Allison's decision to stop trying," added Mark. "She'd had enough; she was punched out. Her body was a mess. She'd had raging hormones for five years with all those chemicals flowing through her, and she was emotionally destroyed."

"Right away I tried to talk to Mark about adoption," said Allison, "but he said, 'Let's take six months off, relax, and stop thinking about all this.' We took six months off. It was then that I began to grieve the loss of my fertility. And during that time I also thought, *I need to give equal time to the idea of not having children. I need to try on childlessness,* which was how I saw it. I didn't see it as childfree; I saw it as childlessness. Mark was able to comfort me a little bit, but not to the extent that I needed. During this time some of our marital struggles began to surface. I wondered, *Is this going to work? Is there anything left of this marriage?* It felt like a shell. Seven years of having one sole focus had consumed me. I was not balanced, and I did not have perspective on it.

"Somehow the six months stretched into a year, and I was just about ready to bring up the subject of adoption again when suddenly Mark's brother was killed in an accident. His death brought us back together in a way that nothing else could have. I really identified with Mark the night that he got the phone call, and I watched him free-fall. Witnessing his reaction made me realize there was nothing I could do except to be there when he hit bottom and help him pick himself up again. I felt more needed, which was gratifying and drew us closer. I felt we were more of a couple and there was more unity."

Mark explained, "My brother's death was a turning point for me. It shattered me and the whole family. Initially his death froze me in my tracks on every level. But several months later I was able to look at his death and say to myself, *There's a gift here that he's giving me if I choose to see it, and that is that life is terribly short* (I was forty-four at the time), *and if you're going to have a child, you'd better get going!*

"For a lot of men, letting go of the desire of leaving progeny is a real issue. I had a dream about having a male child. I'd lost my brother, and my father was an only child; there was a sense of the family line dying out. I had a fantasy of witnessing the birth of my own child. I used to play over and over in my mind the scenario of the birth of my biological child—it was a really clear image for me. It was going to be a very big moment in my life; I had all that set up. I had to let go of that fantasy. Everybody has a lot to let go of in the adoption process.

"Allison convinced me to go with her and talk to an adoption counselor. I went in there and raged for an hour about infertility. I said, 'I've just been through all these years of doctors controlling my life, and now I'm supposed to turn it over to lawyers and agencies? I don't think so!' To his credit, the counselor just listened to me and then said, 'Absolutely. Those are very legitimate feelings. You're right and you're entitled to those feelings.' He let me go and I just punched myself out. When we walked out I felt very agitated but agreed to return the following week.

"On the way to the next appointment I turned to Allison in the car and said, 'I don't know why, but I don't feel the same way I felt last week. I think I'm ready to talk about adoption and go to work on it.' The counselor (who had been adopted) was very skilled and empathetic and helped me cross through. It was cathartic."

Because of his brother's death, Mark's family decided not to celebrate Christmas that year, but his parents invited Mark and Allison, together with their daughter-in-law and granddaughter, to go on a cruise with them. That Christmas was the tenth anniversary of Mark and Allison's engagement, so they decided to have a private celebration of their own during the cruise. On Christmas morning Allison opened a gift from Mark. It was T. Berry Brazelton's book *Touchpoints.* Inside the front cover Mark had written the following:

Will our little person be born this year? Boy or girl; how strange to contemplate, how scary to await. May we embrace his or her life with all the passion, intellect, patience, understanding, and love that we can summon. It doesn't get much more serious than this.

Love,

Mark

"He also gave me another diamond ring," said Allison. "We went up on deck and told his parents that we were going to adopt a baby. They went crazy and we went crazy! That was how we got there.

"When we arrived home I bought several books on adoption and began to devour them. I realized that I had the preconceived notion that kids who were adopted are screwed up because they were given away, that someone didn't want them. I thought that someone who was adopted must always have a desire to know who their parents were and what they looked like. The books I read about open adoption really made sense to me. They gave me a new perspective about adoption and how it could be different; it didn't have to be the old secretive way.

"It seemed wise not to have any secrets; secrets breed dysfunction in a family, and I thought, *Perhaps if there are no secrets, there won't be dysfunction. If my child knows from the very beginning about his birth parents, maybe it won't be a big deal. It will be a fact of life, like having freckles. If there's any kind of adoption that makes sense to me, it's open adoption.*"

For Mark the concept of open adoption was not easy to embrace initially. "Open, to me, was an open concept," said Mark. "I was ready to consider an open adoption, but I wanted to control the parameters of how open it would be. I didn't like the idea of anyone coming and taking the child away or feeling that they could drop in anytime. I wasn't going to have my life invaded like that."

Allison contacted a friend who worked for a West Coast law firm specializing in adoption. This firm placed group ads in national publications on behalf of people interested in adopting. Prospective parents were required to fill out detailed questionnaires and work with local adoption agencies to do a home study and fulfill the legal provisions of their state. Within a short time, Allison and Mark had completed their forms and found a local agency to work with. The law firm also asked them to produce a brochure describing themselves, their lifestyle, their hopes for their child, and so on.

This brochure, complete with photographs, would be mailed to any candidate who had responded to the group ads. The firm pooled a group of people, bought ad space, and divided the cost among the participants. A typical ad would read, "Adoption: Ready, willing, and able couples wish to be loving family for your newborn. Make this a year of love and opportunity for your baby. Please call our attorney at the following 800 number. Void where prohibited." Calls would come in from birth mothers, who would be asked the date of the ad they were responding to. In that way the firm knew which group of brochures to send. Monthly bills for the law firm's services included extensive reports regarding the responses received for each ad and a tally of the brochures mailed to birth mothers.

Mark elaborated, "What we were really paying for was their ability, based on more than ten years of experience, to screen out women who would probably change their minds, who weren't really serious about giving their child up for adoption, who had various other problems, or who imposed conditions that could hinder the desired outcome. The law firm sifted out the variables for us. We were told they had a success rate of more than ninety percent.

"I wrote our brochure for the law firm to mail out to birth mothers. I regarded it as my ultimate public relations assignment. There's no tougher selling job than trying to convince someone you've never met to give you their child. I started by looking at a lot of other people's brochures. Most of them seemed to dwell on the material things a couple could offer a baby. We didn't like that approach and didn't want to be chosen for those reasons. We're not wealthy, we're comfortable. We wanted to be chosen for the type of parents we felt we would be."

"The law firm warned us that it would probably take six to nine months before we got a lead," said Allison. "They defined a lead as talking on the phone with a birth mother who had requested a conversation with us. We were told that talking with a birth mother did not mean everything would work out. It was just a first step. We started advertising on the Fourth of July weekend in 1994. We put our real names and real phone number on the brochure.

"Responses started to come in, and we received reports from the law firm saying, for instance, '9/23 screened lead from birth mother Kimberly of Virginia in response to *USA Today* ad run 9/20—client brochure sent; 9/25 screened lead from birth mother Alicia of Georgia in response to *TV Guide* ad run 9/19—no brochure sent because birth mother has religious preference.' It was good to get all this information. We knew our ads were going out and people were responding to them. The firm had a policy not to send brochures to any woman who was less than six months pregnant; they didn't want to get hooked up with a birth mother who might change her mind."

Mark and Allison began their home study with a local adoption agency. "We didn't have the best relationship with our social worker," recalled Mark. "She wasn't very sensitive. She knew her business, but she didn't convey warmth. Maybe we were needy, but she should have realized that. She was unavailable for a lot of our questions. The woman was basically a cold fish.

"I think everybody has this notion that a social worker comes to your home looking for dust, and of course that's not what happens. I didn't find it terribly threatening. This process did not pull us apart the way infertility treatments had. But my response to things over which I have no control can go one of two ways: I can go insane and try to control it, or I can wait for the situation to play itself out. I tried for the latter. We had a great summer; we went on a nice vacation and tried to relax."

On a Sunday night in January, six months after they had begun to advertise for a baby to adopt, Mark and Allison were reading in bed and were just about ready to turn out the lights when the phone rang.

"Mark answered the phone," said Allison. "I heard him say, 'No, no...' and he hung up. I asked him who it was. 'It was a wrong number;

somebody named Charlene calling collect.' A few minutes later the phone rang again. Mark sounded really annoyed when he answered. Then I heard him say, 'Wait—wait!' He turned to me and said, 'Allison, run in the other room and pick up the phone. This is a birth mother! She says she wants us to have her baby!'

"My hand was shaking as I picked up the phone and said hello. I heard a young woman say, 'My name is Charlene; I'm from Kentucky and I'm nineteen years old. I'm six-and-a-half months pregnant, and I've just looked through a stack of brochures sent from your law firm. I just want to tell you that you're going to have a baby boy.'

"I said, 'What?' She said, 'I've had an ultrasound, and they're ninety-nine percent sure it's a boy. How does that make you feel?' The only thing I could think to say was, 'I can't begin to describe my feelings, Charlene, but this must have been a hard phone call for you to make.' She admitted that it had been."

Mark added, "I felt like I needed to be scraped off the ceiling! My heart was racing and I could barely talk, but I said, 'God, we've been waiting for this call, and now I'm speechless!' I could hear Allison jumping up and down with joy in the next room. 'Let's keep talking now,' I said, 'but can we also agree to talk again tomorrow night, because I don't think we're going to make too much sense tonight.' Charlene said sure. She sounded confident, like she was getting a big kick out of our reaction. I could hear her laughing. Then she said, 'I guess I made your day, didn't I?' All I could think to say was, 'How did you select us?'"

Charlene said, "I read nine brochures and I just loved yours. That picture of you with your dog was great. The Dalmatian is the dog of my dreams. My boyfriend, Jason, the birth father, picked you too. I toyed with the idea of keeping the baby, but my family came down on me like a ton of bricks. They said, 'You can't keep this child. You can't afford it, you don't have a job, and we're not going to do it for you.'"

Mark continued, "Our hearts were pounding as we hung up the phones. You think you're ready for that call, but when it comes you find that you aren't. It is a unique experience. I had an incredible adrenaline rush; I felt giddy. When we got back into bed we were laughing and holding each other. We said, 'Do you believe it? It finally happened!' We didn't sleep at all that night."

"I went to work the next day but didn't make it through the whole day," said Allison. "I had to come home and sleep. I was so exhausted! After I woke up from my nap I worried, *Will she call again?* I talked to the law firm and to our social worker, who asked me a thousand questions for which I didn't have answers. Charlene had said she would call at eight o'clock, and when eight-thirty came and went without the call I felt my stomach begin to churn.

"At eight-forty-five the phone finally rang, and it was Charlene and Jason. They apologized for being late. We asked them a lot of questions, which they answered. Charlene had had no prenatal care for the first five months because she didn't know she was pregnant! We said we'd love to meet them, and they said they'd like to meet us too. Before I knew it, Mark had jumped in and said, 'Well, we could fly out this weekend.' I remember thinking, *Okay! Here we go! It's beginning to take off.*"

The next morning Allison phoned the law firm and was informed that Charlene needed to do a fair amount of paperwork before this could be called a solid lead. They advised Mark and Allison against meeting with Charlene and Jason before her paperwork had been returned to them. The information they sought included a letter from a doctor confirming her pregnancy and a detailed medical history. A few of the documents had to be notarized and sent back to the law firm via overnight courier. Charlene managed to get everything done and met their deadline, so Mark and Allison booked flights for the following weekend.

Mark explained, "We flew to Cincinnati and then drove for about an hour to a little town in Kentucky. It was the middle of January and twenty degrees below zero. We checked into a Holiday Inn where we had agreed to meet Charlene and Jason for lunch. I took a picture of Allison before we went downstairs to the cafe. She was completely rigid. When we walked into the cafe it was empty. We ordered some coffee, and all of a sudden in walked a young girl with a big coat wrapped around her; she was accompanied by a sheepish-looking young man. We knew it was them. They'd seen our photos on our brochure, so they walked right up to us. My first thought was, *She's attractive looking and he's a handsome kid. This is going to be a beautiful child.* We shook hands and invited them to sit down. We all acknowledged that we felt pretty nervous."

Allison continued, "We decided first to order some food. Charlene said, 'Since I've been pregnant I crave steak all the time.' She ordered a hamburger, French fries, and a coke. She reeked of cigarettes. I thought,

She should be drinking milk! And she obviously smokes, but we can't control every-thing. We're going to have to deal with this.

"Mark was great. He got the conversation going by pulling out some family photos we'd brought with us. I was much more nervous than he was. Mark told them about his parents and his childhood, and then Charlene asked me about mine. I didn't know how I was going to tell her about my mother. I started, but then I broke down and cried. The situation was so emotional, and it was hitting something in me. Mark sat there patting me while I blurted the whole story out. I think my honesty was okay with Jason and Charlene."

"We sat in the cafe for a couple of hours with them," said Mark, "and then I said, 'Let's go out and see your world. Let's go for a ride. Show us your town, where you live, what you do.' They were happy to do that.

"We realized very quickly what a desperate place it was—just fast food restaurants and gas stations. Jason's father was fairly successful; he had a large trash collection business, but Charlene had nothing, and it showed. She was dressed rather shabbily. We cruised around and visited some friends of theirs at a dilapidated house. People seemed thrilled to meet us; they gave us big hugs and were very emotional.

"By now the glaze was wearing off a bit, and Allison and I were look-ing around and thinking, *Okay, we can deal with this. We wouldn't want to spend the rest of our lives here, but we'll check it out.* By late afternoon we were burning out on the place. It was pretty depressing. I looked at Charlene and thought, *This girl needs to eat!* So we took them to a steak house (a twenty-four-hour truck stop) for dinner. Their conversation consisted of fragments like, 'I really want a new car' and 'Me and Jason was really partying heavily the other night.' I kept telling myself, *We're not adopting her, we're adopting her child.* It was a dose of reality. When we got back to our hotel Allison and I looked at each other, and she said, 'Oh my God, this is so desperate. I don't know if I can handle much more of this.'"

Allison continued, "I told Mark, 'I'd like a helicopter to pull up out-side right now and take me out of this town. I never want to see these people again.' It was suddenly too close. Suddenly I didn't want any part of it. I couldn't deal with it. I was depressed by the environment they lived in, at the hopelessness and lack of opportunity and their lack of awareness of any other kind of life. I'd never before imagined a life like theirs. There was nothing for them to do. There wasn't even a movie theater in the town. There were no resources for kids, and Jason and Charlene had no internal resources, no idea of other options people have in life. Both were high school graduates, but seemed to have no aspirations or desires. There was no parental support to foster ideas and no financial support for any kind of extended opportunities.

"Before going to bed I took out Charlene's medical report and noticed that she hadn't answered the questions about using drugs. My heart stopped. I said, 'Mark, why didn't we notice this before? What are we going to do?' We decided we had to ask her about drugs. I knew I'd be too nervous, so Mark said he'd do it.

"We had agreed to have breakfast with Charlene and her father, Jim, the next morning. Her parents were divorced, and her father had remarried and had two young children. Jim was great. He said, 'I just want you to know how happy I am for you and how happy I am for us. You are the answer to our prayers.' He got choked up. He said, 'I envisioned a nun in a black habit whisking away my first grandchild and I would never know where he went, but now I'll know.' It was touching."

Mark added, "Jim was very nervous at first. But he was a sweet guy, and we bonded with him immediately. He was a recovering alcoholic and had been a drunk when Charlene was young; she paid the price for that. He worked as a vending machine repairman. I was amazed to learn that he was younger than I was."

After breakfast Mark asked Charlene about drugs. She admitted that she had used drugs in the past but said, "I did not use them since I've been pregnant. Maybe I've had a beer and a glass of wine. I do smoke, you know that."

"We had no choice but to accept what she said at face value," conceded Allison. "I wasn't sure, but I felt fairly confident that she wasn't using anything then. I realized there was nothing I could do about it. I told myself, *You have to abandon your sense of the ideal and hop on the reality bus.*"

Mark continued, "Charlene didn't hesitate or look away when I asked about drug use. We weren't prepared to take on a child with health problems. I felt we had rights. It may sound cold, but I wanted to adopt and raise a healthy child. I didn't want a child who would need to be institutionalized."

The next meeting took place with Sam and Sheila, Jason's parents. "When we drove up to their house, I realized this was the better side of town," said Mark. "We walked in, and they looked at us a bit warily. Jason sat down. He was very quiet. I said, 'I guess you know how we all ended up here.' They said, 'No, we don't.' They knew that Charlene was pregnant and that we were going to be the adoptive family, but they didn't know how it had come about. Jason hadn't told them anything! So I took out one of our brochures and explained. We spent about forty-five minutes playing catch-up with them. They seemed very tense. We learned that they had three grandchildren from two daughters whose marriages had broken up. I thought, *This is not a family that has a good track record. How will they come to terms with saying good-bye to their next grand-child?*"

Jason told Mark and Allison that he felt a responsibility toward his child, but he also said, "I'm too young, and there are too many other things I want to do with my life." He told them that he and Charlene had broken up for a while when she told him she was pregnant.

Later that day Charlene told Allison and Mark that her mother, Stella, didn't want to meet them; she hated Jason and refused to be in the same room with him. Apparently Stella had been pregnant with Charlene when she and Jim got married. Charlene explained that she was living with her grandparents (who didn't know that she was pregnant) and that she planned to go to Georgia to have the baby. Stella had a friend there who had agreed to let Charlene stay with her until the baby was born.

Mark said, "During the flight back home I thought about the weekend and realized it was a blur. But now we had vivid impressions of where this baby was coming from and who the players were. I knew we had moved to a new level, and the bottom line was that our child was going to be born of these two people. I thought, *They come from tough circumstances, but they seem intelligent. They're attractive, but they're kids who would make the best commercial ever for the value of education. They're not stupid kids, they're very wily, they're survivors. We'll take our chances here.*"

A few days later Charlene left for Georgia. Mark and Allison set her up with an adoption agency and an obstetrician there. Allison talked with her several times and felt things were going reasonably well. But suddenly Charlene got very homesick and cried on the phone to Allison. She admitted that she called Jason frequently. Their social worker warned Allison and Mark that the situation in Georgia was not auspicious, that Charlene clearly missed her support system in Kentucky. Then Mark and Allison received a disturbing telephone call from Charlene's mother. She blurted out, "I just want you to know that my daughter is a pathological liar. She changes her mind at the drop of a hat, and I hope you don't get burned by her. I wouldn't trust her any further than I could throw her."

"It was confirmation of our worst fears," said Allison. "We hung up the phone and looked at each other. We were scared. We couldn't understand why a mother would do that to her daughter. Why would a mother jeopardize her daughter's opportunity to get out of a mess? Our social worker speculated that it was because no one had helped Stella out when she was pregnant with Charlene, and she probably felt resentful and jealous."

Allison had plans to travel to Hawaii with a friend, but the uncertainty with Charlene made her hesitate. Mark urged her to go and promised to monitor the situation in Georgia and keep Allison informed.

"Mark called me every day and reported the horror show that was unfolding," said Allison. "Charlene wanted Mark to send her money for food; she said the woman she was staying with had asked to be reimbursed. It turned out that wasn't true. Apparently Charlene was plotting to get money so she could go back to Kentucky. Mark called me and said, 'It sounds like this adoption is unraveling. It feels like Charlene is unraveling.'

"All of a sudden Charlene flew back to Kentucky. Jason picked her up at the airport; she thought they would get together again, but he dropped her off in the center of town and drove off, abandoning her. Her parents were furious about her return; they didn't want her. No one would take her back. She had burned some bridges. She had used a lot of people and borrowed money that she'd never paid back. She stayed with a friend one night and then spent two nights in a truck because we couldn't get approval to pay her living expenses in Kentucky.

"Four days before I was to return home, Mark called me and said, 'Allison, this is getting too crazy. I think we'd better back out.' I told him, 'Mark, I appreciate that you've dealt with this all by yourself, and it's been really tough. But please wait until I get back.'"

Within a couple of days the situation improved. Mark and Allison found a Kentucky agency that was willing to take on their case and recommended a judge, who authorized them to pay living expenses for Charlene for the remainder of her pregnancy. These included heat, housing, utilities, food, and clothing. All monies had to go through an escrow account set up by the agency. Charlene had to submit receipts and get reimbursement for her expenses. A social worker assigned to Charlene found her a motel room to rent on a monthly basis, set her up with a doctor, and got her Medicaid application started.

Allison elaborated, "There was definitely a power struggle going on; it was not clean and simple. But the one thing that stayed constant was that Charlene was positive toward us. She was only slightly apologetic about all the problems, but she never wavered in her intention to give us the baby. She never threatened. If that had been unclear, or if she had wavered, we might not have hung in there. But she always said, 'This is Mark and Allison's baby.'

"I think we understood her background well enough to be able to tolerate her acting out. According to our social worker, her behavior was typical of pregnant teenagers planning to give up their babies. Charlene did have a survival instinct. She thought she could get receipts for bikinis and jeans and pretend they were maternity clothes. She had pinned all her hopes on going to Florida after the baby was born. She was going to go with a friend, lie on the beach, work on a tan, and get her body back. That's what got her through.

"We sent her a box of steaks. She loved them. She sent us a card that read, 'I'm so excited about your/our pregnancy,' and she included her ultrasound photo. Things smoothed out. We got through February. Her due date was in early April. I started working on a room for the baby. It felt like such a leap. I took down the wallpaper and painted the room yellow. My dad and stepmother came with us to pick out baby furniture. It was fun but still scary. I kept thinking, *Is this going to work?* It was a very awkward time. I felt like I didn't have enough time to get ready emotionally. I was going to be a mother in a month-and-a-half and I didn't feel ready to be a mother. I suddenly felt very unsure whether I could be a good mother. I didn't have a good mother; I had no role model. I thought, *Why did I ever think I wanted to do this? How am I going to know what to do?*

"When a woman is pregnant, she might be nervous but she knows she's going to be able to keep her baby. We didn't know whether Charlene would change her mind. We lived with that fear. I thought, *If she changes her mind, what am I going to do? How am I going to handle that?* You can't really prepare for it. We had told the whole world that we were adopting. Our families were extremely anxious that it wasn't going to work.

"I forced myself to control my fear and went out to buy a car seat and a layette. I remember washing those baby clothes in Ivory Snow and folding them, smelling them, reveling in them, holding them up for Mark to admire. I would stand in the baby's room at night. A street light fills that room, and I imagined myself sitting in a rocking chair in the middle of the night, holding my baby by the light and looking down on his face. The thought of that image never coming to fruition was terribly painful.

"As time wore on, our social worker drove me nuts. She took a negative, suspicious tack about Charlene. She told us she was convinced it wasn't going to work. Finally I said to her, 'Listen, I get it! Charlene can change her mind. I understand that and accept it. Now can we move beyond that? I've got questions I need answers to, and all you keep talking about is the possibility that Charlene will change her mind. I'm sorry if your personal bent is toward birth mothers, but right now you're supposed to be here for us. You're our social worker. Can we talk about how I'm feeling, about how hard this is for us?'

"In the first week of March, Charlene began to dilate. The doctor told her the baby was going to be small and that she might deliver early. When she and I talked on the phone she told me she wanted us to be in the labor room with her. I thought, *This could be pretty weird. If she changes her mind when we're there it's going to be really strange.* Part of me didn't want to be in the labor room. As a nurse I'd attended many births and knew how emotional they were. I was still trying to keep myself somewhat emotionally separate and disconnected from Charlene because I didn't want to get sucked in and then dropped."

At the end of March, Charlene reported to Allison that her doctor thought the birth was imminent. When Allison told Mark he said, "What? What do you mean, *imminent? Imminent* means very soon!" That night he packed a suitcase. Allison chuckled. She thought it was ridiculous to start packing. But the next day she told her boss that she might go to Kentucky that weekend.

On Friday evening, Charlene called them to report that she was having contractions. Allison remained calm; she warned Charlene that it might be false labor. "Why don't you walk around," suggested Allison, "see if the contractions increase or stop, take a bath, have a glass of wine. We'll call you after dinner." During the next call Charlene told them she was going to the hospital. Allison asked Charlene to phone them later from the hospital, but Mark had other ideas. "Allison, we're leaving! We're going to Kentucky now. This is it!"

"What do you mean? It's ten o'clock at night!"

"Make me a thermos of black coffee and give me a couple of your herbal diet pills."

"This could be false labor, Mark."

"No, Allison. We're going!"

"We put our plan into action," explained Allison. "Luggage was flying out of the house. I called a friend who had agreed to housesit for us. Watching Mark drive was like watching PacMan eating miles! There was a full moon. We said, 'It's like the star over Bethlehem.' We made all sorts of references. We sang songs. I kept looking at the car seat in the back and thinking, I can't believe we're doing this!

"At one point I implored Mark to stop and call the hospital. 'If she's having false labor, we can turn around and go back home,' I reasoned. He wouldn't do it. He didn't want to call. He wanted to get to Kentucky; he did not want to miss that delivery. It wouldn't have killed me to miss it. I was ambivalent about it. I thought, *I don't want to get more attached to this baby than I already am. If Charlene changes her mind, what am I going to do?*"

Mark continued, "When I get my mind set on something, I do it. She's in labor, we're packed and ready to go—let's get out of here! My heart was racing. We flew out of the house and drove all night. We drove into town, went straight to the hospital, and ran inside—no Charlene! They had sent her home; it was false labor! I realized I had really blundered by rushing out there, but Allison was kind enough not to rub my face in it. She said, 'Let's get some breakfast, check into the Holiday Inn, and go to sleep.'"

Allison continued, "The phone woke us up at eleven o'clock that morning. It was a friend of a friend who lived nearby, but the last thing on our minds was socializing. I heard Mark say, 'You want to give us what?' It turned out they offered to let us stay at their parents' house; they were in Florida for the winter. We visited Charlene at her motel apartment; then we met our friends, who drove us to their parents' house. It was a gorgeous house, and they were such nice people. We moved our stuff in that afternoon. It was wonderful.

"The next day we had lunch with Charlene and her mother. We were exhausted, but we both realized Stella was not someone we wanted to be enemies with, so we made a big effort. She was open and honest about what she thought Charlene's shortcomings were—right in front of her! Stella had brought some baby pictures of Charlene, which was a good ice-breaker, but she clearly was very nervous. At the end of the meal Stella said, 'I'm glad I met you. I feel much better. My parents would like to meet you, too.' So we went to meet Betty and Sal and fell in love with them. They were wonderful to us, gave us cookies and coffee. We sat around their kitchen table and talked and talked. Betty packed up some homemade cookies for us.

"On Monday we took Charlene to lunch, a movie, and out shopping. Then I told her she was going to go for a walk. I don't think she had moved off the sofa for most of her pregnancy. We were trying to get her to go into labor! I was very clear with her. I said, 'Honey, we're going to get this labor going.' She went along with me."

Mark added, "We took her on mall walks and walks in the woods. I thought, *What do we have to do to get this labor going, rent a pogo stick? For us the clock doesn't even begin to tick until she has the baby. We've been out here for four days and nothing is happening!*"

Allison said, "I had sent Charlene a book on childbirth. As the days passed I reviewed it with her and read some parts aloud to her. I talked to her about the different stages of labor and some breathing routines she might use. It was clear that I was becoming her labor coach, because the friend she had chosen didn't show any real interest.

"Finally she called us on Wednesday morning and said, 'This is it! It started at five in the morning and hurts like hell!' We rushed over to her motel. Several of Charlene's friends were there, including Jason. Mark timed her contractions while I walked with her up and down the corridors of the motel. She got to the point where she couldn't walk through the contractions anymore, and then I knew it was time to go to the hospital."

At the hospital, Charlene was surrounded by her mother, stepmother, and several friends. Mark remembered, "For a while they let me stay in the labor room. I was given the task of rinsing facecloths in cold water to put on her forehead. It was a good task; it gave me something to do, and yet I could still watch what was going on. I remember thinking as I watched the three women dealing with Charlene that it was a beautiful sight . . . the women gathered around the woman. I know it sounds hokey, but it was beautiful."

Allison continued, "The doctor came in and said, 'There are too many people in here. I need to have two other nurses, and there's not enough room. You can choose three people.' Charlene looked around. 'Well, I want my mom, I want Allison, and I want my stepmom.' She turned to me and asked, 'Do you think Mark will be sad?' I said, 'He'll be sad, but he'll be okay.' I offered to leave and let Mark take my place, but she wanted me to be there.

"I was given the job of holding one of Charlene's legs up when she delivered. Her stepmother held the other one, and her mother stayed near her head. We started to see a little bit of black hair every time she pushed. I couldn't quite believe that our baby was about to come out. I kept asking myself, *What am I going to do if she changes her mind?* I had to keep that in mind; there was no choice."

"Suddenly Charlene said she really wanted to push. I remember looking down and seeing the baby's face looking up. The cord was wrapped once around the neck, and the doctor slipped it off. Then he said, 'Okay, we have a shoulder . . . ' and then the baby just slipped out. Everyone said, 'It's a girl!' I had wanted a girl so badly that my first thought was, *Maybe there is a God!* After all the years of sadness and feeling like I was getting ripped off, this girl meant that someone had heard my unspoken prayer. I'm not religious, but for that moment I thought, *Maybe there really is . . .*

"They put the baby on Charlene's stomach, and she reacted very tenderly toward her. She seemed very proud. Everyone oohed and aahed. After a couple of minutes the doctor clamped the cord and looked at me. He said, 'Well, this honor should be yours,' and he handed me the scissors. I was shaking. I couldn't believe it. I separated the baby from Charlene; when I did that I knew that, for me, the gesture would hold symbolism for the rest of my life. I was crying.

"After they cleaned the baby off the doctor asked, 'Who should hold her?' Charlene said, 'Allison.' But I said, 'I'm going to hold her for the rest of my life. Why don't you hold her, Charlene?' I think I was afraid to hold her—too shocked and too scared. And I truly believed that my gesture at that time was important. It was important for Charlene to hear me state that I believed that this was going to be my child. I stayed aware of the fact that she could change her mind at any moment, and I was never unaware that I had some power to influence whether that happened or not.

"For one hundred percent selfish reasons I wanted that baby. I wanted that baby more than anything else in the world. I was willing to do anything to make that happen, even if it meant that my initial desire to hold the baby had to be shelved. I felt, having been through labor and delivery with her, a real bonding and an attachment to Charlene and began to have little inklings like, *How are we going to separate and go on to live separate lives? How will this baby become my baby and not Charlene's baby?* She felt very much like Charlene's baby. She did not feel like my baby."

"I sat with Jason in the waiting room for two nerve-wracking hours," said Mark. "Finally I saw Allison running down the corridor. She said, 'It's a beautiful baby . . . girl!' It was supposed to be a boy. I remember doing a little cognitive shift and thinking, *Okay, I can deal with that!* Allison gave me a big hug and asked, 'Are you disappointed it isn't a boy? We were going to name him after your brother.' But I said, 'No, Allison, I'm so happy for you. I know how much you wanted a girl.'

"She went running back right away but called out over her shoulder, 'You can come down in a minute.' I turned to Jason and gave him a big hug. I called my parents and he called his. Then I went down the hall; a curtain was drawn across the entrance to Charlene's room. While standing there I heard the baby cry, and I surrendered. Tears streamed down my face, tears that welled up from the deepest part of me. Maybe it's different when you have a biological child, but I can't imagine that. Is it any more profound or deep? How can it be?"

Allison remembered, "When Mark came into the room, the first thing he did was hug Charlene and say, 'I hear you did an extraordinary job, Charlene. I want to see this little girl.' We went over and looked at her. The baby was under some lights on a little birthing table. She was stretched out like she was sunbathing and looked completely relaxed. Mark said, 'She's just beautiful. What fine little features!' He counted her fingers and toes. We stood there and held each other. When Jason came into the room Mark put his arm around Jason's shoulders; Jason was astounded. He looked as though he couldn't believe there was actually a baby! I don't think he was prepared to have any emotions or feelings about this at all. So when the feelings hit him, he was overwhelmed; there were tears in his eyes.

"After about half-an-hour a nurse came to take the baby down to the nursery. Mark watched through the window while they checked and weighed her. He came back to report that she weighed seven pounds and five ounces. By this time Charlene was on a post-delivery high. She kept saying, 'I can't believe how great I feel! I can't believe it's a girl!' She asked me if I was disappointed that it was a girl. I said, 'Charlene, I really wanted a girl—more than anything!'

"I think Charlene was prepared to give up a baby boy but not a baby girl. Somehow the sex changed everything. She seemed amazed by the adulation she received from Stella, who told her what a great job she'd done. Clearly she had never received this much praise from her mother before. She was finally getting approval for something that she was going to have to give up. The internal struggle must have been hell for Charlene. Apparently Stella had never been a gushy person, and now she was gushing over this baby . . . finally gushing to Charlene about something Charlene had done. It made me feel very anxious."

After a while, Mark and Allison wheeled Charlene to the nursery to get another look at the baby. The pediatrician came up and said, "Oh, I think this is so wonderful when the birth parents and the adoptive parents know each other. The baby's fine; her Apgar scores were great. She's got wonderful tone and she's very relaxed, which is rare. Everybody gather round and take some pictures." Mark and Allison went home about midnight. The baby was now three hours old.

"The next morning I was awake at five," recalled Allison. "I was very excited but nervous that Charlene might have changed her mind overnight. Mark and I didn't really talk about it; I think it was too scary to contemplate. In my heart of hearts I thought, *This is still her baby. That bond and that feeling may be stronger than everything else, and it may break through. This is not a decision based on logic.* I made a lot of phone calls that morning. My father seemed pleased, but I knew he was still scared that this might not work out. He wasn't going to let himself go.

"We bought flowers for Charlene and went to the hospital. The baby was not in her room. She said, 'Do you want to get the baby?' I think she was afraid to get her without us. But they wouldn't release the baby to us from the nursery; they had to release her to Charlene. The nurse said it was time for her to be fed. Mark gave her a bottle, and we took turns holding her.

"We had to visit the adoption agency that afternoon; the staff told us it would take a full week before they would accept Charlene's surrender. The social worker said, 'We feel comfortable with you taking an at-risk placement, unless you want to put the baby in foster care. How do you feel about that?' I had never thought that we'd be allowed to take her home from the hospital, so I was ecstatic. The social worker added that she had already cleared this with Charlene, that Charlene preferred to have us take her. She didn't want the baby to be put in foster care.

"We went back to the hospital and had dinner there. Lots of people came to visit, including Jason's parents. I think they felt that the situation was bizarre. Sam kept saying, 'I can't believe she'll be leaving.' It was hard to hear. Charlene's father came and started crying. I don't think Charlene had expected her parents to be emotional about this baby. It was very odd to watch those dynamics at work. I wanted the adoption to go through, but knowing that it was causing so much pain for so many people was hard."

Mark said, "It frightened me whenever I saw Charlene holding the baby. You can never watch that without feeling threatened. She behaved naturally toward the baby, which was scary to me. But to her credit, Charlene seemed always to be thinking of us. She'd periodically say, 'Mark and Allison, you hold her now.' There was a parade of people passing through her room. When I watched Jason's parents hold the baby I thought, *They're having trouble with this.* I knew they had other grand-children that they were very much involved with. And this was one beau-tiful baby! It's one thing when a child is abstract, but an actual child presents an entirely different situation."

"By about ten o'clock that night we were just beat," said Allison. "When we got up to leave I said, 'Well, tomorrow's discharge day. We'll see you tomorrow!' Then I asked Charlene, 'Do you want me to take the baby back to the nursery?' I was beginning to feel that I wanted the baby to spend less time with Charlene; it was beginning to make me anxious. Each time she held the baby it was getting harder for me to watch. I thought, *She's getting more attached to this baby; she's bonding with this baby. How is she going to be able to make this decision? How is she going to sign those papers? This is scaring the life out of me, but there's nothing I can do except be gracious.* I started to take the baby to the nursery, but Charlene said, 'Leave her here for a little longer.' As we got into our car I thought, *I hope all this works. This is really scary. How can she hold this baby and be ready to let her go tomorrow?*

"We went to the house, made some phone calls, and fell into bed. The next morning when we got up I knew it was going to be an emotional day. We drove to the hospital with the expectation that we would bring the baby home by about two in the afternoon. As we got off the elevator, Charlene's stepmother approached us. She said, 'Mark and Allison, come here for a second. I wouldn't go down to see Charlene right now. Her social worker is with her; she's really upset and had a rough night.' I looked at Mark and he looked at me. I felt as though my stomach had been sucked right out of me. I thought, *This is it! Here's my worst fear. We're going back to Philadelphia with an empty car seat. She's changed her mind!*"

Mark asked, "What's going on?" Charlene's stepmother said, "Well, I guess Charlene has been dumbfounded by how her mother reacted to the baby, and by how she and Jason feel about the baby. I don't think she's going to change her mind; I don't know. I just know she's upset and she's been crying all night." Mark replied, "I don't have to tell you that this is our worst nightmare! This is absolutely terrible for us." She said, "I know. I just didn't want you to walk in there right now. I think you should wait here for a while."

Mark continued, "Allison and I sat down, and I felt the blood go out of my face. I said, 'This is it! We're going to have it right in the face!' All of a sudden I was paged over the intercom to come to the nurses' station. I said, 'Allison, you wait here.'

"I walked down the hall and was met by Charlene's social worker. Allison came up right behind me; she wasn't going to wait. The woman said, 'Everything's okay. Charlene's been very upset all night; she's grieving. She's letting her child go today, and this is normal. It's going to be okay. She's preparing to say good-bye and realizing how hard it's going to be. She knows this is the right decision. She hasn't changed her mind; she doesn't want to change her mind. She just feels terribly, terribly sad. She felt sad yesterday but didn't feel that she could show it in front of you. She was afraid that you would think that she was changing her mind.' With that, my heart just about broke apart."

Allison said, "We walked into Charlene's room, and she said, 'I'm sorry I'm crying. She's so beautiful and I'm so sad. I want you two to have her, but this is really hard for me.'

"I said, 'Charlene, we've all been crying a lot; it doesn't get any heavier than this. Your feelings are normal. I think this is the right time to give you a gift we brought for you.' We had bought a little pendant with an amethyst set in the center and a little diamond set off to the side.

"I was crying so hard that I couldn't speak, so Mark took over. He said, 'Charlene, the amethyst symbolizes your dark hair and eyes, and the diamond symbolizes your little girl, who will always be a part of you and will always be attached to you in some way. When you wear this, think of your daughter and know that she's loved.' Charlene was very touched. The timing was absolutely perfect. It was a bonding moment for all of us . . . so emotionally charged. It definitely felt like the climax of the day, and from then on the emotions were out and Charlene could begin to get herself together. The baby would have her final checkup, and we'd all leave the hospital around noon.

"Lunchtime came and Charlene didn't make any moves to get ready to leave. It felt awkward. I didn't think I should say, 'Don't you want to get ready now?' Instead I asked her, 'What time is discharge?' She said she didn't know. A medical records person came in to take two sets of footprints of the baby, and Charlene told her she wanted a third set for Jason. The hospital's policy was that they made one extra set. They wouldn't make two extra sets. Charlene said she wouldn't sign the release papers until she had two sets of footprints. I felt she was getting unnecessarily worked up about this and told her I could buy a stamp pad and make another set for Jason. But she was adamant about it. I felt some of the problems of the day were beginning to escalate.

"Mark and I left her and went down to get some lunch. We came back up and sat there waiting. At about three o'clock a nurse came in and said they had to do a blood test on the baby at nine that night (it had to be done at least forty-eight hours after birth). She said we could leave that night after the test or leave now and bring the baby back the next morning, but that Charlene would also have to come back with the baby. Charlene said she wanted to stay and do the test at nine.

"I thought, *Oh, God, we have to wait six more hours before we can leave this hospital? I'm going to lose my mind!* At that point I felt certain that Charlene was going to let us take the baby—the crisis had passed—but it was such a frustrating situation. We left and drove around to eat up the time. This gave Jason and Charlene some time alone with the baby. Mark and I went shopping for formula and diapers. We would alternately cling to each other and vent our frustrations. I don't know whether I was feeling more anxious than Mark, but I felt like my stomach was being eaten up. I kept thinking, *All I want to do is get this baby home! I want to begin to be her mother, and I can't do that when I hold the baby in front of Charlene. I am so self-conscious; I am so cognizant of the fact that this child did not come from me, that she is not mine. I don't feel bonded to this baby.*

"There was never one moment in the hospital when Mark and I were alone with the baby. The course of emotions that went through me was profound. I thought, *How many more ideals do I have to give up? How much do I have to give up to get what I'm really going to be good at and what I really want? I can't stand this one moment longer. I can't do it, I'm too frustrated.* These were thoughts that I didn't share with Mark because I was afraid that if I started to express my fears, they would get out of control and I would explode."

Mark continued, "Allison and I were both getting irritated. We didn't know what was going on, and we didn't think it was our right to say, 'Can we have the baby now?' We were waiting for somebody to take charge. At the hospital some of the staff were really nice to us, but another group did not treat us nicely. They acted as though we were the rich couple from Philadelphia who had come to steal the baby. We were treated brusquely and cruelly by some of them. I kept saying to Allison, 'Let it ride. We'll ride through this storm.' We came back to the hospital and had some dinner; there was still nothing going on."

Allison and Mark were talking to Charlene's father when a nurse came out and told Jim that Charlene wanted to see him. After he left, the nurse turned to them and said, "I don't think there's any way that baby's going to get discharged tonight." Allison became hysterical. She started sobbing and said, "I can't take it. I want to go home." Mark said, "What do you mean? Back to Philadelphia?" She nodded yes. Mark told her, "Do me a favor. Go to the ladies' room, take all the time you want, but we're in this. We're not walking away. We're just going to roll with the punches."

Allison said, "I went in the ladies' room and sobbed. Tears were flying out of my eyes. I buried my face in my hands. I thought, *I want to be under general anesthesia. Wake me when this is over. I can't bear it one moment longer. This is too painful. What do you mean they're not going to let her go tonight? I can't go home without that baby tonight. I've waited all my life for this!*"

Mark walked down the corridor and saw Charlene talking with her parents. "I told them Allison was beside herself and we needed some answers. The head nurse walked by, and I asked her for some information. I said, 'My wife is in the middle of a breakdown; this has been a very stressful day, and no one has told us anything. What's the plan?' She explained that if the baby's blood test was given at nine o'clock, we'd still have to wait an hour for the results, and it was unprecedented for an infant to be discharged so late at night."

Meanwhile, Allison continued, "I splashed some water on my face and went back out to join Mark. We seemed to reach a kind of peace at that moment. I had let all this out and felt better for it. Charlene's parents were there, the baby was there, and we all passed her around and talked. Charlene's mother was rubbing her back, and a sense of calm seemed to come over everybody. It was dark, it was late, and everyone was exhausted. It had been a very long day. Finally the doctor came in and said the baby could go. Then Charlene got a call from Jason and started to cry. He was screaming at her for choosing her mother to be with her during the delivery instead of him. That's just what she needed to hear at a time like that! I tried to comfort her."

Mark continued, "It was time to spring into action. I thought, *Wow, this is finally going to happen!* The discharge nurse came in. I had dubbed her Nurse Ratched [a character in *One Flew over the Cuckoo's Nest*]. She turned to Charlene and started giving her instructions for the baby. Charlene said, 'I think you'd better tell Mark and Allison.' Nurse Ratched said, 'What you do with the child when you leave this hospital is your business. I am legally required to give you this information.' She turned her back on us. I whispered to Allison, 'Just remember, she's a jerk. She'll soon be out of our lives; don't let her get to you.'"

Allison admitted, "Mark was a rock. He usually takes everything very personally, but he knew that I was falling apart and he had to be strong. The nurse kept reading a list of instructions to Charlene: 'You are to feed her every three hours; if she doesn't wake up at night, that's fine. She'll probably need a diaper change every three hours. Next, cord care: apply alcohol after every diaper change.' The woman was cruel. Charlene's mouth began to quiver, and it was clear that she was about to burst into tears, but this woman persisted with her instructions. Mark said, 'I'll get the car seat.' The nurse turned to him sharply, 'Don't bring it into the hospital; just wait in your car under the canopy at the emergency entrance.' Charlene went into the bathroom to get dressed; she was sobbing. The nurse said, 'I haven't finished yet. I need to give you more instructions. Will you please come out?' She was awful!

"After Charlene got dressed and came back into the room, the nurse continued, 'Charlene, you will carry the baby in the wheelchair. The baby must leave the hospital in your arms. What is the baby going to wear?' I had an outfit from Mark's brother's wife and a baby blanket that my grandmother had knitted before she died. The nurse said, 'Is this the only blanket you have? This isn't warm enough for a baby at this hour of the night.' I said, 'It would have been if she'd been discharged in the afternoon.'

"Charlene held the baby as Nurse Ratched wheeled her down the corridor. She was sobbing. Her parents walked behind her with me. It felt like a procession. We had to walk through the emergency room, which was teeming with people. They all stared at us. Cold air hit us outside. Charlene stood up from the wheelchair and turned to me. Mark jumped out of the car and rushed over to us."

Mark said, "That damn nurse gave us all the wrong feelings for this beautiful moment. She made us feel filthy. And she was rotten to Charlene. The poor girl had tears running down her face when she handed Allison the baby. She was completely unraveled. We put our arms around her and said good-bye. She said, 'Please take good care of her.' Her parents helped her over to their car."

"Mark and I got into the back seat of our car. I was holding the baby, and he sat beside me on the hump on the floor. I was sobbing. We put our arms around each other. Mark said, 'I feel so dirty. I feel like I'm stealing a baby.' And that was exactly how I felt, too! I felt so awful; that nurse was so mean. Maybe she touched on feelings that we all had; we *were* taking someone else's baby. That was the reality. But we knew the only way we were going to have a child was if somebody gave us theirs.

"We put the baby in her car seat. I was still crying. I kept looking at this fragile little being and thinking, *I didn't think I was going to begin being a mom at midnight!* After we had been on the road for about five minutes, Mark said in a shaky voice, 'How's the baby back there?' I hadn't taken my eyes off her. 'She's just fine, Mark,' I said.

"We got to the house exactly at midnight. It was pitch black. We had been up since six in the morning and were absolutely exhausted. It had been the most emotional day of our lives. I paused at the door and told Mark we should both carry her over the threshold. I was still overcome with emotion, and when we got inside I fell to my knees and said, 'I think we need to say a prayer.' Mark gave me a strange look as I said, 'I think we need to acknowledge the people who were important to us and are no longer living.' I talked about my mother and Mark's brother and all the people who buoyed and supported us through this process of becoming a family. I needed to stop for a moment and recognize how long it had taken us."

Mark and Allison fed the baby together, and for the first time began to call her Christina. Then they settled her into a lovely wicker bassinet, which their friends had kindly left beside their bed. "I agreed to get up with her that first night," said Mark. "I heard her crying at three in the morning, so I took her downstairs, gave her an ounce-and-a-half of formula, and changed my first diaper. I was scared to death! She was such a little thing—like a little bird. I was afraid that I was going to snap an arm off. I put her back in her bed, and she went right back to sleep. At six Allison got up for the next feeding. She woke me at about seven and said, '*Shhhh*, don't roll over.' I looked and there was Christina. We were in a beautiful, sun-filled room with the baby in bed with us. It was wonderful. We knew we were still at risk, but we had our baby."

The next day Mark and Allison stayed at the house alone with the baby. "We didn't see anybody," said Allison. "We just wanted to be by ourselves. I cuddled Christina and carried her around all day. Even when she was asleep I was checking on her every five minutes to make sure she was still breathing. I'd had a fair amount of experience in handling babies, but Mark had none, and he would panic when trying to dress her. I still felt she wasn't ours. In some ways I felt like a foster parent; I was caring for her, nurturing her, loving her, but I wasn't letting myself fall in love with her. I was but I wasn't. A part of me was holding back.

"On Monday we took Christina to the pediatrician. Charlene had to go with us. The doctor said the baby was fine. Afterward we took Charlene to lunch. She looked pretty horrible; there were dark circles under her eyes. She wanted to hold the baby. I wasn't feeling nearly as threatened as I had been in the hospital, but there was still a tug. I thought, *Who's the mom here? Who calls the shots?* Before she left the hospital Charlene had asked us if she could see the baby, and we had said she could see her anytime she wanted. But that turned out to be hard for me. I didn't want to share Christina. But I forced myself to say again, 'I'm going to hold her for the rest of my life, and you're only going to hold her for a week.'

"Charlene and Jason had a counseling session with a social worker on Tuesday. This was required before the release could be signed on Thursday. I talked to Charlene every day. I told her how the baby was doing, how she slept, how she was eating, and how she burped. We told her to feel free to call us. Mark said to her, 'You're clearly going through a time that we can't imagine; we'll take our cues from you. When you want to talk, call us. The same goes for Jason. And if you want to come and see the baby, call us.'

"I woke up on the day of the signing feeling nervous. Mark said, 'Allison, it's going to be fine. Charlene seemed fine when we talked to her last night. Everything she said makes me believe she intends to follow through.' We drove to the adoption agency and sat down in the waiting room. The social worker came right out and told us that Charlene and Jason had already signed their papers! Mark and I stood up and shared a high five, then a huge hug. There was a sense of relief, but we were so tapped out emotionally there wasn't a lot left inside of us. All we could think about now was going home.

"The social worker asked if we would let Charlene and Jason have some time alone with the baby before leaving the agency. We were happy to let them do that. She took the baby away; Mark rushed off to make some phone calls. I was left sitting in a little playroom on a couch; the sun was shining through the window on me. I closed my eyes and fell asleep!

"I was awakened by the social worker, who took us into a room to sign our papers. Then she suggested that Mark and I sit down with Charlene and Jason and talk about what would happen next. She stressed that it was nonbinding, but thought it would be helpful for all of us to express our expectations and needs about future interactions. We worked out an agreement about frequency of letters, phone calls, photos, et cetera. We agreed to send a letter and photos every three months for the first year and on Christina's birthday and at Christmas each year after that. We said that Charlene could call us anytime she wanted, but that there could be no meeting until Christina was old enough to request it and if we agreed that she was emotionally capable of handling it. We stipulated that they could not show up at our house—that would not be acceptable, ever. But they could always call.

"After the surrender I felt more comfortable with Christina. That time was blissful. There was no family to drop in, no visitors. It gave the three of us time to be alone together. The day before we left for home we took Christina around to visit everyone. We stopped at Jason's parents' home; they gave Christina stuffed animals, blankets, outfits, and a baby mug. Then we went to Betty and Sal's house; Charlene and Stella were there. Everyone held the baby and said how beautiful she was.

"The last night we took Jason and Charlene out to dinner; then they asked if they could come back to our house and spend some time alone with Christina. We left them in the den with the baby, and Mark and I waited in the kitchen. I paced back and forth and realized, *I can't share this baby anymore; I'm done sharing this baby. This is the last time that Charlene has to hold her. I can't wait for this to be over. It's just torture . . . agony.* After thirty minutes Mark decided it was time and we walked into the den. Jason said, 'We've got to go, Charlene.' She was sobbing and clinging to Christina. When she handed her to me she whispered to the baby, 'I know you're going to be fine, but I feel so sad.' We said good-bye and then Jason led her to the door. When they were gone Mark walked over to where I was standing holding Christina. He put his arms around both of us and we began our life."

Mark reflected, "I think open adoption is like a great ride on a roller coaster. It's frightening, exhilarating, and uncertain, but the outcome was so positive for us. I don't know how I would feel about open adoption if Charlene had changed her mind, but fortunately we don't have to answer that. We took part in something so moving; you don't get many human experiences like that."

Allison added, "The difference between a closed adoption and an open adoption is that in a closed adoption all the same feelings are there, but neither party sees the other side of it. The open adoption was honest but incredibly painful, and that was something we absolutely were not prepared for. I was not prepared to witness Charlene's struggle with the loss of her child. No one addressed that. We weren't prepared to witness the birth parents' pain of surrender. Because we grew close to them, it made it harder in some ways.

"I still advocate open adoptions despite the pain we went through. Most of my reasons for feeling this way have to do with what it will mean to Christina. I feel that to have witnessed that pain and to be able to tell her the story in detail is a gift for her. We will tell Christina about the people she came from and that there's nothing to be embarrassed or secretive about. Three generations of wonderful people opened their hearts to us and let us walk out of their lives with a child they loved. That's the essence of an open adoption, which makes it worth it. It was hard, but I don't think anything in life is pure roses. It was the bitter with the sweet. But I'm so glad we have this wonderful story to tell Christina. We will truly be able to say, 'It was not easy for your mom to let you go. It was incredibly painful. We were there; we witnessed it.'"

"I also believe that open adoption is good for the birth parents," said Mark, "because I suspect Charlene has as much peace of mind as any mother could have in her situation. She knows where her child is."

"One unexpected difficulty with open adoption was the responsibility we continued to feel for Charlene after we came home," admitted Allison. "Her plans to go to Florida after the birth fell through, and she crashed. She went on a downward spiral for a while. She called often and I felt responsible for her. There was such a close connection that I didn't have the ability to distance myself from her. I kept calling our social worker to talk about it. I was having trouble reaching out to Charlene. I think Charlene felt I was abandoning her. In fact, I think I was.

"The social worker said she thought Charlene would be less clingy if she had some spontaneous contact from me. So I made attempts to reach out to her. I wrote her a couple of letters and always thanked her for her gift to us. I called her and asked her how she was doing, and I think that made a difference. And time began to do its work; her hormones went back to normal. For the first six months Charlene called us collect. It was hard for us. We wondered at what point we should tell her not to make any more collect calls. We decided, *If she needs to do this, it's not that much money for us, so we won't say anything about it.* In time she started calling us on her own nickel and the calls became less frequent."

"I often think about what Christina's life would have been like if she'd stayed with Charlene," said Mark. "I think she would probably be just as sharp and funny, but she wouldn't be getting the stimulation she's getting and the security of two loving parents. One of the satisfactions for me is realizing we've given her a nice little garden to grow in. She's really flourished. One of the things I love about being an adoptive parent is that I can look at my daughter and, with all objectivity, say that she is a beautiful child. She's an angel. I just get such a kick out of her. We'll take credit for what we can, but we'll never actually know what we've done. She's a great mix."

Allison concluded "I still look at this child every day, and I am absolutely astonished by the fact that she was given to us. I am so proud that we adopted her. And I believe I love her more because she was adopted. I feel I worked so hard for this. Because I have an appreciation and a remembrance of the longing I had for a child, I embrace even the difficult parts of being a parent. I'm so amazed that Charlene and Jason gave her to us. They trusted us. They said, 'We don't really know you, but we know you'll do a better job than we can. Here is our child.' What an amazing gift!"

2/ Zachary and Hannah
Adopting a four-year-old Romanian boy

"When Hannah put him down I got down on one knee and held out my arms. He said, 'Poppa!' and ran and jumped into my arms. It felt like he was saying, *Where have you been for four years, Dad? I've been waiting for you!* It was instant love."

THE CHIEF reason people decide to adopt is infertility. Occasionally, however, people are touched by the plight of a specific child or group of children and, somehow caught unawares, are moved to embrace a child without a great deal of forethought or planning. People captivated by a child in this way often feel instinctively that fate has brought them together and that adoption is the right thing to do.

Zachary and Hannah are such a couple. Although they had been married for only three years and had not given much, if any, thought to starting a family, the photograph of a Romanian orphan inspired them to become parents.

Hannah is a slender brunette whose soft voice belies great inner strength and determination. She grew up in a Jewish family in New York, the youngest of five children. "My parents loved everybody's kids," she said. "They always had kids around—neighbors, cousins, everybody. They'd travel with anybody's kids. Some cousins lived with us for a while. There were a lot of pets in my family; we had a cat who kept having kittens. We always had a dog of one type or another. And I had a pet iguana, a turtle, and some goldfish. It was very open; everything was acceptable."

Zachary is tall with curly dark hair and a warm smile; he speaks candidly in a commanding voice. "Like Hannah, I'm also the youngest child in a Jewish family," he related. "I have two older sisters. Our family was always close; we still are. My father owned a small hotel in Colorado and I grew up loving the mountains."

After college, Zach took some time off to work as a waiter at a ski resort in Vermont before starting graduate school. One night, just before closing time, Hannah walked in. "I was with my sister and a friend," said Hannah. "Our flight was late in arriving, and we realized immediately that the waiters weren't too happy to see us show up at the end of the evening. They were already setting up for breakfast."

Zach explained, "It was ten minutes before closing, and the other waiter and I had plans for the evening. While he served them I finished setting up for breakfast. I was so upset that at one point I accidentally dropped a whole tray of dishes as I walked by their table.

"The next night the maitre d' said, 'I've got a present for you, Zach. You can wait on the three girls. But just invite me to the wedding.' (We rarely had single women staying there; that's why he said it was a gift for me.) During the meal one of the girls asked me how they could get into town after dinner. Immediately I seized on the opportunity and offered to drive them when my shift ended. We went to a bar; I asked Hannah to dance but she turned me down. So I danced with her sister. Finally Hannah agreed to dance with me, and that was it. She made a big impression on me. Two nights later I asked Hannah to marry me!"

Although Zach and Hannah fell in love quickly, they didn't get married until three years later. During that period Zachary completed an M.B.A. in Boston and began a Ph.D. program in New York. Hannah worked as a graphic artist in New York City. "We decided to have a double wedding with my sister and her fiancé," said Hannah. "Our parents had died, and my sister and I thought it would be fun to plan it together. Also, we thought it would be easier for our relatives to come to just one wedding instead of two; I think a lot of them enjoyed the spectacle of a double wedding.

"Zach and I were still such kids. We didn't talk much about our future or having children. I was enjoying my job and he was going to school."

Hannah enjoyed a close relationship with her cousin, Sarah, who lived in New Jersey. Sarah and her husband had been trying to have a child for years but without success. "Fairly early in our marriage I asked Zach how he would feel about me being a surrogate for her," said Hannah. "He said, 'Do you think I would want to go through nine months of pregnancy with you to have somebody else's baby? Maybe if we already had a couple of our own . . .' I thought about it—I don't know how seriously. I guess just thinking about it is serious enough. I knew how unhappy Sarah was, and it didn't seem like such a foreign idea to me. That was one of the only conversations Zach and I had about having children.

"Then Sarah saw a program about Romanian orphans hosted by Barbara Walters on '20/20.' She called ABC and was given the phone number of Lena, a Romanian woman who had been interviewed on the program. Lena lived in New Jersey and was helping Americans adopt Romanian orphans.

"With Lena's help, Sarah and her husband, Lenny, traveled to Romania and visited several orphanages and hospitals. No one in the family knew a thing about it. It was the summer of 1990. Lena took them under her wing; she just loved my cousin. She took them all over the country. Sarah hoped to find two babies to adopt. But at some point during the trip she realized that she felt more drawn to the three- and four-year-olds; the number of orphans in this age group was staggering. Sarah and Lenny took photographs of dozens of children. They were particularly drawn to a little boy in one orphanage (who reminded them of Lenny's brother) and a little girl in another orphanage."

By late autumn Sarah and Lenny had adopted the little girl and brought her to the United States; at Thanksgiving she was introduced to relatives, including Zachary and Hannah. In December Hannah went to a birthday party for Sarah's daughter, who was turning four. "During the party I looked through my cousin's photos of their trip to Romania," said Hannah. "I kept returning to one particular picture. It was of a little boy named Sasha, who lived in the same orphanage that Sarah's daughter had come from. I don't know what it was about this child; he touched something in me. I asked my cousin whether he was still available. She said she thought so and offered to ask Lena. I took some photos home to show Zachary.

"I said, 'Zach, look at these kids. Look at this little boy. I can't get him out of my mind.' Zachary looked at me like I had two heads!"

Zachary elaborated, "My first response was, 'Are you nuts? You want to fly to Romania and adopt a little boy you've never seen before? No way! We're not going to do this.' Hannah said, 'Fine. Okay. I'd really like to, though.' It was the smartest thing she could have done. She didn't push it. A few days later she brought the pictures out again. She pointed to the one of Sasha. 'Isn't he beautiful?' she asked. 'I really think that we should adopt him.' I told her, 'I'm not ready to adopt a child.'"

"I don't really take no for an answer very often," said Hannah. "I just let it sit. For me the thought of adopting Sasha grew to an all-encompassing desire. I became completely obsessed with him. I was dreaming about him . . . and at that time I didn't know anything about him. Then '20/20' did another program about Romanian orphans; I made Zach watch it with me. He was moved by the program. It was so touching. They took cameras inside the institutions and showed the children—there were so many children—strapped in their cribs, in horrible conditions. It was heart-rending. When the program finished Zach looked at me and said, 'Well, why don't you at least find out if Sasha's still available?'"

"Hannah changed my mind in a month," admitted Zachary. "Our discussions proceeded to the point where I was ready to look into it, but I didn't want to rush things. I felt a combination of emotions. First, I wanted to do it for Hannah. Second, I had always entertained the notion of adopting a child some day. I knew there were kids out there who needed homes and families. Third, I knew it was the right thing to do. I was thirty years old, and I can promise you I wasn't ready to become a parent. What really turned me around was that it was the right thing to do. I knew I wanted to have a son someday and realized this would be a challenge for me; it would push me to grow up. Actually, there were a lot of different reasons, and Sasha's picture didn't hurt! His smile was amazing."

Hannah called Lena's home. Her husband told her that Lena was back in Romania, but he invited Zach and Hannah to drive to New Jersey to discuss their interest in Sasha. "I needed a lot of assurances," said Zachary. "After we met Lena's husband I insisted on calling Lena in Romania. I asked her, 'Are we going to be able to see Sasha? Has he been cleared for adoption? And are you going to be there for us when we fly into Bucharest?' She answered yes to all of my questions. Lena explained that Sasha was already one of her kids; she had pre-adopted Sasha, along with several other children, and was busy sorting through paperwork in preparation for their adoptions. She assured us that Sasha had tested negative for HIV and hepatitis B and that his birth parents had signed a release freeing him for adoption."

Hannah continued, "Lena's husband gave us information about adopting in Romania, what documentation we needed, and about the home study process in New York. My cousin told us that Lena was a savvy, bright business lady; she had no legal expertise but she knew Romania inside and out. She knew how to get through their red tape. Things began to happen. It wasn't easy for Zachary. He was not as confident about this child as I was. He was worried about going to Romania; it was a pretty desperate place. It had only been a year since Ceausescu had been shot; the country was in turmoil.

"I understood all this, but I also felt strongly that we had to find Sasha, to see that he actually did exist. I needed the tangible reality of him. I remember Zachary begging me, 'Can't we just slow down and think about this for a while?' But I said, 'Now that we know this little boy is sitting over there in an orphanage, how can we take a couple of months to see how we feel? Two months is forever to a child! If we're going to do this we should go now.' Zach continued to be nervous, but I felt that I was being guided from above. I heard the child's voice, saw his expressions in my dreams.

"We made arrangements to travel to Romania in February; because the Gulf War was going on, Zach decided we would fly Swiss Air through Zurich. We were inoculated for hepatitis B, knowing that it was widespread in Romania. An independent social worker came to do our home study. I was nervous; it was difficult to be judged by a total stranger. But she was pleasant and it was relatively easy. Zachary was very cooperative. We got our paperwork finished and had it translated. Sasha's INS [Immigration and Naturalization Service] documents were in the pipeline before we left for Bucharest, but we'd been given no idea when they'd be completed. We hoped to spend a week with Sasha so we could get to know him. Zach worried about the Romanian bureaucracy. Lena had warned us that the situation was starting to get difficult over there; Romania was flooded with people trying to adopt children, and a crisis seemed inevitable."

Zach narrated, "After an exhausting flight we arrived in Bucharest in the middle of February. It was late afternoon, gray and dismal, freezing cold, an awful place. I was scared to death. Soldiers met the plane and

marched us across the tarmac. I was the last passenger in the line waiting to go inside the terminal. I noticed that one of the soldiers was staring
at me. He finally asked, 'Do you have any cigarettes?' I said sure and gave
him a pack. Lena had told us to bring lots of cigarettes.

"Inside we were asked where we'd be staying. I had no idea! Lena
was supposed to meet us, but she wasn't there. I started to get nervous,
but finally a man showed up to meet us. We stuffed our enormous duffel bags filled with toys, children's clothes, and medical supplies into his
tiny car. He told us we'd been invited to stay at Lena's apartment with
her. As he drove us through Bucharest I saw nothing beautiful, just concrete, cloudy skies, and dirty snow everywhere. It was a scary place. I
wondered if we could trust Lena."

Hannah explained, "We spent three anxious days in Bucharest waiting for Lena to finish up with some other people before she could take
us north to the orphanage where Sasha lived. We walked around, we ate,
we talked to other people who were trying to adopt. There seemed to be
hundreds of people waiting to see if they could get out of the country
with babies. It was a fury of baby seekers. People accosted us with questions: 'Are you adopting? Who is your liaison? Who's doing your legal
work?'

"After a while we didn't even want to speak English in front of anyone. We were embarrassed by the behavior of these people. I felt angry
knowing there were so many beautiful older children, and most people
cared only about the babies. We learned that people were paying nurses
in hospital corridors for information about newborn babies. It was unbelievable. Zach and I felt extremely uncomfortable when we realized what
was going on."

Zachary elaborated, "Lena seemed overwhelmed. It wasn't just us she
was helping; she was juggling several other parents as well. I felt she was
out of control; she was trying to do everything herself. I worried that she'd
never get around to taking us up to see Sasha."

Hannah had promised her cousin, Sarah, that they'd check on the little boy she and Lenny had found on their first trip to Romania. Despite
her overwhelming desire to see Sasha, Hannah insisted they take care of
her cousin's boy first. "After all, we wouldn't even be here if it weren't
for Sarah," she said. So before they went to see Sasha, Zach and Hannah
went off with Lena and her driver in a different direction to visit the

little boy and to try to expedite his adoption on Sarah and Lenny's behalf.

"We drove out of Bucharest in a dense fog at five-thirty in the morning," said Hannah. "Lena called the area we were driving through Gypsy Land. Odd-shaped trees loomed over the icy roads, and high snowbanks created a narrow passage for the driver to negotiate. We saw horse-drawn carriages and wagons laden with people and goats. The houses had a Turkish look about them, with strange columns and shapely arches painted in a variety of colors. It was a real adventure! Along the way the driver had to stop to change a flat tire. We prayed that the other tires would hold out because in Romania if you can't change a tire yourself, you have to abandon your car."

Zach continued, "There was only one kind of car in Romania, and none of them worked! We arrived at a city in western Romania just after noon. I thought it was awful. This probably had more to do with my state of mind, but it was not a pretty place. The people looked mean and very strange. When we checked into our hotel we found there were no light bulbs in our room, no soap, and no toilet paper! On top of that, the towels were dirty. I went down to the front desk to complain, but no one spoke English. I realized that Hannah was very unhappy; she was on edge. When I got back to our room she had opened one of the packages of cigarettes we'd brought along and was smoking. Neither of us smokes, but I joined her!

"Later that afternoon we went to visit the orphanage where the little boy lived. It wasn't as terrible as I had anticipated, but still it was pretty bad. It had concrete floors. The only room they let us see was the playroom. I thought the child looked sickly."

Hannah continued, "The child wasn't afraid of us, but he didn't speak. He was wearing mismatched sneakers with no laces; they were on the wrong feet. He was clean but had a skin rash. I held him for a few minutes and gave him little presents that Sarah had sent with us. The orphanage wasn't horrible, just deprived of warmth and comfort. Its bare, institutional feeling overwhelmed us. I went with Lena to pick up the boy's birth parents for a court appearance. While we waited for them to come out to the car, a dozen Gypsies stood around staring at us; they came toward the car, crowded around the windows, and reached out their hands. We gave them gum and candy. As we drove away, the ones who didn't get anything screamed and pounded on the car. My heart was racing."

Despite Lena's best efforts, the local bureaucrats refused to expedite the little boy's paperwork. Zach and Hannah were forced to spend another night there before appearing in court on behalf of Sarah and Lenny; however, the next day they were successful and finally able to shift their focus to Sasha.

"We drove twelve hours to travel three hundred miles," explained Zach. "The roads were in terrible condition—icy and full of potholes. We had another flat tire, which the driver quickly replaced. One other problem with the car was that it had no windshield wipers, and for a while the driver had to stop every ten minutes to wipe off the windshield and headlights. I didn't feel that we were going to die or that our lives were in peril, but I was full of anxiety. I thought, *We're never going to get to see this kid!*"

Hannah continued: "Zachary and I tried to be supportive of each other during the long drive, but it was hard for us to be at someone else's mercy. We finally pulled into the little town at eight o'clock at night. Instead of checking into a hotel, we went straight to the orphanage. Lena felt that if we had to wait even five more minutes we'd explode. When we got to the orphanage the person in charge told us that all the children were asleep. Lena knew the director and called her at home; she gave permission for Sasha to be brought down to us. We finally, finally, got to see him! Our sleepy little boy barely resembled the tan, smiling face we had stared at for two months in Sarah's photograph. His hair was darker, and since it was six months later, he'd lost his baby looks and appeared older than we had expected.

"The woman holding him said, 'Here are your Momma and Poppa. They came to see you.' I was completely overcome; it was such a relief to abandon all my anxiety. It was incredible to look at this living, breathing, warm little boy and know that he was going to be ours! Sasha reached his arms out to me. The feeling was unbelievable. The woman holding him began to cry when she put Sasha in my arms. He felt heavy and solid. The shock of feeling him and hearing him whisper 'Momma' and his expression of intelligent understanding made me wonder what he thought of us and whether he approved. I felt dizzy. He was just perfect!"

"The reason Sasha got adopted was his personality," said Zach. "He was so happy, outgoing, and unselfconscious. Without words we knew he was saying, *Hi! How are you? Here I am! I'm Sasha! I love life!* That's him . . . and that's probably why his picture was taken; that's what caught our eye. When Hannah put him down I got down on one knee and held out my arms. He said, 'Poppa!' and ran and jumped into my arms. It felt like he was saying, *Where have you been for four years, Dad? I've been waiting for you!* It was instant love. My pockets were full of matchbox cars and lollipops for him. Hannah gave him a bracelet with our pictures on it. When it was time to leave, I didn't want to go.

"I had a hard time sleeping that night. What I really wanted to do was go to a bar! It had been one of those days—a long, tiring drive culminating in this incredibly emotional meeting."

"I felt like a mother right away," Hannah admitted. "It was amazing to me, because I'd had such fear. I was thirty-three and I had become the instant parent of a four-year-old. I didn't know anything about raising a child, and it had all happened so quickly! I'd had only a few months to prepare myself mentally for the concept of motherhood. But Sasha made it so easy. He was perfect in every way. I couldn't wait for the next day so we could see him again.

"When we arrived back at the orphanage, the children were just finishing lunch. We peered through lace curtains into the cafeteria and saw over one hundred three- and four-year-olds eating from metal plates. The sight of so many young children on their own in the world broke my heart. Soon Sasha came marching out with his group. He signaled the kids to follow him over to us and seemed proud and happy to show us off. He pulled out the matchbox cars Zach had given him; on his wrist, already broken and disassembled, was the bracelet with our pictures on it.

"Lena persuaded the director of the orphanage to allow Sasha to stay with us at our hotel for two nights. Sasha fell asleep in the taxi on the way to the hotel. When Zach opened the taxi door, Sasha woke up and started to cry. He must have thought Zach was going to leave him again. It was touching. I thought, *This is true love!* In the lobby, Sasha seemed a bit frightened and started rocking back and forth and crying a bit. The rocking tore our hearts out; we knew this was typical behavior for institutionalized children and were reminded that during his four years of life Sasha hadn't received enough love and attention.

"When we got to our room we changed him into new clothes and sneakers. He was very independent and wanted to dress himself. He got a big kick out of combing his hair and brushing his teeth. He seemed to love the taste of the toothpaste and giggled when I tried to brush the back ones for him. His teeth were beautiful and even but not very well cared for.

"We took him out to eat and he was a perfect little gentleman. He behaved so politely and ate carefully and neatly, smiling all the time. The waitress teased him, and he laughed and shook his finger at her. I thought his gestures were funny and sweet. Zach and I were as delighted as Sasha was when the waitress brought him an ice cream soda as a special surprise.

"Before bed I tried to give him a bath. He cried hysterically, 'No bai!' But he was happy to let me bathe him while he stood at the sink on a stool. Afterward he played with our cassette player and put all his books and cars next to him like a little squirrel. Sasha piled everything up neatly just like he'd found it and finally fell asleep at about nine o'clock. Zach and I ate in the room and watched our perfect little boy sleep like an angel."

Zach continued, "Our room had two single beds pushed together. We let Sasha sleep between us. Hannah and I kept leaning over to give him kisses. I woke up once in the night. It was pitch-black. I thought, *Where am I? Wasn't there a little boy sleeping between us?* Sasha had slipped down between the beds and was sound asleep on the floor! I scooped him up and put him back in bed. He slept restlessly and kicked a lot."

"Sasha seemed happy when he woke up; he immediately brought all his new toys into bed and played with them until it was time for breakfast," said Hannah. "We were fascinated by his intelligence and wit. At breakfast he displayed perfect manners and charmed the waitress. Afterward we put a new winter coat on him and went out for a walk together. He squealed with pleasure when we swung him off the ground between us. He repeated everything we said and kissed me whenever I asked.

"Lena and her assistant, Casimira, came to have lunch with us at the hotel. They told us they were impressed with Sasha's manners. He sat at the table for two hours and didn't make a single complaint. Before we got up to leave, Lena asked Casimira to explain to Sasha that he'd stay with us for one more night and then we'd have to take him back to the orphanage, assuring him that very soon we'd come back to take him home with us. Tears welled up in Casimira's eyes when she finished talking to Sasha. He nodded that he understood. Sasha was fine; he had no tears."

"I felt confident that we'd be able to adopt him," said Zach. "After following Lena around for a week I realized she knew how to get through the system in Romania. I had been wearing a money belt containing thousands of dollars in cash. It was all for Lena; she took care of the distribution. I gave it to her that evening. We bribed a lot of people there, not with money but with cigarettes, candy, gum, and cosmetics. Bribing, in that situation, was not even a moral judgment for me. We simply wanted to make people happy so they wouldn't make things difficult for us. Lena had brought a computer for the director of Sasha's orphanage. The director allowed Sasha to come out with us for two days. That's supposed to be against the rules, but Lena knew how to make things work there."

"As the day passed, the idea of leaving Sasha loomed above us and weighed us down," admitted Hannah. "Every time I thought of being without him my eyes burned."

Zach continued, "It was obviously dramatic to have to take this little boy back to the orphanage after spending two days with him. I felt very protective of Hannah and worried about her—more so than about myself. When we first went to Romania I didn't feel any pressure. My life wasn't dependent on whether we had a child. But after we met him the pressure started to build inside me. I was anxious about the paperwork and worried whether things would work out so we could adopt him.

"Sasha fell asleep in my arms while we were driven to the orphanage. It was very hard to leave him, to say good-bye to him. By the time we dropped Sasha off I was getting to the point of very high anxiety. I feared we might never see Sasha again, and I was increasingly nervous about Hannah."

"When Lena said good-bye to Sasha she reassured him that we would come back soon and take him to America," said Hannah. "Then she said, 'Sasha, when you miss your Momma and Poppa you can kiss their pictures on your bracelet.' He said he would and demonstrated his understanding by kissing our pictures. He was smiling. It was obvious that he was happy to be back at the orphanage, and that made us feel so much better about leaving him there. After all, it was the only home he knew. We went inside; Sasha hugged us and then sauntered into the director's office. He was so proud of his new sneakers and coat. He was fine . . . so beautiful, happy, energetic, and healthy. I knew he would be okay there for another month or so. The director of the orphanage took his hand,

and Sasha proudly walked down the corridor taking our hearts along with him. Zach and I were in tears. I sobbed in the car; I was a mess. We missed Sasha already."

"Immediately the pressures of traveling took over," said Zach. "Flying in Romania was quite an adventure. We were on a big old two-prop plane, divided into two sections; smoking was on the left side and nonsmoking on the right! I noticed that one of the stewardesses was smoking! It was bizarre. But we made it back to Bucharest in time to catch our flight to Zurich."

While Zach and Hannah were en route to Switzerland, Lena went to court and successfully completed Sasha's adoption for them. They talked with her from their hotel that night. She said, "Congratulations! You're the momma and poppa of a little boy!" Zach suggested to Hannah that they celebrate by going out to dinner in Zurich. "We were so excited," said Hannah. "It was the ultimate confirmation. I can't remember what we ate. It had been such a blur and we were exhausted. We called Zach's parents. They said they were so proud of us and that it was a great thing we were doing."

Zach added, "My parents were enthusiastic. I'd told them about Sasha only a week or two before we left for Bucharest. I was apprehensive; I thought they'd think it was a crazy thing to do, irrational, irresponsible. And of course they didn't. They responded appropriately."

"When we got home I started to get a room ready for Sasha," said Hannah. "We owned two studio apartments that we'd made into a duplex. It had a little garden in the back and stairs to the second floor. We converted a small study into Sasha's room. We bought a little bed, bedding, clothes, and books; friends and family gave us lots of other things for him. Sarah and I talked on the phone almost every day. We were both so excited."

"We had a huge problem with the INS in New York City," said Zach. "It's still hard for me to talk about it, because the woman I had to deal with there was absolutely the meanest in the world. She just didn't care! I met with her several times, begged her to speed things up. She held the key. The problem was that our fingerprints had already been sent to the FBI, and this woman refused to expedite their return. I became like a maniac. I waited outside this woman's office, and once I went in the back way. I had on a suit and tie, so nobody bothered me. She screamed, 'What are you doing in my office?' Another time Hannah came with me and started crying when this woman rebuffed us yet again. We began to fear that we'd never get Sasha.

"Lena phoned to tell us that the adoption frenzy in Romania was beginning to spin out of control. I called [Senators] D'Amato's and Moynihan's offices. Their staffers told us we should have expedited our fingerprints, and since we hadn't we'd just have to wait for them to go through the system. The situation was horrendous. A friend at work kept telling me that this would all pass and I'd soon have my son. But I'm not someone who anticipates: I'm a Red Sox fan! I thought, *No, I won't believe it's true; not until Sasha's home and in my hands. And once we've got him, nobody's going to take him away!*

"Then Hannah came up with a brilliant idea. We had our fingerprints taken again, and she had them shipped overnight to the FBI in Washington, D.C., herself. Within two days we got them back!"

Hannah continued, "I called Lena and told her to get the kids ready. I planned to bring my cousin's little boy back with me, too. It hadn't even been a month since we'd come home. I was actually still a bit jet-lagged when I flew back to Bucharest! At the last minute Sarah's husband decided to come with me. Lenny had only an Israeli passport, and this was a bit risky because of the Gulf War, but he insisted on coming along.

"When we arrived in Bucharest, a car and driver were waiting for us. I looked inside and saw Sasha and his new cousin sleeping in the back seat. The driver took us to a hotel. Sasha seemed a little confused when he saw Lenny instead of Zach. But he seemed to get a real kick out of the other boy. They were fast friends already. All the new clothes we had given Sasha were missing. He was back in his orphanage gear. Luckily I had brought more new clothes with me.

"The next day was Sasha's fourth birthday. I bought some pastries and candles, and we had a little party in our hotel room. Later we took the boys down to dinner. A band was playing in the dining room. After the meal I took Sasha's hand and walked onto the dance floor. I picked him up and danced with him. He was delighted; people were smiling at us. When I tucked him into bed that night, I realized it was probably the first birthday party he'd ever had.

"Our three days in Bucharest were hectic. Lena talked to us on the phone and guided us through the bureaucracy. The boys had to have checkups and we had to pick up their passports. It was difficult, but we got everything done. The important thing was that the boys were with us; everything else was a blur.

"This time we flew on Air India, and our flight took us back through London. One of my sisters lived there, and I had planned to spend a week with her before taking Sasha home to New York. Unfortunately, I didn't know ahead of time that Sasha would need a visa to enter England. At Heathrow Airport there was a big fuss about Lenny's Israeli passport and the two boys with no visas. Lenny got the immigration officials into a big uproar. At one point I was terrified that they were going to send the boys back to Romania; they wouldn't let us in, and they didn't let us pass through to get on a flight to the States. I tried to calm Lenny down, but he was out of control. Finally the officials gave us emergency twenty-four-hour visas and allowed us to leave. My sister and her husband were anxiously waiting for us. They dropped Lenny and his son off at an airport hotel, and drove us to their home in London.

"The next morning the problem with Lenny's passport continued. Immigration officials wouldn't let him get on a flight to New York. Lenny caused another commotion. I said, 'Lenny, I'm taking the two boys. If we don't get them out of here today, we're going to be in limbo. You get back when you can.' I was really upset. You can't have an arrogant attitude with immigration people. Lenny was responsible for himself, but I wasn't going to take a chance with my cousin's son.

"The boys were great on the flight. Sasha seemed to enjoy my cousin's boy; he was sweet with him, completely animated. Every time one of the boys had to go the bathroom the other one decided he needed to as well! It wasn't a big problem; we were in business class and the stewardesses were helpful. The difficult part was at Kennedy Airport in New York. Getting through immigration with two newly adopted boys and dragging all of our suitcases, strollers, and so on, was a nightmare. Nobody wanted to help me. The boys were tired and cranky. It took over an hour to get through. We sat, we waited, we stood in line; the security systems were still in war mode. After they finally waved us through, I put all our luggage on a big cart and sat the two boys on top of it. When I pushed them through the door I spotted Zach; he was waiting for me with a group of friends. I was so relieved! I said, 'Get me out of here!'"

Zachary noted, "I was actually quite sick. I had a high fever and felt dazed. Sasha called me Poppa and then fell asleep immediately!"

"Sasha walked into our apartment and was completely at home!" said Hannah. "For the first five minutes our dog frightened him, but they quickly became friends. Sasha was jet-lagged and a little confused, but he slept pretty well the first night.

"My company had no policy on adoption. I had already used up ten vacation days on the two trips to Romania. I begged, borrowed, and stole some more time off so I could be with Sasha at home. Everyone at my office was sympathetic, but the situation was political. They said if they made an exception for me, it would set a new precedent. I thought, *How am I going to do this?* Luckily the YMCA near our apartment had a nursery school. The director was a kindhearted older woman who told me she had come to the United States during wartime as a little girl. She welcomed Sasha warmly. The nursery school seemed friendly and well run. On his first day I was supposed to stay in Sasha's classroom for a couple hours so he could settle in, but soon after we arrived he told me I should go. He was happy. He wanted to pass out the juice and joined right in.

"Once we brought Sasha home, Zach and I had a new relationship . . . a new life. The transition was hard for Zachary. We had no idea what the responsibilities of marriage were yet, let alone of parenthood. Neither of us was very mature in our marriage. Sasha's arrival caused a lot of tension between us. It was quite trying; there was a lot of push-pull going on. I felt protective of Sasha and thought Zach was too strict. We experienced a lot of conflict in the beginning, especially the first few months. Sasha was never the worse for wear, however. He was never in any situation where he didn't feel inundated with love and affection from us, from cousins, aunts, uncles, and grandparents. The problem was between Zach and me. There were so many new things we had to decide together about raising this child.

"It took Sasha only about two months to learn to speak English fluently. At one point I set up a meeting with a Romanian man so Sasha could hear his own language again. I thought that was important for him, and I also wanted the man to explain a few things to Sasha that I was having trouble making him understand. The man was sweet and there was nothing off-putting about him, but when he began to speak in Romanian Sasha became frightened. Maybe it brought back painful memories. I wanted the man to explain to Sasha that Zach was going away on a business trip but that he would come back in a few days. I was worried that Sasha would feel we'd been deserted. I'm not sure whether he listened carefully enough to take that in."

Zach admitted, "My reaction to having Sasha in our home was not completely positive. When I first met Hannah I was living by myself with a dog in the middle of Vermont. I went from almost total isolation to living with Hannah, a dog, and four cats in a small apartment in New York City; suddenly there was a little boy with us as well. I thought I was going to go over the edge! There was a lot of tension.

"I never second-guessed it; I certainly never entertained the idea that I should undo it somehow or that I should leave Hannah. But I was miserable. When Sasha first came I was thrilled to have him. But our apartment felt overcrowded and our lives had changed overnight."

"It took about two years for everything to calm down and fall into place," admitted Hannah. "We had a lot of issues to resolve while becoming a family. I guess for every new father there is the sudden realization, *Now I have to share you with another person.*

"Zach came from an affectionate family; being affectionate with Sasha was easy for him. My family wasn't particularly affectionate, but after becoming a mother it felt completely natural to lavish affection on Sasha. The first year he wanted to be held all the time. After constantly carrying him around for a few months, I had to go to a chiropractor.

"As soon as his English was good enough, Sasha began to ask questions about being adopted. The first one was, 'Did I come from you?' He was still only four years old but was, in some ways, like an old soul. I told him the whole story about seeing his photograph and falling in love with him. At one point he asked, 'Why didn't my parents want me?' I explained that Romania was such a poor country that a lot of parents couldn't take care of their children; that the best thing parents could do was to let their children be cared for in orphanages. He absorbed what I said and seemed satisfied with my explanation.

"Sasha is nine years old now, and Zach and I are expecting a new baby in a few months. For years Sasha had been begging us to have a brother or sister for him. He loves to be with other children. Truthfully, if he were our only child Zachary and I would be content. But since I came from a big family, the thought of Sasha being an only child bothered me. By the time I was thirty-eight, Zach and I had decided that we'd better try before it was too late. After we knew the pregnancy was viable, Zach and I sat down with Sasha to tell him.

"Zach said, 'Sasha, we have some really exciting news.' Sasha looked at him expectantly. 'What would you like more than anything in the world?' 'A new skateboard?' responded Sasha. 'How about a brother or sister?' asked Zach. Sasha looked at me in astonishment and said, 'Mom, you made a baby?'

"He was so excited! He just couldn't believe it. A neighbor of ours had had a baby recently, and someone in our building asked Sasha if he heard the baby crying. He replied, 'Not much, but when I do it's music to my ears.' He's an incredible kid! I've never met a kid like him; he's the light of our lives.

"Now that I'm pregnant, Sasha has started asking a lot more questions about his adoption. He told me he feels embarrassed that he didn't come from my tummy. I told him I believe that children who were adopted are the luckiest kids there are. He asked why. I explained, 'Most people who want to *can* have a baby, and some people have babies they don't even want. But people who adopt a child have to want that child so much and go through so much to get him that there can never be any doubt that the child is loved.'

"I tell people there is nothing more satisfying or joyful than adoption. I'm more proud of adopting Sasha than of anything I've done in my life. It still amazes me that we managed to get there and do it! When I think how short the period of time was—from my first reaction to Sasha's photograph in December to bringing him home in March—I have no idea how it all happened so fast. It was just miraculous. It was meant to be."

Zach related, "I picked Sasha up from school one day recently and said, 'Let's go to the movies, Sasha.' He smiled and said, 'Great!' As we were walking across Eighth Avenue, Sasha put his arm around me and said, 'I love you so much, Daddy. I love you more than my birth father.' I chuckled to myself, because I knew that Sasha had no memories of his birth father. But I said, 'That's nice, son.'

"If I were Sasha, I'd want to go back and visit Romania. I told him we'll take him back when he's older. We know the village where his birth mother lives. We could probably find her if he wants to. Romania was so devastated when we were there. I hope it will improve. I think we should take Sasha in the summer; the winter was so cold and dark. The Carpathian

Mountains are gorgeous, and there are some great places to see there. I want Sasha to be proud of who he is and where he came from.

"I think his adoption sets Sasha apart in a good way. He's an extra-ordinary kid; he's got more self-confidence than I had at his age. He's more comfortable with himself, too. I find him amazing. He's a happy kid who's comfortable with his body; he's a good gymnast. I don't have any fears about Sasha. He's clearly a survivor. He always says, 'Go ahead, Dad. I'll be fine.' Sasha's a born leader; all the kids love him. He'll be great with the baby. Hannah and I have been blessed with this boy."

Hannah concluded, "People say, 'You're so lucky that you got such a great kid!' They're right! It's all fate; I'm a great believer in fate. I always have been. Everything in my life has happened this way. I have strong beliefs. I have no doubt that God led me to this child."

3/ Gina and Tom
Two miracle babies

"Our adoption agency's policy was that you couldn't adopt if you were pregnant. But we didn't know if this pregnancy was viable; none of the other six had been. So we decided not to tell them. There was no doubt in our minds (although I certainly would have convinced my wife otherwise if she'd had a fit of honesty) that we were just going to keep our mouths shut and play it straight through."

IT'S NOT uncommon to hear of a couple who have adopted a child only to find out that their long-awaited pregnancy has finally occurred. In fact, this happens in only about five percent of adoptions, but it's a phenomenon that gets a good deal of attention. The difficulties that Gina and Tom experienced in trying both to give birth and to adopt made having two babies arrive within a few months of each other seem like a fitting reward for them.

Tom is a tall, trim man, casual yet confident; his conversation is permeated by an appealing dry wit. "I'm one of four kids," he volunteered. "I had an unemotional Irish upbringing. My family is warm but not fuzzy. Everyone gets along wonderfully, and no one has moved away. We all live in the San Francisco Bay area. None of the four married siblings has gotten divorced. We've each had two to four kids, my parents are healthy, they've had decent success in business, and they live a comfortable life."

Gina is fine-boned with dark hair and large, dark eyes; she is intense, astute, and delightfully sincere. "I grew up in a small town in northern California," she related. "I'm completely Italian—second generation—from a traditional household. I was the second of four children; my parents were always very hardworking people. My grandmother lived with us and provided the stability we needed. I went to the public school behind our house and came home for lunch with my grandmother. I was always afraid she would die alone. I was extremely close to her. I still am. Noni is now ninety-eight years old.

"Later I went to a small Catholic college near home because they gave me a scholarship. After two years I transferred to a college in San Francisco. I majored in accounting, even though I hated it, because I thought it was a safe bet that I could get a job when I got out of school. In my first year out of school—1978—I made more money than my dad.

"Tom was in my class. I was very impressed by his comments to the professors; Tom had no fear and always had something worthwhile to say. He was tall and good-looking, but he wore a strange coat, and I thought he looked homeless! I ran into him a few months after graduation while walking to my apartment in San Francisco. He was sitting at a little side-walk cafe with a girl. I said, 'Hello, aren't you Tom?' and he said, 'Do I know you?' I told him we'd been at school together and that was that. Two weeks later I saw him sitting there again (with a different girl), and we said hello again."

Tom recalled, "I called a mutual friend and said, 'Who is this girl, and how do I get in touch with her?'"

"He called me at work and wanted to know if I would go to the symphony with him that night," said Gina. "I told him, 'I can't. I guess I should tell you, I'm engaged.' I was actually in the process of breaking off my engagement to someone I'd gone out with for five years. A month later, Tom called me at home and said, 'I was wondering if we could have dinner tonight.' I thought, *This is an impulsive guy!* I said, 'I really can't answer that question right now; do you think you could call me back in an hour?' At that very moment my ex-fiancé was in my apartment moving his things out! Later when Tom called me back I finally agreed to have dinner with him.

"On the way to dinner we got into a minor car accident, and I immediately started crying. I said, 'I'm really sorry. Maybe you should just take me home. I feel like my life is under a black cloud right now.' He said,

'You know, Gina, I don't believe in things like that. Let's just go have dinner!' We got married four years later.

"Tommy is a very aggressive, determined, and focused guy. He was in real estate development when I met him. I had no idea what that was; the only thing I knew about real estate was the agents you used when you moved. But no one in my world ever moved—you bought a house and stayed in it until you died! He had huge dreams and believed in giving credibility to those dreams. He was the exact opposite of my father in every way."

Tom said, "One of the things I was most attracted to in Gina was her openness and emotions; my mother didn't show her emotions. This quality of Gina's was something new to me, and I liked it."

Gina and Tom planned their wedding for May 1983. On the day before their wedding Gina experienced severe abdominal pains. Tom explained, "I have a specific memory of talking to Gina on the phone that day. She called me from her doctor's office. He was advising her to postpone our wedding because he'd discovered a large ovarian cyst that he thought was ready to burst. My reaction was a combination of feelings; I was crushed, disappointed, sad, and worried. After all, we were about to be married and go off on our honeymoon!

"Gina said she wanted to go ahead with the wedding. She negotiated with her doctor that she would limit herself to just one dance at the reception. We asked a doctor guest of ours to bring along his black bag just in case. We had a brilliant day, wonderful weather, and everyone had a lot of fun. I have no sense that our wedding day was at all hampered by Gina's physical condition—and all of that credit goes to her! However much pain she was in, she just smiled and enjoyed her day. The next morning I took her to the hospital."

"During that surgery part of one ovary was removed," continued Gina. "After that I expected that having children would be difficult for me."

Tom said, "We did not try to have children for about three years into our marriage. Gina got pregnant in 1986 and had an early miscarriage."

"That was no big deal," she remembered. "I'm a pretty resilient person and I just thought, *Next! We'll move on from here.*" Gina got pregnant again a year later, but it was ectopic. "I had to have surgery and it was scary," she said. "I was in agony!

"Two and a half months later I was in pain again. I thought, *I can't believe this, but it feels like another ectopic pregnancy!* At that point I owned a small restaurant. I called my staff and said something I never say, 'I need some space today; I'm going to go shopping for a couple of hours.' I went to Saks Fifth Avenue (I never go to Saks Fifth Avenue!), and I was getting dizzy from the pain, so I asked a clerk to get me a chair. She said they didn't have one! I told her if she didn't get me a chair I was going to fall over. She got me one! I sat there for about five minutes and then drove myself to the hospital. By this time I was out of my mind with pain. I got to the parking lot, and the guy said, 'No, lady, there's no room!' I threw my keys at him. 'You can have my car!' I met my doctor in the emergency room and had surgery again on the same side. That was not fun! Tommy was pretty upset."

"Gina is a very determined person," said Tom. "It's not her worst trait, but I've tried to encourage some moderation in her. Driving herself to the hospital when she had that kind of pain and was in that kind of danger. Ectopic pregnancies can be fatal! It's not cookbook surgery, it's major; she was in the hospital for about a week. At that point having a baby was obviously going to be a bigger issue. It was getting to be pretty discouraging.

"My reactions to all the unsuccessful pregnancies were considerably more muted—certainly externally—than Gina's. It's not that I was trying to hide it; I just don't emote. I don't ever want to concentrate on the bad. I'd think, *Okay, the bad just happened, now how do we get better?* But there came a point where I got concerned not about starting a family but about the health of my wife—my life partner."

Gina's doctor told her, "I can't say that you'll never have a child, but your organs function rather strangely."

"After that I started to see a fertility specialist," said Gina. "I started to bring up the idea of adoption at that time, but Tommy wanted to have nothing to do with it. He said, 'Look, I don't want to adopt. We have a long way to go before I think we need to be in the adoption mode.'"

Tom elaborated: "To me, choosing to adopt meant accepting the failure of having our own child. And accepting failure is not something I'm very good at or willing to do without more fighting. I was a resister, and that caused a fair amount—if not the most amount—of friction that we've ever had in our marriage. I was against adoption, but I'm sure the way I was delivering it to Gina was, 'Let's just wait—let's keep on trying.' Of course, it was her body that was taking the punishment . . . and her mind. She takes everything more to heart and is more emotional about things. She's Italian—God bless her!"

Despite Tom's attitude, Gina started to call adoption agencies. She explained, "Initially I thought an international adoption would be preferable to a domestic one, because then the whole issue of 'does that baby look like you?' goes away. Friends of ours had adopted two Korean children, and I thought they were the most beautiful children I had seen in my life. But Tommy was just not into it—he's an absolute and complete optimist, and he was not ready to accept that he wasn't going to give birth to an heir. A lot of tension was building up because I thought Tommy was not interested in starting a family. I said, 'What's the difference between pursuing infertility treatment and pursuing adoption? Let's talk about starting a family; let's not talk about how it happens. Are we interested in having a family now or are we interested in giving birth now? Because for me, it doesn't really matter.'"

While the debate continued, Gina switched to a well-known fertility specialist, who told her that she was a good candidate for in vitro fertilization because she obviously was able to get pregnant. He prescribed a course of daily injections.

"A nurse showed me how to give Gina the shots," said Tom. "I was incredibly nervous about it, but it turned out to be quite easy. It goes on for thirty days, so you get used to it. There was one funny incident. I had had a couple of drinks, and when we went home it was time for her shot. To give the shot you pulled the serum up into a vial through a thick needle; then you took that thick needle off, threw it away, and put a thin needle on to do the injection. On that day I forgot to take off the thick needle. Gina looked down and saw this needle—which must have looked like a fire hose—about to go into her! Then she looked at me and said, 'Hey, pal, how about sobering up just enough before you shoot that into me!' We'll probably always giggle about that.

"We finished the series of shots and went through the in vitro procedure. I remember one lazy Sunday when we were alone at home waiting to hear if Gina was pregnant. The phone rang, and I picked it up. I heard the nurse from the clinic say, 'It didn't take.' I remember the disappointment—the feeling of failure was a tough, tough thing. It may be that this in vitro thing, being a collaborative effort, got me over the hump and able to say, 'Sure, I'll look into adoption. Let's walk through what needs to be done.'"

Gina knew a woman at her health club who had adopted two children. The children had come from private placement adoptions through two attorneys in San Rafael. Gina said, "We met the two attorneys, who explained that they had both adopted children, with their respective spouses, and had been through traumatic experiences with adoption agencies. So they decided to get into a legal practice doing adoptions only. The attorneys were kind and seemed to make the process less daunting for us. After talking with them, we decided to try a private adoption."

In the meantime Gina's fertility doctor told her, "I've just learned about a blood foundation in Los Angeles which is doing infertility research; I think your profile may match the kind of people they're looking for. They have a theory that women who have multiple miscarriages may be genetically so similar to their mates that when they get pregnant the fetus is not protected. So they inject you with your husband's white blood cells, and you then produce antibodies to protect your fetus.

"It sounded a bit like hocus-pocus to Tommy and me, but we were told there were no side effects, so we flew down there and did it," said Gina. That was in the summer of 1990.

"A month later our attorneys told us, 'We've been working with a family for four or five months, and they have just backed out on a young woman who is about to give birth in Oregon. We were wondering if you were interested.' We told them, 'Absolutely!' We quickly had to initiate a home study; we found an independent social worker and told her we needed to accelerate the process because there was a possibility of adopting a baby right away. We asked her if she could jam this through. I think from the social worker's point of view we were an easy couple to accommodate. We had been married for seven years, we were economically stable, we owned our own home, we were the right ages, and there were no problems with us. And we had gone through the infertility thing; she understood that we really wanted to be parents. So we completed the home study quickly."

Gina started having regular phone conversations with the birth mother, who was twenty years old and named Elaine. "It was terribly difficult the first time I called her," said Gina. "What do you say to a birth mother? I told her all about our problems having children and why we wanted to have a child so much. I asked her questions about how healthy she was and whether she smoked. She told me about her background and a little bit about the birth father. It was an uncomfortable conversation at the beginning. I remember having a tingling feeling on the back of my neck. I was afraid she wouldn't like me and say no. It was hard to imagine that all of a sudden we might have a baby. The reality that this process might actually work was astounding to me, just overwhelming and exciting.

"We talked to Elaine almost every day; the baby was overdue. All of a sudden we didn't hear from her for a couple of days, and then one of the attorneys called. He said, 'Elaine has had a baby girl, but she's not sure what she wants to do right now.' Tommy and I were devastated! It felt as though someone had died. It was the Fourth of July weekend, and we had friends visiting us."

Tom added, "The tension that was in the house! I remember our friends being as glum as we were. Finally the attorney called back and said, 'Elaine has decided to give the baby up for adoption but through an agency. Apparently she was recruited by someone while in the hospital.'"

"We were so upset!" said Gina. "All of a sudden we realized how naive we had been, that there was a weakness in the situation that we had no control over. We realized this was not going to be as easy as we had hoped. You just don't know everything that's going on, and that's one of the problems. We started to realize how out of control you are in a private adoption.

"If I knew then what I know now I would not have gotten involved in a situation where a family had backed out on a birth mother at the last minute. It's such an impossible decision for a young woman to make. She had found some haven of comfort and trust, and then the family had backed out on her. We were brought in to save the day, but in this young woman's mind there must have been the worry that this could happen again and she'd get stuck with the baby. What could she do? So she turned to an agency.

"Unfortunately, we felt she would have made a great decision had she chosen us as adoptive parents, but she didn't know that. We could have protected our emotions, our own fragile condition, by staying out of this situation. I was pregnant again and had another miscarriage that month. I had started to get physically tired of being pregnant."

Gina and Tom continued to work with their adoption attorneys, who advised them to place ads stating their desire to adopt a child in newspapers around the country. Gina said, "I liked the idea of a baby being born in Texas; I don't know why. We advertised a lot there. The attorneys gave us a list of every publication in the state. The list included the tiniest Texas town newspapers. I looked at a map and decided to choose places that were within an hour-and-a-half's radius of Dallas. I sort of got funny with the names. I loved the idea. I picked Temple, Texas, because my husband has a good friend from there; I thought, *There must be good stock in Temple.* You need to have a sense of humor about all this. We placed ads in Illinois, too. We ended up getting a birth mother on the line from Illinois.

"Her name was Adelle; she was twenty years old and not due for two or three months. She was nice, and the talks were much the same as with Elaine. But Adelle was better; she'd call me after she had visited her obstetrician and tell me how everything was going. She wasn't Catholic or even religious; she had simply denied her pregnancy until it was too late to get an abortion. Adelle was going to be induced, so we made plans to fly to Illinois. There was no commitment, nothing in writing; it was all hope. Our attorneys had been talking regularly with her as well. They're seasoned to hear things that might mean trouble, and they thought things were going fine with Adelle."

Tom remembered, "We got out there to a small Midwest hospital; we walked in late on a Friday afternoon while Adelle was waiting to be wheeled into the delivery room. I don't remember it as a particularly awkward meeting. Her mother and sister were there. They were pleasant and incredibly supportive. Adelle introduced us to the hospital staff. She said, 'Here are the parents!' A social worker assigned to the case held us by the hand as we got waltzed around. My feeling was that it was warm and very okay and the decision was made. Adelle was induced at about seven in the evening, and the social worker suggested that Gina and I go out for dinner. We were excited and spent the entire meal talking about what to name the baby.

"When we returned to the hospital they said, 'Congratulations, you have a girl!' We saw the baby through the nursery window. Gina was jumping out of her skin! We rushed back to our hotel to call our parents. As I was talking with them on the phone, pressure was building up inside me. I was thinking, *Oh, my God! We're this close! We're here. There's a baby. The baby's healthy. The birth mother says she is giving her to us . . .*"

Gina said, "When we walked with Adelle to the nursery the next morning, she wanted us to hold the baby. She asked us what we were going to name her, and I told her we'd chosen Catherine Nicole. Adelle said, 'My middle name is Nicole, too!' I thought, *The stars are aligned right here!* It was so exciting!"

Tom added, "We held the baby and fed her. We got instructions on folding and changing diapers. The hospital people were great. We met with a local attorney to get all the paperwork processed. He told us the surrender couldn't be signed until the following Friday and that we might as well go back to San Francisco. He said the baby would be put into a foster home; we couldn't have kept her with us in our hotel during that time, but we could have visited her at the foster home. I knew the pressure was building every time we were with the baby. There was a waiting period that we had to live with and that would drive us completely mad, especially if the rug were to be pulled out from under us. This was not because of anything specific that I saw, but because I'm someone who anticipates. Our investment in this child was growing exponentially, and six days is a long time. So I encouraged Gina that we go back home on Sunday, which is what we did."

Gina added, "The last day we were there we brought Adelle a lobster dinner, and the three of us ate in her hospital room together with the baby; everything was fine. Then we left and flew home."

Tom said, "Adelle was due to be released from the hospital the next day, Monday. I called the Illinois attorney from my office at noon on Monday to see if everyone was released, because that was an important point. Mother gets released and goes this way; baby gets released and goes that way. I asked, 'How did it go?' He paused, then said, 'There's been a problem, Tom. Adelle has changed her mind. The baby is going to be adopted by her sister.' I leaned forward and put my head between my knees as I felt the shock of what he'd just said. I didn't cry, but the pain was unbelievable! After a few minutes I sat up and tried to pull myself together because I knew that I had to tell Gina. Her restaurant was near my office."

Gina said, "I saw Tommy come around the corner and walk in. He said, 'Let's go outside for a second; I have bad news for you.' Once outside he said, 'We're not going to Illinois this weekend. Adelle has given the baby to her sister to adopt.' In a daze I stuck my head into the restaurant and told my staff I'd be back in a while."

"It was a beautiful October day," said Tom. "Gina and I hugged each other as we walked across the street to a park. We sat on a bench and I cried like a baby. I cried more than she did."

"Tommy and I were both struck with grief," said Gina. "We had met Adelle's sister. She had told us that she had an unreliable husband, several children of her own, and no money. That poor baby! I'm sure Adelle and her sister must have been talking about it. I don't think you decide to take a baby at the last minute. It was so traumatic for me! I blamed myself and said I shouldn't have left Illinois. I felt I had made a wrong choice. This was way too close for me. We'd spent three days with this baby! I told Tommy, 'We need to talk about this . . . I don't know if I could ever do this again.' I think Tommy and I both consider ourselves people of action who have a fair amount of control over our lives. We just instinctively want to solve problems; and this was the most hopeless feeling we'd ever had."

Shortly after this terrible loss, Gina had two more early miscarriages within a three-month period. "I was ready to look at adoption again," said Gina, "but we decided to use an adoption agency. The reason we came to that conclusion was that I couldn't expose myself anymore. I needed a buffer between my emotions and the reality of what could or could not happen. We hadn't used an agency before because I had a problem with spending thirty thousand dollars. It made me sad to think that a lot of people can't afford that kind of money to adopt a child. From a value standpoint, I had a hard time with that.

"I went to a therapist to talk it through. She said, 'Gina, you've been through several years now of unfortunate situations. Don't you think you've paid your dues and deserve to have things work out for you? The reality is that you have the money and other people don't. Does that mean you shouldn't adopt a child?' She helped me sort it out.

"We looked at two or three adoption agencies and then signed up with an agency that had been recommended by a friend. We were looking for a relatively quick route, and this agency was supposed to be fast. The director, Miriam, was a woman whose appearance was a mess; she was outrageously overweight and had a crazy mane of hair. She did not make you feel secure, because she didn't give off any sense of being pulled together. We told Miriam that we didn't care what it cost or what we had to do, but she should understand that we had been through a long and painful ordeal and needed to be protected. I was not comfortable with

Miriam, but Tommy said we should keep ourselves focused on the baby (Miriam said we could be parents in three to six months) and just put up with the situation."

"I thought Miriam was a wacko lady," said Tom, "but we were so beaten, so callused by what we had already gone through that her craziness was like background music to us. We had our eyes on the prize, and we would have put up with worse things than Miriam if we'd had to. We were getting very clear about what we wanted to accomplish and what we were willing to do. Our contact with Miriam was only for three or four sessions. We often dealt with other people at the agency; Miriam would occasionally flit into the room, sprinkle her pixie dust around, and go off to another room.

"My overall impression of the social workers we met in the adoption world was poor. We met social workers at several different agencies, and I didn't like these people. The industry of adoption seemed to be full of do-gooders. They think things should be done a certain way, and since they're in charge they're going to make sure you do it their way! After meeting the social workers, Gina and I would come out of some of these agencies, look at each other, and say, 'Oh, my God! How do these people get dressed in the morning?' It was a very unimpressive group of professionals; in fact, I'd say *professional* is a stretch of the word."

Gina continued, "Meeting Miriam turned out to be the beginning of an unruly and wild ride. We were able to use our old home study, so we started off okay. They found us a birth mother quite quickly, but a few weeks later Miriam called us and said she'd discovered that this birth mother was an intravenous drug user and had taken drugs early in her pregnancy. She recommended that we not work with her. We said, 'Absolutely! Thank you very much!' That was comforting. I was grateful; I felt that Miriam was doing her job."

Tom added, "We were relieved and disappointed at the same time. It seemed as though nothing was ever going to work for us. But I will give Miriam credit; she recognized that she was in a service business—a transaction business—and a customer relations business. She said, 'We're going to put you at the top of our list. We're going to salve your wounds very quickly.'"

"Miriam was definitely a wheeler-dealer," said Gina. "She owned apartments all over the area and put up birth mothers for the last trimester of their pregnancies. The agency's policy was that you'd meet with the birth mother before the baby was born. The first one had fallen through in early March. A month later Miriam called with the news that she had a birth mother in South Carolina. She wanted to know what we thought about that. I said, 'We need more details; what's going on?'

"Miriam said she would fly there (on our nickel). We asked her to stay in very close contact with us. But thirty-six hours later we still had no word from her! We had no idea where she was or what she was doing. When Miriam finally called, she told us that the baby had been born but that she hadn't met with the birth mother yet; she said she didn't know how things were going to turn out. I told her, 'Look, Miriam, we haven't spoken to you for thirty-six hours! This can't happen to us again; we are sitting here by the phone!' She got quite defensive. Then the same thing happened again; another day went by with no word from Miriam.

"She finally came back without the baby and called us into her office. She told us that while she was down there she was looking around for other birth mothers. I thought that sounded like a witch hunt! I told her it was unacceptable. I said, 'Your primary concern right now is Tom, me, and the baby. You shouldn't have been looking around; you should have been paying attention to us.'

"Miriam starting screaming at me. She accused me of being mentally unstable! I thought Tommy was going to reach across the room and choke her! She said she was going to have me thrown out of the agency; she was crazy! I don't know what happened to Tommy, but he ended up being the facilitator and calmed everybody down. Maybe it was one of those spiritual things where he knew he was hanging in there for the right reasons. I honestly don't know, because that is not in his nature."

"A few weeks later Miriam called to say that she had another birth mother, the perfect girl for us," said Tom. Her name was Cindy; she was twenty-one years old and from the Midwest.

When Gina and Tom met Cindy, they thought she was great. "The scary thing was that Cindy knew what a jerk Miriam was, and she told us a lot of things to confirm this from the other side," said Gina. "She told us about little lies Miriam told the girls, and that she charged us for taxi rides Cindy never took. But Cindy was such a doll; Tommy and I just loved her. When we met her I thought, *I don't care what Miriam does as long as I get Cindy's baby. It will all be worth it.* We spent a lot of time with her, and after our first meeting she told us, 'I think this agency is horrible, but I think you're great!' She loved Tommy! Cindy was an art student, so we took her out to places where she could sketch. She told us that the birth father had been her boyfriend since they were in junior high and that he was in his first year of medical school. She really loved him. I think if he had asked her to marry him, she would have done so in a second!"

Tom added, "Cindy was intelligent, a college student, very pretty, with wild blond hair and a great personality. We were thrilled. We had two or three long sessions with her. The purpose was to form a bond that would make the birth mother comfortable with us and continually comfortable with her decision, at least long enough to sign off and say good-bye. We went into it wanting to sell ourselves, but we could tell this woman was intelligent enough that a sales pitch wasn't required or appropriate. She made us feel comfortable.

"All the birth mothers we'd met seemed incredibly young. Here I was thirty-six years old, and I'd seen a bit of the world. These birth mothers all seemed to be from Nowhere, USA, and so innocent. We felt beholden to them, hopeful for them, sympathetic toward them—a great mixture of emotions."

Just before Cindy's due date Gina learned she was pregnant again. Tom said, "Our adoption agency's policy was that you couldn't adopt if you were pregnant. But we didn't know if this pregnancy was viable; none of the other six had been. So we decided not to tell them. There was no doubt in our minds (although I certainly would have convinced my wife otherwise if she'd had a fit of honesty) that we were just going to keep our mouths shut and play it straight through."

On a Monday afternoon, two-and-a-half weeks past Cindy's due date, the weather was incredibly hot and humid, and Gina was feeling anxious. The wait was becoming unbearable.

Tom remembered, "I was in the CFO's office at a hospital where I had done a large development, when I got a phone call from Gina telling me that I had a daughter. I turned and shared the news with everyone, waved good-bye, and headed for the hospital where Cindy had given birth. It was a small hospital, but driving up to it (knowing what was inside) made it seem like Versailles!"

When Gina and Tom walked into the hospital room, Cindy was in bed and the baby was near her in an isolette. Gina said, "I had a physical reaction when I saw the baby (similar to the way I'd felt in that Illinois hospital eight months before). I thought, *How do I control my feelings? Do I sell out?* My heart was pounding inside me, but a reality check was holding me back. The baby seemed quite tiny, and I was surprised that she had so much hair. She was lying on her side, sound asleep. Cindy invited me to hold the baby and give her a bottle. I picked her up, but I felt the baby was not mine yet, and I felt I was being intrusive. I was trying so hard to be respectful of the birth mother. This was not my child yet."

Tom said, "The feeling I remember when I first saw the baby was protectiveness, that the responsibility to take care of this baby was already mine. I felt like a father! I wanted to show how happy I was but it seemed inappropriate to express possessiveness in front of Cindy; it felt like I was tearing apart inside. It was as though we were onstage and knew we should not overact. We couldn't express our joy."

Gina continued, "When we went back the second day, Cindy was holding the baby and didn't offer to let Tom or me hold her during our visit," said Gina. "I started to feel that things were going in the wrong direction. I couldn't help having flashbacks to our time in Illinois. After four days, Cindy still hadn't signed the surrender. She was having a tough time. So we sat with her in the hospital. That's the way she wanted to do it; this situation illustrates our lack of control. You either get help from the agency or you don't; and then it's just you and the birth mother. That's the way it was; it was incredibly hard.

"Cindy wanted us to take the baby home, but she still hadn't signed the surrender and didn't plan to leave the state for another two or three days. We called our social worker and asked her to help us. Tommy said to her, 'Look, we'll pay for the baby to stay in intensive care, or we'll hire an army of private nurses and rent the top floor of the Ritz-Carlton, but we don't want to take this baby home without Cindy's signature on the surrender. We've been through too much.' And I'll never forget this; the social worker said to Tommy, 'If you two can't deal with this emotionally, then maybe you shouldn't be parents.' Tommy started to cry. It was the cruelest thing that anybody had ever said to us! We took the baby home. She was with us for two nights. We were completely numb."

Tom said, "I stayed home from work with Gina. It was still incredibly hot and wildly humid. I was both on cloud nine and nervous; the pressure was unbelievable. None of our family came to see the baby. I suspect both sets of parents and siblings sat in their houses holding their breaths and praying. They didn't ask us what they could do to help. They weren't going to add to our tension.

"When the first birth mother fell through on us it was a minor nick in one's soul. But back then we had no idea what minor and major was! We were hurt by it, but we were far away from the flame compared with when we went to Illinois and got completely burned. I'm in a business where we do deals, and this was a very big deal! The corollary of deals is that deals fall apart, even at the last minute when everything is written down; then there's no one you can blame because it gets sprinkled around. You can't grab anyone, and even if you can blame that very obvious person, you can't solve the problem by choking them (which is where, sometimes, your emotion is!). When a business deal falls apart, you get someone on the phone or in a meeting and start convincing him or her— or standing on your head! You offer the person more money or a compromise. But you can't do that in an adoption.

"The worst thing about adoption is that there are three parties to it— the birth mother, the child, and the adoptive parents. It's probably appropriate that we (as adoptive parents) are third in line in people's concern, but we always got the impression that we were twelfth in line. That's pretty disappointing. It was as if they thought we were incapable of being hurt or that it was okay to hurt us. Some sensitivity is required, because frankly the child isn't really in the game. The child is in the process of being passed around somewhere, and wherever the child ends up, chances are it works out for him or her, whether it stays with the birth mother or goes to adoptive parents. Because we had been so burned and were so sensitive, I felt the agency should have helped us to keep our distance and not get fully invested. But the bottom line was the agency wouldn't let us do anything like that. They insisted on a full buy-in from us.

"Cindy didn't sign the surrender when she checked out of the hospital on Thursday because, she said, she didn't feel like it. She was supposed to go to the agency the next day and sign it. Late on Friday we got a phone call from the agency saying she hadn't shown up. I was all but ranting and raving. Then they told us, 'Cindy wants to see the baby again before she signs the surrender. She has a two-thirty flight scheduled tomorrow to go back home, so bring the baby to the agency in the morning.' I said, 'You've got to be kidding! The baby's been with us for two days now, and Cindy could just say thanks for taking care of her, but I'm taking her home.' But they said, 'Those are the rules she's decided to play by, and we can't do it any other way.'

"That night we probably slept some but obviously not much. The next morning was unquestionably the worst morning of our lives. We were just wet noodles—absolutely, positively beside ourselves!"

Gina said, "Our next-door neighbor, Robin, had been through all of this with us. She was a wonderful friend and understood our situation. She had two children of her own. She had seen us go out to Illinois; she knew about the ectopic pregnancies and the miscarriages. She came over that morning and just couldn't believe what was happening. She was in tears. She walked out of our house and said, 'I can't deal with this—I have to leave.' Tommy and I put the baby in the car to drive to the agency. As we drove away, Robin stood at the end of her driveway sobbing! It was awful. We were certain we were going to lose this child.

"At the agency Miriam rushed out of her office and told us immediately, 'Cindy has just signed the surrender form! But she wants to spend some time alone with the baby to say good-bye.'"

"We were probably there for an hour-and-a-half," said Tom. "Cindy spent about twenty minutes alone with the baby. At some point we were all in the same room together. Cindy handled herself well. She gave us a handwritten note saying she was sorry. I don't recall it entirely, but she told us how difficult it was for her and how hopeful she was for us and the child."

"She was clearly upset when she handed the baby to me," said Gina. "She was weeping. I gave her a hug. Cindy is a wonderful person, and she did a courageous thing for her baby."

Tom added, "Cindy gave us a hug and a kiss and said good-bye. When she walked out of the agency I was flooded by a sense of relief. I don't recall the drive home. When we got there, Robin was out, so I put a big sign on her garage door. It read: SHE SIGNED!!"

Gina continued, "When Robin got home she came running across the yard screaming with joy. It was wonderful! But I wasn't completely relieved until ten o'clock that night, when we got a phone call from an attorney in the Midwest; he confirmed that the birth father had picked Cindy up at the airport and they had come directly to his office, where the birth father had also signed the surrender. Now we could finally name our baby: Melissa Rae.

"Everyone was joyous about Melissa; she was a beautiful baby with blond hair. I don't think our families understood the struggle we'd been through to get her. I think Tommy and I did a relatively good job of sheltering them from all our pain.

"We had a basket for Melissa to sleep in and some diapers—that was it. I had refused to set up a nursery in advance. I was spooked by the idea of buying furniture, painting a nursery, and all that. It was great fun to finally go out and buy baby things, but it always felt so weird. I kept thinking, *Should I really be doing this?* I thought that even when I was standing in a store holding Melissa in my arms!

"About two weeks later I started to feel really pregnant; I was completely exhausted. The doctor said, 'Let's just see where it goes.' Soon after that I had an ultrasound and saw a heart beating! I couldn't believe it. For the first time I had a viable pregnancy! All of my miscarriages had happened so early that I'd never heard a heartbeat before. But I couldn't even let myself think about being pregnant, because so much was going on with Melissa and we'd been through so much before that. I thought, *Whatever happens, happens.*"

Tom said, "It was like having two eight-hundred-pound gorillas on our backs. We had this brand new baby with all of the joy, continuing trepidations, and the operational difficulties of looking after her, and we had this pregnancy. We started to get more confident as the weeks passed. Gina was consumed by Melissa—as she needed to be—physically, mentally, and emotionally. There was little room for her to give of herself to this being growing inside her."

"What was astounding to me after we brought Melissa home was the lack of freedom," admitted Gina. "I don't mean that in a bad way, but it was just amazing that from that point forward I could not do anything without taking care of someone else first. I'd been married for eight years, I'd run my own business, and I was thirty-six years old. As much as I like to view myself as flexible, I had my own routine. Tommy and I are terribly independent but wonderfully close. Then all of a sudden I had this baby, and I had to learn to prioritize."

Tom continued, "The adoption agency sent a social worker over for follow-up visits with Melissa, and each time she came, Gina was looking more and more pregnant. The attitude from the agency was that they were delighted that Gina was pregnant. They knew that when we started the process with Cindy, Gina was not pregnant. If anyone from the agency had given me any lip I would have choked them! I'm sure I gave them that impression."

Gina added, "I didn't suffer from morning sickness; I was tired for two weeks and that was it! I did get a little frightened at one point because now I understood the responsibility of having a baby. I was worried that if this turned out to be another ectopic pregnancy, I'd be hospitalized again for four or five days and would need a month to recover. It would be much more complicated now. Until the middle of my eighth month I still couldn't believe that I was going to have a baby! It was wild."

Just before it was time to go to court to finalize Melissa's adoption, the adoption agency forwarded a letter to Gina and Tom from Cindy. It read:

Dear Gina and Tom,

I just wanted you to know that I'm doing really well. I'm really happy. You've probably been worried about what's going to happen and I want you to know that you have absolutely no reason to worry.

I know that I made the right choice. And I know Melissa will be happy for the rest of her life.

Sincerely,
Cindy

"That made me feel great," said Gina. "Cindy wanted us to know that she wasn't going to do anything to prevent us from adopting Melissa."

Tom explained, "Gina was completely worried for six months until we went to court to finalize Melissa's adoption. The child could have been removed for two reasons during that period: one, if it can be proven that you are bad parents, and two, if it can be proven that the birth parents signed the surrender under duress. And as long as there are lawyers . . . When I see what goes on every once in a while in the newspaper with these birth parents and adoptive parents fighting for two or three years, I think, *There but for the grace of God go I!* It's heart-wrenching! Anyone can understand it, but it just goes through our bones. If my daughter were ever threatened with anything like that I wouldn't dream about what I would do. I would do anything in my power, and we would probably find ourselves living in a foreign country with different names! I suppose there are instances where adoptive parents win in these situations, but you don't hear about those cases."

"One of our most joyous days was when we went to court with Melissa," said Gina. "It was extremely cold, and I was hugely pregnant. Melissa looked adorable, and the judge fell in love with her instantly. She had Melissa dancing on top of her desk throughout the procedure. It was so sweet. I walked out of the courthouse thinking, *Oh, she's ours!* To me, that was the most fantastic day."

Tom added, "That was a great day because it was getting home free for Gina, and for me that was as satisfying as anything. I was already there; I wasn't really worried. But I felt relieved as we left the courthouse."

When Melissa was seven months old, Gina gave birth to Max. "After ten hours of labor and three hours of pushing, I ended up having a Cesarean section," remembered Gina. "Max had a wrecking ball for a head—just huge! And he weighed eight pounds and twelve ounces. I was so happy to have a boy. I had wanted this baby to be a boy, but I didn't want to wish for it too much! I didn't think we'd ever have another baby and I felt it would be a lot easier if our children were two different sexes. I felt that a boy was our reward for all we went through before, that God took care of me."

Tom remembered, "A couple of hours after Gina was admitted to the hospital I looked down at a rolling tray of equipment in the birthing room and saw a tiny bracelet. It read MALE. I gasped! Gina had had an amnio, but we'd chosen not to know the baby's sex. I was excited because we already had our girl, and our druthers, after happy and healthy, were to have a boy. I was thrilled but decided to repress my joy because I didn't want to blow the surprise for Gina. But my knowledge became a big annoyance because he wasn't born for six more hours!"

Gina said, "When I had Max, I grieved for Cindy because then I understood how hard it must have been for her to relinquish her baby.

"Max was a difficult baby. He never slept, was never happy. He had colic for six months. Melissa was great. I put them in different bedrooms. Having two little ones was hard on Tommy. I think it was hard for him to understand that our life was no longer our own. Sometimes I felt he couldn't wait for Monday morning to come around so he could go to work. I don't think that's atypical for a man, and I don't hold it against him. In fact, I felt bad for him."

"Life with two babies was trying, that's for sure!" explained Tom. "We'd just moved to a new house and were still getting used to it. Max was spitting up half of everything he ate. We laughed because there were white stains on all our shirts. For the previous twenty years I had slept through the night every single night. It was a huge shock for me to wake up suddenly because one of the babies was crying. I'm sure Gina got up most of the time, but that still left some turns for me. We walked around like zombies for a few months! But I couldn't imagine myself not being a father and not having kids. Initially most of my joy and satisfaction had to do with achieving this for Gina; I feel that to have deprived her of that would have been horrible. She has so much fun with them. I have just as much fun, but it's a different kind of fun. I think mothers are more special than fathers in some respects."

Gina said, "After Max got over his colic and became a real human being, Tommy and I were able to take a deep breath; we sat down and talked about trying to have another child. Part of me wanted to try, for Max and Melissa's sake, because Tommy and I both grew up in families with four children. And the whole ordeal we went through with them seemed as though it had robbed us, in some way, of the joy. I told Tom, 'If we're going to do it, I want to do it soon because I don't want to get out of the soup. I'd rather just be in the soup for a little longer.'

"I had sold my restaurant and I thought, *If I'm home full time, I might as well have another baby!* But Tommy told me that he'd thought about it and realized he didn't want another child. He was embarking on a big career push and wanted to be able to work like a maniac for a few years. I told him that was fine. I didn't have a problem with it. It was the sort of thing that I definitely needed him to be on board with me, and there was ambiguity in my own head. Having a boy and a girl made it easier. I wasn't committed enough to try to convince him. I'm happy to think that we have two very special children.

"People have said to me, 'Oh, which one is yours?' I say, 'Which one is mine? They're both mine!' People are so stupid, it's scary. One day we were in the checkout line at the grocery store. Melissa and Max were bantering back and forth, and both of them were calling me Mommy. Max looks Italian, like me, and Melissa is a blue-eyed blonde. An old lady in front of us said to Max, 'Oh, you have your mommy's big brown eyes.' I knew where this was leading. Then the old lady turned to Melissa and said, 'Now, where did she get those eyes?' I said, 'Obviously not from me.' And I just left it at that. I used to feel the need to explain to people that Melissa was adopted, but I don't do that anymore. They ask, 'Why is her hair blond?' I say, 'Because her father's hair is blond.' I don't believe people are mean; they just say things that they don't stop to think about.

"I have no fears for Melissa; she's a great little girl. She's happy, and I think she knows how much she's loved. I fully anticipate that she will want to meet her birth mother one day. I believe that Cindy is part of the reason why Melissa is such a wonderful person, and I want Melissa to understand that; not because I'm not important—I think I'm tremendously important—but Cindy is part of Melissa. She's not a figment of someone's imagination.

"I'm not going to push Melissa to find Cindy, but I don't want her to think it's something she shouldn't do or shouldn't feel good about doing. I think there may be a part of her that will want to see what her birth mother looks like. That's my dream: that the desire would come from a curiosity, a life circle, to create some closure on unanswered questions. When she's old enough I think it could benefit Melissa to know that her birth mother is a nice person who did a courageous thing for her. I look forward to seeing Cindy again one day—I really do."

"When I look back on this whole thing, I'm glad it's not a part of my life anymore," Gina admitted. "It went on for years and years and, in a way, controlled our existence. We didn't even realize how much it controlled us until it was gone. I think Tom and I did a terrific job of dealing with an impossible situation. Tommy always had a great way of keeping my spirits up. He'd say, 'Just keep your eyes on the prize.' Anything in your life that you expend a lot of energy working on, something that's obviously meaningful to you, whether it's a professional endeavor or a personal goal, usually comes with a lot of sacrifice and pain. And, to me, adoption is clearly much more important than any of those other things.

"Melissa asked me recently if I came from Nonnie's (my mother's) tummy, and I said yes, so I knew more questions were coming. It was nice the way it happened: It was a Friday night, and the four of us were sitting on the couch before bedtime and talking. Melissa said, 'Mommy, did I come from your tummy?' I said, 'No, sweetie, actually you didn't.'

"She looked at me with a sad expression on her face. I said, 'You know, Melissa, not all babies come from their own mommies' tummies. Sometimes they come from other mommies' tummies. You came from another mommy, and I want to tell you a story. I had a boo-boo in my tummy and couldn't grow a baby. But after you came I used to hold you on my tummy and you made my boo-boo go away—that's why Max could grow there.' She loves that story! And I truly believe that that's what happened, that it's part of the reason Max is alive. If Melissa and Max grow up believing it too, that's fine with us."

Tom added, "I don't fear Melissa's questions about her adoption, because the strength of the bond between Melissa and us has something to do with where she came from and how she came to us. We hope that her understanding will be gradual, started by us, and very consciously done to build that bond—as opposed to needing to rush in at the last moment and repair."

Gina said, "If I were asked to do it again, I would do it again in a second. I would do it the same way in a second. I would experience as much pain if I had to, even knowing how bad that pain can be. The first two years of Melissa's life, having just gone through this crazy adoption routine, being pregnant, owning the restaurant, having Max—honestly, I don't know how I lived through it. It was absolutely insane. I know that life is not always easy; there are times when things get really tough and you wonder how you're going to make it through. Well, I have complete confidence that whatever happens to me, I will figure it out! That's what I've learned from this whole experience."

Tom concluded, "A number of our friends and acquaintances are experiencing infertility problems. I give out advice fast and furiously—in fact, I'm more forceful than sensitive, although I remember my own reluctance to welcome the adoption process. I'm very quick and eager to say to people, 'Get off it! Adoption is tremendous! There's no difference. I happen to have one of each. There is absolutely no difference!' I couldn't be a bigger advocate of adoption. As you can see, I'm an enormous beneficiary of it.

"For me, adoption cured—in a spectacular fashion—the unsuccessful adoption tries and the difficulties with infertility. It may be a tougher thing for women, because they miss out on the birthing process. Obviously, we as fathers are a lot more outside the birthing process. But I'm a huge advocate of adoption. I'm sure some people try the adoption process, as a function of infertility, fail repeatedly, and give up. That I would not wish on my worst enemy. I think one would carry those scars forever.

"We made an agreement with the adoption agency to provide them with photographs and a letter every year on Melissa's birthday for five years. Cindy can have access to them if she wants to. I've thought a little about the possibility of Melissa's meeting her one day. If everyone is happy, I think it would be fine. I would be very concerned, cautious, and nervous, but not in the sense that Melissa would fall out of love with her parents. I think if we have done a good job of raising our child and if Cindy is happy, satisfied, and complete, it could be a good experience. I feel an affiliation with and compassion for Cindy because of what she did for Melissa. After Max was born, I was more acutely aware of what she did and how difficult it must have been for her. It is our hope and duty to let her know that she made the right decision, that this person she set free turned out great!"

4/ Meredith
An adult adoptee builds her family

"A nun came up to me and said in English, 'You must be Meredith.' I nodded, and she picked up a baby from one of the cribs. Then she turned to me and said, 'She's been waiting for you all day.' As she handed Caroline to me, my father and I dissolved into tears. She said that normally the baby was very calm, but she'd been fidgety all day. I sat down and fed her a bottle. There's no way to describe what I was feeling."

SINGLE MEN and women who wish to parent children are now able to create families through adoption. Although it is necessary for single people to be fairly selective when choosing an agency to work with, there are plenty for them to choose from. In international adoptions certain countries, such as China and Peru, have made it clear that they welcome single-parent adoptions. In this story, a single woman who had been adopted in infancy offers a unique perspective on adoption and shares her childhood experiences when explaining her approach to adopting and raising her own children.

Meredith is a slim, fair-haired woman who projects an air of inner strength and confidence. She grew up with her devoted parents in an affluent Boston suburb, where her father owned a successful business. "I had a great childhood," Meredith said. "We were very close. I don't think my parents ever took a vacation without me. They used to say that they wished they'd adopted more than one child. I missed not having siblings, but I grew up in neighborhoods with lots of kids, and a lot of them were adopted also. I don't think it was as much the exception even then [in the 1940s] as people thought. I always knew I was adopted and never had any trouble with it. I don't think adoptees have trouble with it. I think some people have trouble with it—they're uncomfortable, which can create problems for adopted children.

"I was always crazy about kids, and when I was in college I decided that I wanted to teach." After graduating from college Meredith found a teaching job near her parents' home and moved back in with them. They were now spending the winter months in Florida, so she had the house to herself for the best part of the school year. Meredith bought herself a house on Cape Cod where she enjoyed summers on her own. Her life settled into a comfortable routine and she enjoyed teaching first and second grade for many years.

"After nineteen years in a classroom I decided I didn't want to deal with other people's children anymore. I wanted my own. I almost got married—twice—but then I decided I didn't want to. I thought about adoption after I decided not to get married." In 1978 Meredith took a leave of absence from teaching and went to work with her father, Tom. At this time Meredith began to look into adoption. "After the Vietnam War I'd heard that a lot of war orphans were being adopted by Americans. I had a friend of mine call a United Nations high commissioner about the possibility of adopting there. But it was discovered that a lot of the children were not actually orphans, so the whole operation was shut down."

In 1986 close friends of Meredith's adopted a baby girl from Chile. "No one knew they were doing it," said Meredith. "They went away on vacation and came home with this gorgeous six-week-old baby. My father said to me at the time, 'If you would like to do that, I'll go to Chile with you.' And I said to him, 'You're seventy, and I'm not sure that with all the trouble down there you need to be trying to dodge bullets.' So I let that rest, but in the meantime I did some investigating. When you can see that it does happen, you get a little bit more courage to go ahead, which is what I did."

A few weeks later Meredith's friend Denise called. "She asked me if I was still interested in adopting, and I said yes. She said she had met a Peruvian man at a conference who'd told her that single parents were welcome to adopt in Peru. So I asked her to get some more information from him, and I thought, *if it happens, it happens, and maybe it will."*

Meredith waited for her parents to leave for Florida that November before she began the adoption process in earnest. The parents of the adopted Chilean baby had recommended their agency, and it was a good match. "I thought the social worker was wonderful," said Meredith. "She was very sincere about how she dealt with me. I felt she would let you talk, but she was never invasive. And she was very prompt about getting my home study done." During the home study interviews, Meredith felt that a unique friendship was developing between her and the social worker. Because her agency had recently placed two children from Peru, they were familiar with the rules and regulations there. After speaking on the phone with the two families, Meredith decided that Peru was the right choice for her.

Denise's acquaintance in Peru referred Meredith to his best friend, Juan, a prominent attorney in Lima. "Juan was wonderful," said Meredith. "I liked him from the first phone conversation. He told me he'd never done an adoption before but that he loved children and would be happy to help me. He said if he could not help me within three months, he would find me another attorney." Juan was an invaluable contact for Meredith, and she began to believe that something would happen.

The amount of paperwork needed for the adoption was enormous. "From November until February I did nothing but paperwork. I was in the office, but I did nothing as far as business was concerned. One day I went to the Peruvian consulate in Boston because I needed the consul's signature on a paper. I waited for him from nine-thirty in the morning until five in the afternoon. I sat there and he did not show. His secretary knew exactly how I felt because she had a little boy she'd brought home from Guatemala. She said, 'The consul's going to Peru tomorrow.' So I said, 'If he doesn't sign these papers, I'm going to be at the plane.' But he came in the next morning and signed them."

At Christmas Meredith flew to Florida to be with her parents. "We always opened our presents at midnight on Christmas Eve. The last present I gave them was a pair of baby shoes. My mother screamed and woke everybody up in the building. My father just sat there smiling smugly. I said, 'You knew. You figured it out.' He said, 'I could tell you were doing something. When I talked to you on the phone, I could tell by your voice that you were up to something.'"

Meredith didn't tell anyone else about her adoption plans. "I just did-n't want anybody to say to me, 'When are you going? What's happening?' I thought that nobody should get into it at this point, because then it's all over the place. And you never know what can happen, although one friend of mine figured it out in February." By then Meredith's paperwork was completed and she sent it to Juan in Lima. There was nothing more for her to do but wait.

Two months later Juan called Meredith to tell her about some nuns in southern Peru who were caring for infants. The nuns had seven babies: five boys and two girls. Juan told Meredith he would fly down the next day to see the babies and would call her as soon as he got home.

"Naturally, I couldn't work all day," remembered Meredith, "and I couldn't wait for him to call me, either. I called him at home that evening just as he was coming through the door. 'There's a baby girl, and she's three weeks old,' said Juan. He told me I could come for her in May—just one more month to wait. I left for Peru on Mother's Day, which was nice. My father came with me."

When Meredith and her father arrived in Lima they checked into a hotel suite. They met Juan and Mariana, his wife, and felt an instant rap-port with them. Two days after Meredith visited a police station to establish residency in the country, they flew to southern Peru. "I had brought a whole suitcase of stuff for the baby. She and my father were the only ones who had clothes, because my suitcase went to Chile for a week by mis-take. During those first two days in Lima I ran around like a lunatic buying clothes and toiletries for myself. We flew down near the Chilean border and then drove for a couple of hours. I don't remember much about the ride. All I could think about was the baby.

"When we finally got there we found out it wasn't really an orphan-age, but a temporary shelter. It was a rather odd-looking place but very clean, and there were lots of little kids running around. When we went through the door, I almost died. I thought I was going to split in half! A nun came up to me and said in English, 'You must be Meredith.' I nod-ded, and she picked up a baby from one of the cribs. Then she turned to me and said, 'She's been waiting for you all day.' As she handed Caroline to me, my father and I dissolved into tears. She said that normally the baby was very calm, but she'd been fidgety all day. I sat down and fed her a bottle. There's no way to describe what I was feeling. I think my father was overwhelmed. I said to him, 'Do you want to hold her?' and he said, 'I don't want to drop her.' I said, 'I've never seen you drop one yet!' So he held her for quite a while. It was rather late in the day by that point, so we decided to leave the baby there one more night. The nun told me they'd be up and moving by about six, so I told her we'd be early.

"The next morning Juan drove us back to pick Caroline up. We took her to the hotel and I dressed her in a white two-piece suit. It was adorable. She weighed only about eight pounds; she was really small. I had brought several sizes; I didn't know what she was going to wear. It's a wonder I didn't bring shoes for first grade! I have a cute picture of my father and Caroline that I took that day. She was on the bed, this tiny baby, and my father, who was a big man, was sitting beside her and leaning on his elbow. She was sound asleep, and he just stared at her for a couple of hours."

At two o'clock that afternoon Meredith, her father, and Juan went to court. Meredith was holding Caroline. Also present were the district attorney and the nun from the shelter. "The judge had decided that we'd have to stay there for fifteen days until the adoption was final. Juan told him we wanted to take the baby back to Lima, but the judge was definite that we would have to stay.

"I just sat there; I couldn't say anything to him; I don't speak Spanish. Caroline coughed a couple of times, and Juan suggested to the judge that the damp climate was bad for her, that it would be good if he'd allow me to take the baby to a doctor in Lima. He pointed out that the papers could be flown up to Lima at the end of the fifteen-day period. The judge looked at me and said, 'That's a happy mother, and that's going to be a happy baby. I think that baby should go to Lima to see a doctor.' When we got out of the courtroom Caroline was silent. She never had a cough after that!

"The first night with Caroline was wonderful, just wonderful. I don't think I slept. I think I looked at her all night long! She was a breeze of a baby. She'd have a bottle about every four hours. Oh, she was marvelous. She's still the same way!"

When they arrived at their hotel in Lima the next day the bellboys made a big fuss over Caroline. "Those Peruvian men, they love babies," said Meredith. "They were all excited and hovered about. The guy from behind the desk came out, and the girls came out. After that they never said hello to me. They always said, '*Hola*, Caroline.' They were wonderful. They went out and bought formula and diapers for her a couple of times when we weren't supposed to be on the street because of problems with the Shining Path guerrillas and a police strike."

Meredith took Caroline wherever she went. "I had been told by the hotel that they could provide baby-sitters for very little money. And I thought, *No, I didn't come down here to have anybody baby-sit.* I never put her in a stroller. I carried her everywhere, took her to every restaurant. We were glued at the hip."

After nearly a month of living in a hotel suite, Meredith and her father began to get anxious to go home. On the day that the papers were due to arrive from the southern district where Caroline had been born, Meredith was pacing back and forth in her suite. Juan had been expected to bring the papers at about two o'clock, but it was now six and Meredith was getting exasperated.

"After almost thirty days, I said I was going to shoot my way out of this place! Finally the doorbell rang; my father answered it, because I was feeding Caroline. Juan was at the door and I turned. He had the most magnificent roses, of a color that I had never seen and have never seen since. He handed me the flowers and said, 'These are for you.' Then he gave me Caroline's adoption papers and said, 'And these are for her.'

"It was a Thursday night. We decided to have a farewell dinner together the next evening with Mariana. As he was leaving our suite Juan turned to say to me, 'I want you out of town by Saturday night!' I had everything done the next day and off we went. When we left the hotel I told the bellboys that I'd be back in a year, because I had already decided to return for another child.

"Our flight wasn't due to leave until eleven-twenty at night, but I insisted that we be at the airport by nine. Juan and Mariana were with us. I had to go through a holding area to get Caroline's papers stamped . . . again. Mariana said, 'If the baby cries, don't try to quiet her, because Peruvian men don't like to hear a baby cry.'

"As I was going through, Caroline, my baby who never cried, started to shriek! I handed her papers to the first man I saw. She was just screaming, and he stamped everything quickly. Then I went to the next table and handed her papers to another man. By then Caroline was crying so loudly that I started to cry. The man just looked at us, stamped the papers, and said, *'Pasa, pasa, pasa.'* I turned around to look back through the glass wall at Mariana and Juan. They smiled and Mariana gave me a thumbs-up sign.

"When we finally sat down on the plane and it moved back from the jetway—it must have been about twenty minutes later—my father said, 'I think that you can probably begin to breathe now!'"

During the flight Meredith talked to her father about her plans for the baby. "My father said he would add on to the house, and I said to him, 'No, I think I should get my own house now.' 'Oh, don't do that,' he said. 'We've waited all these years; don't take her away.' I knew what having Caroline there would mean to my parents, so I never mentioned leaving again.

"When we came through the jetway in Boston I heard my mother saying, 'There they are!' She had a big banner that read WELCOME HOME CAROLINE, TOM, AND MEREDITH. Caroline cried when I handed her to my mother. My mother put the baby's face right up to hers and started to cry too. One of my friends was there, and a friend of my mother's had come as well. It was a nice welcoming committee.

"My mother had mailed out my announcements two days before our return. By the time we got home there were about thirty-five people there! Everybody was so excited! There were so many presents that the place looked like a department store.

"On one of those first days at home somebody asked me if Caroline had any siblings in Peru, and I said, 'That isn't anything I will tell anybody. That's only for her.' I was surprised by the question. I know people are interested and don't mean to sound insensitive, but I had decided from the beginning that I wasn't going to give anybody any information. And it has worked out very, very well.

"Motherhood hasn't been a big surprise for me. It was everything that I have ever dreamed it would be and more. I don't think I was ever tired. I hated having to put Caroline to bed at night. I used to hold her when she went to bed. And I'm glad that I didn't do it sooner, because even though I would have felt the same way about another child, I would never have wanted to miss her. This one was meant to be for me."

Meredith enjoyed the follow-up visits with her social worker. "I was happy to have her come and see the baby," said Meredith. "I never felt that I was on trial. One thing was funny. The standardized checklist asked what the baby's favorite toy was, but Caroline was only a couple of months old, so I said, 'I guess it's her bottle!'

"Since I had legally adopted Caroline in Peru, it wasn't necessary to do it again in Massachusetts, but I decided to do it anyway, because then she would get a birth certificate with our names on it. When Caroline was about eight months old, I took her to court. The judge signed all the papers in about two minutes, and then said, 'I have to come around and kiss that face.' She got up and kissed Caroline. 'That face was made to be kissed and pinched,' she said. It was wonderful."

Meanwhile, Meredith updated her paperwork in preparation for another child. She asked Juan to find her twins this time. "Mariana said to me on the phone, 'You know we love you like our family. I want to tell you that now I know you're insane!' Shortly after Caroline's first birthday I finished everything and Juan worked at locating another baby. In Peru they do what they call a search for a baby who has either been abandoned or relinquished by the birth mother."

Meredith also decided to pursue a domestic adoption. She had learned about a birth mother who was five-and-a-half months pregnant and living in New York. Meredith spoke to her on the phone. "She was about twenty-five years old," said Meredith. "She had made a very good decision, and it made perfect sense to me. It had nothing to do with negative feelings; it just wasn't the right time for her to have a baby. I told her, 'If you're going to change your mind, please do it now, because you can't do it afterwards.' And she said, 'I'm not going to.'"

With two adoptions going on at the same time, the director of Meredith's adoption agency became concerned. "'You're not supposed to have two ongoing,' she said. 'Well, I'm definitely going to go with the Peruvian one, because that will happen. The domestic one I'm not sure of, nor is anybody else,' I said to her, 'but you have to find a way to okay this, because you know I can do it.' She said, 'Well, Meredith, that's a lot . . .' and I said, 'No! You have to, you really have to. You can't stand in my way. The baby in Peru will be adopted before I leave there. It's finalized there. So by the time I get back the only one I'll have ongoing is the domestic one.' She called me back later to say that she had talked it over with my social worker, and they were going to go along with it."

A few weeks later, Meredith received a phone call from Juan with the happy news that he had found another baby girl. Juan and Mariana took the baby home from the hospital and cared for her instead of leaving her in an orphanage.

"I asked Juan to get as much paperwork done without me as was possible, because I didn't want to leave Caroline for any longer than was absolutely necessary. I felt I couldn't take her with me; the food and the water were problems, and the country was unstable. But the main thing was that Caroline didn't have a U.S. passport yet, and I would never have taken her back to Peru without it. I knew Caroline would be better off in her own home with my mother looking after her. I told Juan I wouldn't come until everything was ready for me there. Mariana took care of the baby for two weeks, and every night she prayed, 'Please don't let anything happen to her until Meredith gets here.'

"The first worst day of my life was leaving Caroline, going to New York, and getting on that plane. My father came with me again. Caroline was sixteen months old, and I had never left her before. My pediatrician had told me, 'You'll be okay and she'll be okay, because you won't be gone that long.' It was okay, except that she wouldn't speak to me on the telephone the last week I was there. I was there only nineteen days. I think it was the fastest adoption in the history of the country. Once I got there I never stopped moving.

"We arrived in Lima late at night and went to the same hotel. We couldn't get our old suite, so we took adjoining rooms. There were gorgeous roses in my room from Juan and Mariana. The next morning I went out early to establish my residency in Peru again. When I came back to the hotel, as I was getting out of the cab, I saw through the big glass doors Juan and Mariana inside holding the baby. I don't know if my feet were on the floor as I walked into the lobby. Oh, she was the cutest thing! Some of the bellboys who remembered Caroline came around and made a big fuss again. Upstairs I rushed over to knock on my father's door. 'Dad, open the door. She's here!' He looked at her, and said, 'Oh, Lauren, you're so sweet.' Then he sat down on the bed and held her.

"Lauren was another easy baby. When she cried she sounded like a busy signal, and if you fed her, that was it, she just fell asleep. I worked very hard to get everything done quickly. We were in court three or four times. The political situation had worsened. There were military people all over the streets and guns everywhere. I hadn't been scared the first time I went there, because I knew I didn't go there to die. But I was afraid the second time. I was afraid that if I got killed, what would happen to

Caroline? It was terrible being away from Caroline. After a while Juan said, 'Don't even mention her name, because you can hardly do it without falling apart.'

"I'd had announcements made before I left for Peru. The front of the card showed one baby looking at another. It said, 'Another Blessing' and inside it said, 'Caroline would like to announce the arrival of her sister, Lauren.' My mother mailed them out before we got home; I had kept this second adoption very quiet, too. Only a few people knew about it. By the time we got home a lot of people were at the house.

"I had put Lauren in a beautiful white hand-smocked dress with a matching slip, but I had on a black cotton sweater, so instead of looking perfect for her arrival, she had black fuzz all over her! We drove up, and everybody came outside. I got out of the car and handed Lauren to a friend, because I had seen Caroline on the front stairs. She was wearing a blue dress with a teddy bear on the front and held a blue bottle of water. My mother held her by the hand and brought her down the stairs.

"My pediatrician had said to me, 'She may be angry, so go slowly.' Rather than rush to her I knelt down on the sidewalk and looked at her. I said, 'How's my baby?' She looked up, took the bottle out of her mouth, and said, 'Momma!' Oh, it was wild. I hugged her to me. She said, 'Momma, Momma, baby?' I took her over to see Lauren, and she wanted to give her a kiss.

"About five hours later my father said, 'Don't you think you could put Caroline down now?' Caroline was a little distant with my father during the day, but by that night she was okay. She was saying 'Poppa, Poppa, Poppa.' I think she thought that he was the one who had taken me away, because he said, 'She's blaming me.' My mother told me that she had screamed every night that I was away, but she slept all night the night I came home. The next morning, Caroline was with me in the kitchen while I was getting Lauren's bottle ready. My father came down and she went over to him. He said, 'She's saying something to me, but I don't know what it is.' I listened. She was saying, 'I'm happy!' Dad said, 'Yes, Caroline, you're happy because your mother's home!' It was so sweet.

"A cousin came to visit us the next night, and she wanted to hold Lauren, of course. Caroline grabbed her by the leg saying, 'No, mine. Momma's. Mine!' I guess she was afraid somebody might take the baby away. She had a very hard time when I came home. I couldn't even go to the bathroom without her! My pediatrician had told me to multiply each week that I was gone by two or three, by which time her anxiety would go away—and it did.

"Eight days after I brought Lauren home I got a phone call from the attorney I'd hired for the domestic adoption. He said, 'Meredith, a baby boy was born at ten-fifteen this morning.' I almost went through the ceiling! I called my father. 'Dad, guess what? The baby was born!' He said, 'It's a boy?' I said, 'You've got it!' I knew the girls were going to be thrilled with him. Something really strange happened just before he was born. I'd been in a store at the Cape [Cape Cod] to buy a couple of new sleepers. I don't know how this happened, but when I got home there was a little boy's baseball cap in the bag, which I had not purchased, and I didn't take it back!

"The baby was born on a Thursday. On Sunday I took Caroline with me and flew to New York. Two of my closest girlfriends came with us. We drove to the hospital, and I left Caroline in the lobby with my friends while I went upstairs to the maternity ward. I went up to the desk, gave the nurse my name, and said I was there to pick up my son. She said, 'We're changing shifts right now. Could you wait for half an hour?'

"After half an hour I knocked on the nursery window. I said to the nurse, 'I have a seventeen-month-old downstairs.' She said, 'Alone?' I said, 'No, but it's a hundred and ten degrees in here, and I can't wait around.' She said, 'We have to give you a course on how to take care of a baby.' And I said, 'You do?' She said yes. I said, 'There's a seventeen-month-old downstairs and a nine-week-old back in Boston.' She laughed. 'We'll cancel the course. Give me five minutes to get him ready!'

"I went downstairs to tell my friends about the delay, and when I got back up on the maternity floor I saw a nurse pushing an isolette with my name on it. My knees started to fold. The nurse took me into a room to get him dressed. Oh, I thought he was beautiful! He was small; he was only three days old. He had white fuzz on his head and gorgeous blue eyes. I was crying and the nurse was crying. I said, 'I can't dress him.' I was trembling too much! She dressed him for me in a beautiful blue one-piece suit that I had brought for him, which was far too big! After that, I had to sign him out, and then I picked him up. The nurse said, 'You can't walk with him.' I said, 'Of course not, he can't walk!' She said that I had to go in a wheelchair! Somebody photographed this. I was so thrilled, because otherwise Daniel would never have left the hospital with such fanfare.

"Caroline saw me come out of the elevator in the wheelchair holding the baby. 'Mama,' she said. Then she looked at her brother and said, 'Oh, Danny baby!' We never called him Daniel after that. He was Oh-Danny-Baby. She'd say, 'Oh-Danny-Baby is crying' or 'Oh-Danny-Baby smiled at me.' Caroline crawled up on my lap in the wheelchair, and I held her and the baby while we sat on the sidewalk waiting for our car.

"No one knew that Daniel was coming except one or two people. I called a friend the morning after I got home. 'Jean, I want you to come up,' I said, 'I have something to show you.' 'Bring it down,' she said. 'I can't; it's too big,' I said. 'Oh, all right. I'll be up in a minute,' she said. What a surprise I gave her! And Daniel's godfather knew that he was coming but not when, and did not know that I had brought him home. He came in and saw me holding Daniel. He was surprised by how tiny he was. 'What is he, about a minute old?' he said. Then he looked at me and said, 'What is it, Meredith, one in every room?'

"Lauren and Daniel were baptized on the same day. Daniel, who usually cried constantly, slept through the whole thing. Lauren, who never cried, screeched through the whole thing! Daniel wasn't as easy as the girls. He vomited a lot. But after about six months I got smart and started wearing jeans. He was always hungry, but he was growing beautifully. It's hard to believe, but he's been turning over since he was three days old! He would do it in the crib, and I think he'd frighten himself, because all of a sudden he'd be looking up! By now I had three cribs! Caroline and Lauren were in one bedroom and Daniel was in another. I used to play with him at two in the morning. He slept a lot during the day, and I enjoyed being with him in the middle of the night because I had Caroline and Lauren alone during the day.

"When Daniel was only about a month old, I went back to New York with him to finalize his adoption. My two friends volunteered to go with me, and I took Caroline. I couldn't leave her again, even for a day or two. We were waiting at Logan Airport in the Red Carpet Club. It was a very rainy day with thunder and lightning. I had checked all our luggage except Daniel's baby bag. While we were waiting, I got a phone call from my mother. She said, 'You're not going. Something's wrong in the courts.' I went to customer service to ask these nice people to take all of my luggage off the plane! It was ready to leave in about fifteen minutes, but they got everything off. Then a red phone rang, and it was my father.

'You're going!' he said. I said, 'I just got all my luggage off the . . .' 'You're going. They found a court that will be open. That's what the problem was. The judges don't like to work on Friday afternoons in August.'

"Now we had to get everything back on the plane, and we're downstairs. I looked at the woman from the airline and I said, 'You're not going to believe it.' She said, 'I'll put it back on, Meredith (by this time we were calling each other by our first names!) but I'll tell you, your luggage will get on but you're not going to make the flight.'

"My friend Maureen turned to me and said, 'The hell we're not,' and she ran to the gate. I had Caroline in a stroller, which meant that I had to take an elevator, and my other friend had Daniel in an infant seat. We got through security and went to the gate, only to find that they had posted the wrong gate! So by the time we got to the right gate, the jetway was back and the door to the plane had closed. I recognized the woman at the door and said to her, 'I'm supposed to be in New York tomorrow morning at nine to finalize an adoption.' She talked into her walkie-talkie: 'Bring it back and reconnect the jetway.' Now they normally don't do that! They opened the door and pushed the jetway out. They didn't reconnect it; we had to jump the last few inches! Then the stewardess took charge. It's great the way people are willing to help you out when they know you're adopting a baby.

"The New York judge was wonderful; he had five adopted children of his own. He interviewed my friends, and I had to leave while he talked to them. When I went back in he said, 'Meredith, I've decided that it's in the best interest of this child that I sign all these papers and get you home fast, but I do have one question. You have this little girl right here who's how old?' I said, 'She's seventeen months.' 'And your son is a month old? Well, there's a mistake here. It says there's another one.' 'Well, there is, Your Honor,' I said. 'She's only twelve weeks old, and she's at home in Boston with my parents.' He said, 'Congratulations and good luck,' and we left! We went out for lunch and flew home late that afternoon."

"Shortly after I adopted Daniel somebody said to me, 'You must have paid seventy-five thousand dollars to adopt a Caucasian boy,'" said Meredith. "When I didn't reply the person said, 'Well, isn't that the going rate?' I can't believe how nosy people are. Children hear these comments, too. Caroline came home from kindergarten one day and asked, 'Mom, did it cost you a lot of money to get me?' And I said, 'You know, Caroline, you can buy a car and you can buy a house. Poppa buys airline tickets, we bought a puppy, but you can never buy a person. So don't ever listen to any of that.'

"My basic philosophy is: *Don't tell people too much.* Don't tell your next-door neighbors everything about your children's adoptions. I think the child's dignity and privacy are violated when everybody knows everything about the circumstances of their adoption, and they don't realize it. It must be a terrible feeling to have a best friend when you're twelve or fourteen and to decide to say, 'I care enough about you to tell you this,' and then have your friend say, 'Oh, I already knew.' I believe in giving adopted children their dignity; they deserve the right to tell the people they choose to tell.

"One child taunted Caroline by telling her that I wasn't her real mother. She asked Caroline why her mother had given her away. 'Didn't your mother like you? Or did she die?' When Caroline told me about it she wasn't very upset. I said, 'Caroline, I thought you told me this little girl was smart.' 'Well, she can read, Mom,' said Caroline. So I said, 'Well, gee, Caroline, if she told you I'm not your mother, I don't think she's as smart as you think she is.' Caroline said, 'You know, Mom, I don't think I'm going to talk about it with her anymore, because she just doesn't understand.'

"I said to her, 'Just remember this: I am your mother. What does *mother* mean? *Mother* means the one who loves you best in the world, who's there to take care of you, to drive you to school, and to get your lunches. That's what a mother is. It's only a word and I'm the word.' The next morning when I took Caroline to school this child tapped me on the shoulder and said, 'I know a secret about Caroline.' I said, 'What is it?' 'I know she's adopted,' she said. I said, 'And I know that's none of your business.' That usually stops people cold.

"A neighbor at the Cape made a comment to me recently. He intro-duced me to someone and then said, 'But that wasn't always your name, not from the beginning, was it?' I said to him, 'What does that have to do with anything?' And he said, 'Oh, I was only kidding.' His wife seemed very embarrassed and said to him, 'Why would you even mention that?' He turned to me and said, 'Well, I know that you were adopted and that's probably why you adopted your kids.' I said, 'Boy, you really think you have all this figured out, don't you? Well, you don't have a clue!' I walked away from him.

"I hope my children will be strong enough and like themselves enough so that if they get nasty comments they'll be able to say, 'My mom always said that there are stupid people out there.' On this issue only, and I don't want them to be nasty, but on this one issue, which is their business, I want them to be able to say, 'This doesn't have anything to do with you.'

"I live in a lily-white community, and there's a lot of prejudice, not only because two of my children are from another country, but also because of their coloring. Some of the mothers say, 'Isn't she beautiful with her olive skin,' but I don't think that's what they mean.

"Caroline went to kindergarten and had no problems, although her teacher said she was a bit withdrawn. One day the teacher asked me, 'Do you think she's shy because she knows she looks different?' Now you tell me, how does a five-year-old know she looks different? I find that some teachers aren't very helpful. They want our personal information but I don't give it to them. Some of them are biased. They don't mean to be, but they are. Caroline's teacher said, 'I don't think there's a disability, but you want to watch her. You don't have any background. You don't know if there are any learning disabilities. She doesn't really concentrate.' And I said, 'She's only five years old!'

"When she was in first grade Caroline came home one day and said they'd talked about Peru in geography class. I thought, *Here it comes.* She had told the class that she was born in Peru, and I said, 'Oh, that's nice.' Then Caroline said, 'I'm sorry I said it,' and I said, 'It's a beautiful country, Caroline.' I never want my children to feel that they have to be quiet about coming from Peru. I've decided to send them to a school that has a wider mix of nationalities so that they don't stick out. I've found a wonderful Catholic school with Asians, Colombians, blacks, et cetera, and I hope they'll be more comfortable there."

Tom, who had encouraged Meredith to adopt and had helped and supported her in every way, had only a few short years to enjoy his grandchildren. When Caroline was seven, Tom became seriously ill. Meredith tried to prepare the children for his death. Caroline had said to her mother, "I want to be home when it happens." Meredith answered, "If you're not, I'll come and get you."

When the time came, Caroline was at school, and Meredith went to pick her up. "I stood at the door of her classroom, and she looked up and saw me. She came rushing over and whispered, 'Did he die?' I said, 'No, but I think it's going to be very soon.' As we were driving home she said, 'Do you know, Mom, I'm really going to be very sad, but it isn't going to be anything like what it'll be for you, because you and Poppa *really* love each other.' I said, 'Yes, we do, but he'll always be my father, even after he's dead.' And Caroline said, 'Yes, and he'll always be my Poppa.'

"So my children know that they're in the same situation that I was in," said Meredith, "and it's forever. We take care of each other. I think it's an advantage that I was adopted. The children saw how much my father loved me, and he told each one of them how much he loved them before he died. We all miss him. The children are a tremendous comfort to my mother and me now. I tell them that this is the way it was meant to be. We were meant to be together."

5 / Rachel and Scott
A baby girl from China

"We knew exactly what would happen on this day. Everything was very well organized. After breakfast we were to go back upstairs and wait for the babies to be brought to us in our rooms. Scott and I went back to our room and started pacing back and forth. I kept thinking, *Oh my God—this is it!* I kept peeking out into the corridor, which was T-shaped. Finally I saw a string of nurses carrying babies coming up the hallway and turning the corner—what a picture! Our room was second to last, so I knew we'd have to wait a bit longer. I closed the door and turned to my husband. 'Okay, Scott, this is it. They're rounding the corner!'"

INFERTILITY is not the only medical problem that can dash a woman's hope of becoming pregnant. Some women adopt because an illness prevents them from bearing a child. For Rachel that illness was lupus. The disease had damaged her kidneys to such an extent that pregnancy would have been life-threatening to her. Unwilling to take that risk, Rachel and her husband, Scott, turned to adoption.

Scott, a trim, fair-haired man, was the second of four children. "I grew up in a lovely environment in New York," said Scott. "My father was not rich, but we had a comfortable life. Our house was next door to my grandparents. The family was highly structured, from Granddad on down. All his sons went to the same boarding school, and all the grandsons continued at that school. I was a rebellious teenager, which didn't sit well with the family.

"When I was a junior in college and my little sister was only sixteen, my mother died of cancer. She was a sweet, loving sort of person. After her death there were some rough years for our family. When your mother dies young, it goes down very hard."

Scott majored in English and decided to become a teacher. After graduation he taught in a private school for a couple of years. This experience led him to an interest in producing audio-visual materials; Scott took a few courses and launched himself into a career writing sales and marketing publications, producing slide shows, and creating promotional materials. He works in a large firm in New York City.

Rachel is a dark-haired woman with wide, friendly eyes that do not completely disguise the physical suffering she has endured. She speaks in a thoughtful manner with a warm, inviting voice and has a melodious laugh. "I was the third of four girls in my family," said Rachel. "We're Jewish but attended a Quaker school as children. I was strongly influenced by the Quaker philosophy. I didn't adopt the religion but learned to admire their practice. Quakers believe that God is in every person and that idea is a strong part of who I am. I have wonderful memories of going to weekly Quaker meetings in which we would sit and contemplate. If you were moved to do so, you would speak."

Rachel's father was an architect. Their home in suburban Philadelphia was filled with art and music. "By the time I was thirteen," said Rachel, "my parents were divorced. This was before divorces became common. I didn't have any friends to share the experience with." After high school Rachel knew she wanted to be an artist but didn't feel ready for college. She spent a few years working as a waitress, first in the Midwest and then in California. When she turned twenty-one, Rachel decided it was time to go to back to school. She returned home and began a four-year studio program at a museum school.

"As soon as I got back to Philadelphia, I met Scott," she remembered. "He was living with a dear childhood friend of mine, but they were not in a good relationship. Over a two-year period Scott and I became good friends."

"After I broke up with my girlfriend, I asked Rachel out and things happened pretty quickly for us," said Scott. "All our friends were artists.

We had a sort of Bohemian existence for a while. After a couple of years we decided to get married. It was 1981; Rachel was twenty-four and I was twenty-seven. We hadn't talked about having kids. In fact, we thought very little about the structure of our marriage or our family. We knew we wanted to be together, and that was enough for us at the time. All our ambitions for our lives were couched in terms of our careers."

Rachel added, "After I graduated from art school I told Scott we had to move to New York City. I'd had marvelous training as a painter but no liberal arts courses, so I was unsure about how to make a living. In New York you can plug into the art scene. I knew I couldn't do that in Philadelphia. It was a quick decision, but it turned out to be a lucky one."

Scott found a marketing job, and Rachel developed a freelance business doing drafting work for an interior designer. A year after their move to New York, Rachel saw her doctor because of flu-like symptoms and discovered that she had tremendously high blood pressure. "She had been having insomnia, was grinding her teeth, and would sometimes wake up singing in the middle of the night," remembered Scott. "It sounds strange, but we learned that this behavior is typical for people with high blood pressure."

Rachel added, "When the doctor told me how high my blood pressure was, I went straight to Scott's office. 'We need to upgrade our health insurance policy,' I told him. My mother had a history of high blood pressure and kidney problems, and I was savvy enough to know that my problem might be serious. Scott changed our insurance that very afternoon. Within the next few days, I talked to a lot of people and found a kidney specialist."

Scott said, "The kidney specialist told us that Rachel had lupus, that her kidneys were failing, and that she would have to go on dialysis for the rest of her life, which is not a nice sentence. We scrambled around madly to find another doctor. My dad helped us."

Rachel added, "I went to see the doctor my father-in-law found for me; he was top-notch. He told me immediately that I was in critical condition and needed to be hospitalized; he said he would have a bed for me first thing the next morning. The news shocked me, because physically I didn't feel anything. I wasn't in pain. In some ways, that's the difficult part about lupus.

"That night was emotional for Scott and me. I realized that I was very ill and didn't know what the outcome would be. In this type of situation you naturally separate, you detach; you gain a whole new perspective and just long for the stupid, everyday business of life. Scott was great. He held me, grounded me emotionally, so I didn't lose control."

Scott added, "Massive injections of steroids saved Rachel's kidneys; she has about half function now. It was a miraculous thing, but we spent an incredibly dramatic three days where she was looking death right in the face. I was sleeping on the floor next to her bed in the hospital. It was serious. She had too much phosphorous in her blood, and her heart was in trouble. The steroids had terrible side effects; Rachel felt nauseous, hyped-up, weird. One doctor we'd consulted had warned us against these treatments because he felt they were too dangerous. He said people could die from them. We knew the risk, but Rachel didn't want to lose her kidneys."

Rachel continued, "It didn't occur to me consciously that I could die when I checked into the hospital. I calmly put on my hospital gown and got into bed. As soon as the medication started, I began to feel high and my mind played a trick on me right away. I looked out the window of my room, thought I was in a prison, and started screaming. I wanted to leave.

"During the next few days my doctor would stop by to talk, and I couldn't always understand what he was saying. There was only so much I could take in; sometimes he would say something that scared me, and I would stop listening. The idea that something could go wrong was shocking."

"Our week in the hospital was a powerful experience that changed us permanently," said Scott. "We were on the edge of eternity together and it cemented our marriage."

"Scott was terrific," said Rachel. "I never felt that my illness threatened our marriage. We'd come through fire together! The medicine made me disoriented, and initially I couldn't even walk around the block without getting lost. I'd get a rush and would have to stop to figure out where I was. So I began taking a cab to my sister Martha's every morning, and I would spend the day with her and her baby until Scott finished work. I had to come to terms with my illness emotionally as well. I thought, *I'm young. Why did this have to happen to me at this point in my life? I'm unlucky. I'm unworthy.*

"On one of my office visits, my doctor told me I'd sustained too much kidney damage to ever carry a child. I thought, *It's okay. That's fine . . . no problem. I'm happy to be alive, I'm happy I don't have to be on a machine. I can deal with that.* To me it seemed a fair trade-off. It wasn't the biggest tragedy.

"It took about two years for me to feel normal again. I was in therapy, and once I began to feel better, I went back to school and completed the liberal arts courses I needed for a B.F.A. I majored in illustration so I could do something commercially."

Before Rachel's health crisis, Scott and Rachel hadn't seriously considered the idea of having children. Scott explained, "We had assumed it would happen when we were ready. Afterward I was quite shell-shocked about Rachel's health, so the decision not to get pregnant was a relief for me. I also had a rather juvenile thought: *All right, I got out of it! Maybe I can continue being like a teenager, not having kids, not having all the responsibilities. I'll have more money to do fun things.* I think there's a part in most males I know that thinks, *If I can wriggle out of this family stuff, I'll try it.* At the same time, I felt a sadness. I'd always pictured in my mind a little girl who was like Rachel. I had the normal feelings of wanting to see my wife, whom I dearly loved, reflected with me in a child.

"Over time, the realization that she couldn't have a child was much more traumatic for Rachel and quite sad. Her sisters had had children. I think Rachel felt left out. When her sister Martha learned that we weren't able to have children she invited us to the birth of her second child. I did the Lamaze training with Martha, and Rachel and I were with her during her labor. Afterward I joked with Rachel: 'Thank God you won't have to go through that! It doesn't look like much fun.'"

Rachel added, "Martha's husband was traveling a lot and couldn't be depended on to be there for her delivery. I saw this invitation as a good opportunity for Scott. I thought, *Why shouldn't he have that experience?* As it turned out, Martha's husband arrived just before the delivery, so we didn't see the birth. But some feelings came out of this experience for me. I felt it was better to take it head-on rather than averting my eyes every time I saw a pregnant woman. I knew it might enhance my feeling of loss, but I decided to see it and deal with it. And it felt good to be there for my sister."

Scott added, "Our involvement in this birth and Rachel's strong desire to have a child got us thinking in a family way and led us to considering adoption as the next logical turn. I was rather passive toward adoption. Our discussions went on for about five years, and during that period we began to feel somewhat confident that Rachel had recovered her health."

Rachel continued, "As soon as I knew that I couldn't have a child, I automatically made the assumption that I was going to adopt. Adoption was not an issue for me. I had intended to have a child biologically and found that I couldn't, so of course I would adopt. I would just follow the course."

Rachel believed that the issue was not about pregnancy versus adoption; it was about raising a child. "It took me a little time to get used to the idea that I couldn't have a child, that I'd miss the experience of pregnancy. My friends and sisters were having babies. I wasn't invited to some of the baby showers because people thought it might be an issue for me. I know they had good intentions, but being left out made me feel hurt and angry. I never felt I was less of a woman because I couldn't experience pregnancy or that adoption carried a stigma. I was quite impatient with women who felt stigmatized. It took me a while to be forgiving of that attitude and to accept it as ignorance, which is what it is.

"Scott had a harder time deciding about adoption, and that's why it took us a long time. I was pushing the idea, but whenever I slowed down, the momentum would slow down. We both had ambivalent feelings. Scott's were due to his concerns about money and the responsibilities of parenthood. My ambivalence was due to my health; I wanted to see what was going to happen with my lupus. I knew I wasn't cured. I thought, *Will I have enough energy to be a mother? What if I'm totally incapacitated or not around? Is it fair to Scott to insist on having a child?*

"The doctor had told me that, typically, if lupus presents itself critically at the onset, it is less likely to recur. I've made a lot of choices based on that assumption. I don't remember ever sitting down and making the decision to adopt. We just had no other option if we were going to have a family. When Scott got comfortable with the idea, we finally went ahead."

Scott and Rachel chose an adoption agency that had been recommended to them by friends. Scott remembered, "The social worker, Gail, was a lovely, kind-hearted woman from whom I felt a kind of instant compassion, which made me a little uneasy at first. I remember feeling that I was an object of pity. Gail was easy to talk to, but I found that all the adoption agency people talked almost in baby talk to whomever they were speaking. They dragged out their words in a certain way. They said, 'Awwwwwwww . . .' a lot! It made me squirm a bit, but I assumed this was to be expected from an adoption agency. I felt a little embarrassed. I had some residual thoughts like, *If I was a real man, I'd have my own babies.* It was a macho reaction to having to deal with what felt like a woman's world with all the social workers talking about birth mothers, babies, and so forth."

Rachel added, "I liked Gail, and I think she liked us. She was comfortable with us, she wasn't snooty, and I think she enjoyed the fact that we were loose and informal."

Scott continued, "The agency had a group training program that was a bit too 'touchy-feely' for me; they wanted us to talk about our feelings and encouraged us to spill our guts about how unhappy we were because of our inability to have biological children. A lot of the other people in the group had been through years of infertility struggles, and since that wasn't our case, I realized I felt a little superior. I didn't have any feelings of inadequacy to bring to the table, but a lot of the others clearly did. It woke me up. I'm glad I went there, because it made me realize how painful infertility is for men and women; I could see the pain on their faces. Some seemed terrified of adoption and showed a sense of hopelessness. I felt they had already reached the end of their rope and had come into the adoption process believing that adoption would also be hopeless. They brought a sense of resignation to these discussions."

"I realized the group meetings were making Scott squirm," said Rachel, "but I thought they were necessary. The real problem was that Scott and I didn't go through infertility and the people who did were wrecks! My heart went out to them, but their attitudes were negative, whereas I looked on adoption as a good thing. Hearing what these women went through made me realize what I had been spared. I found their stories horrendous."

Gail explained to Scott and Rachel that traditional adoptions—in which adoptive parents wait for a child to be chosen for them—were no longer available through the agency. Instead couples were encouraged to advertise in newspapers in various parts of the country and wait for a birth mother to call them. It was a new program, and Gail couldn't accurately predict how long it would take, but she suggested that within a year they would make contact with a birth mother and be on their way.

"The process was weird," said Rachel. "We sent out some ads and had a special line for incoming calls. The first call was from a college student in Arizona. I talked with her for over an hour. She said she was interested in us because our ad stated that we were artistic and she was an art major. While talking to her I felt nervous but excited. I thought, *Maybe this whole thing can be over easily and quickly!* We kept talking and all of a sudden she said, 'Oh, my mom's here. I've got to go!' And she hung up! For a few days, I kept hoping that she would call back, but she never did.

"Another time a birth mother called and seemed to be fishing around to find out how many things we would pay for. Once a man called; the agency had warned us against negotiating with birth fathers. We felt the calls were not always legitimate. I hated the process. It was emotionally treacherous. We'd advertise for a month, stop for a couple of months, then try again."

Scott added, "The ads led to some grizzly experiences. It was horrible for Rachel when the girl from Arizona hung up on her. She was devastated. We got very few calls in the two years we advertised. With some of them we had fears: *her boyfriend is a drug addict; she doesn't know who the father is; the father is mildly retarded.* The agency had told us to budget one to two thousand dollars for advertising. It seemed terrifying and iffy. I didn't like the program. They wanted us to make an active effort, but I felt there was something desperate and needy about this approach.

"The ads are aimed at a teenage audience. A typical one would say, 'We're going to give our child teddy bears with hugs and kisses and pizza.' Apparently this worked for some people! I realized we were trying to appeal to uneducated Bible Belt teenagers and that we should accept the agency's advice of what works with them. But I was uncomfortable with that. I didn't like the process of having to sell ourselves to someone in order to get a child."

Rachel continued, "We got to the point where I realized Scott was beginning to look stunned, and I finally said to him, 'This is ridiculous. Let's look into an Asian adoption.' My father had remarried, and he and his wife had adopted a Thai daughter. I thought she was beautiful and would have loved to adopt a Thai child. Gail told us that the agency didn't have a Thai program but that China had just reopened, so we decided to go for that. I think Gail was happy to see us move on from the domestic program, because at that point we were the slowest ones from our original group. All the other couples had found birth mothers and were on their way. By this time I was thirty-seven and Scott was forty."

"When the China program opened, Rachel and I decided instantly that we wanted a Chinese baby," said Scott. "We were fed up with the domestic program; we'd spent two years and a thousand dollars on advertising, and nothing had happened. I was very discouraged. The China program seemed right for us. We were told it would take about a year. They had a list of people, and we got in line. There wasn't going to be any question about it; it was going to happen. We would be spared the agony of begging a teenage girl to give her baby to us. The China program was very straightforward. For me it was an opportunity to get a dark-haired baby girl who might look a bit like Rachel. I've always thought Rachel looked rather Oriental in her childhood photos. I wanted a little girl. This was all about having a little Rachel."

Scott and Rachel were able to switch to their agency's China program without having to pay extra fees or to rewrite their home study. But they were faced with a daunting amount of paperwork, required by China's bureaucracy. Scott explained, "The agency assigned a new social worker to us. Faith was more reserved, more diffident than Gail. Her job was administrative; she was there to help us with the paperwork.

"The Chinese had several concerns. They had to be assured that we were not criminals or child molesters, so we got fingerprinted and had police records checked; they wanted reassurance that we were who we said we were, so we submitted tax statements and letters from employers; we also needed letters from Rachel's doctor stating that her life expectancy was normal. All these documents had to be translated; they went through the Chinese consulate in New York, the Chinese embassy in Washington, D.C., and then were sent to China.

"I was worried that Rachel's health would somehow throw a kink in the process. Translating information about complex medical matters is difficult; I worried that the Chinese people reviewing her records wouldn't know enough about lupus and kidney function. We hoped they would just trust the American doctors' judgment. It was a bit nerve-wracking. I thought that some little thing might cause a problem, that a piece of paper wouldn't be done correctly.

"It was a tedious process. Once, we had to go to the Chinese consulate during a ninety-degree heat wave and wait in line for three hours only to have them shut down for lunch just before it was our turn. Big stew pots were brought in, and the consular personnel ate right in front of us! The consulate was in an old hotel, and apparently all the officials lived upstairs; they never left the building. It was like being in China."

Rachel continued, "Getting ready to go to China was hair-raising. I put on a lot of weight because I was nervous about the adoption, about becoming a parent. I was making a commitment to the idea that I was healthy and would continue to be in good health. We were going halfway around the world to become parents. It was a big adventure."

Faith explained to Scott and Rachel that once the Chinese approved their paperwork, a baby would be chosen for them at random. They wouldn't be looking at photographs and choosing a baby themselves. A passport-sized photograph of the child and a medical report would be sent to the agency in New York.

"We weren't sure about the kind of baby we would get," said Scott. "We were leaping into a void. When we finally got the photograph, it was an incredibly powerful moment. Faith called me at work. She said, 'I have a baby for you. Her name is Mei-Mei Chen. Do you want to come over and see her picture?' My office was near hers; I rushed over there. I looked at Mei-Mei's picture and thought, *This is the cutest baby I have ever seen!* Faith seemed a bit reserved, and I asked her if the baby was okay. 'Well, she's really small,' she said. 'She's six months old and weighs less than ten pounds.' I thought Faith was saying that the baby's health was in jeopardy because of her size, that she might not make it. I felt instantly paternal. It just poured out.

"The photograph opened a floodgate. It had all seemed abstract before. There was never a time during the paperwork when I associated the process with a flesh-and-blood baby. It wasn't until this little one-inch photograph came that I realized, *This is my little girl.* It was so emotional. I looked at her face in the photo; it was a sad little face, and I thought she looked like she was all alone, that she was waiting for us. I wanted to be there instantly, but I knew it would be a few more months before we could go to China."

Rachel said, "After Scott picked up the baby's photograph, he came running into my studio. I thought she was beautiful. I studied the picture carefully, trying to understand her expression; one of her eyebrows was up. I rushed to make photocopies and faxed them to everyone we knew.

It was a thrill for me to see how excited Scott was. I had done most of the paperwork and the running around up to this point. I had always told him about what I was doing, but I realized that seeing this picture had changed his attitude about our adoption. It pleased me to see his reaction; his reservations about adopting a child and raising a family seemed to vanish.

"Our agency put together a group of parents-to-be to travel to China. I began to buy a few baby things, but I didn't know exactly what to get and was unsure what size to buy."

Scott continued, "We got lots of used baby clothes from relatives and friends, but of course we bought all-new clothes anyway! We had a Goodwill store's worth of baby clothes piling up in our apartment. Rachel decorated the nursery. We met the group of people we would be traveling to China with; it consisted of six couples and one single woman. The agency held a couple of sessions for us. It seemed like a good group; we were all about the same age."

At last, the group left for Beijing, a twenty-hour flight from New York. "Our translator, Yun, greeted us at the airport," Scott said. "We heaped our mountains of luggage into a large van and headed off to our hotel. We entered the city through tollbooths topped off with pagodas. Although it was ten o'clock on a Friday night, the sidewalks were empty and the shops closed. Yun explained that there's not much nightlife in Beijing because there aren't many restaurants or bars; people go home and watch television in the evenings. Our hotel was a nice, Western-style hotel. Physically, we were beyond jetlag.

"At breakfast the next morning we were all as nervous as cats. We knew we weren't getting the babies for two more days; the next day we would fly to a small city in the center of China where the orphanage was. Yun took us sightseeing. Beijing made New York City seem deserted! In contrast to the previous evening, the city was mobbed—thronged with people; the roads were filled with cars, bicycles, donkey carts, and tractors all mixed together. Pedestrians walked right into the middle of this chaos. It was much noisier than New York, and I'd never seen more exhaust smoke in my life. We saw the Forbidden City, Tiannanmen Square, and the Great Wall."

Rachel added, "I felt so excited knowing that soon we would get our baby. I loved Beijing, but I must say that it made New York City seem clean and quiet in comparison! We walked freely among the Chinese people, many of whom could speak English. I realized we stood out, that we were a curiosity."

Scott continued, "At the end of the day we went back to our hotel, and Rachel cried for a long time, venting three years of tension over our search for a baby. We were so nervous. What was about to happen seemed unreal. All we had was a little postage stamp-sized photograph. We wondered whether the baby would like us. *What's this going to be like? Is there really going to be a baby?* Rachel had tears of joy, sadness, and fear all mixed up. I was sad with the realization that our life as just a couple was almost over. I thought about my mother and told Rachel I felt that Mom was watching over this event. It was an emotional night."

The next morning Yun escorted the group to central China in a small plane. "It was a long flight," said Scott, "and when I saw a stewardess use an air-sickness bag I worried about the competency of the crew. The countryside between the airfield and the city was pretty. There were rice paddies and wheat fields tended by people in cone-shaped hats. But the city proper looked like a run-down or half-built version of Newark. There was a polluted lake outside our hotel, and beyond that a massive industrial sprawl of factories and grim apartment buildings, all seemingly poured from the same mold. The sun was hidden behind thick smog, and hovering over the scene was a nuclear power plant in the center of the city."

Rachel continued, "The next morning I woke up excited, but I also felt scared and physically numb. We had breakfast together as a group; all of us were giddy. One woman told us she had stayed awake all night reading the nursery rhymes printed on the diapers she'd brought! We knew exactly what would happen on this day. Everything was very well organized. After breakfast we were to go back upstairs and wait for the babies to be brought to us in our rooms.

"Scott and I went back to our room and started pacing back and forth. I kept thinking, *Oh my God—this is it!* I kept peeking out into the corridor, which was T-shaped. Finally I saw a string of nurses carrying babies coming up the hallway and turning the corner—what a picture! Our room was second to last, so I knew we'd have to wait a bit longer. I closed the door and turned to my husband. 'Okay, Scott, this is it. They're rounding the corner!'"

Scott added, "I paced like I was in a maternity ward. They started the deliveries at the far end of the corridor, so we had to wait an agonizing twenty minutes. Seven nurses were holding babies, accompanied by government officials. The entourage, led by Yun, stopped at each room to deliver a baby and take pictures. Finally they knocked on our door. We opened it to find a nurse holding our baby, a man in uniform, and several other men and women who were local officials. The nurse walked in and handed the baby to Rachel. She was very cute—just like we'd expected—but her hair was raggedy, almost like it had been shaved; she had a big bald spot on the back of her head. I thought she looked angry."

Rachel continued, "The moment was confusing. I was trying to look at the baby, but the nurse kept pointing and saying something to me; I couldn't figure out what she was trying to say. The baby's eyes were open, and she was looking around. She was quiet and subdued. We were distracted from the baby because so many things were going on. The nurse wanted to show us how to make formula and change her diaper. Scott held her while I tried to follow the nurse's instructions."

Scott said, "After the officials moved on, the nurse took the baby back and began ordering us around by pointing and making little clicking noises. She had us install a diaper, and then she changed the baby into the new clothes we had brought. She took care of this efficiently, almost roughly, knocking the baby into sleeves and legs without ceremony, which made me feel ill at ease. She showed no tenderness. My initial feeling was that the baby would break at the touch! But after seeing this no-nonsense approach, I realized these babies must be pretty tough. Although it was a hot day, the nurse insisted on covering every inch of the baby's body with clothing.

"They bring the babies at feeding time so the new parents can calm them down with a bottle. As we were scrambling to get the formula made, the baby started to get fussy. Our first attempt at making formula wasn't satisfactory; the nurse indicated it was too thin. We hurried to add more powder, but the baby's mood quickly deteriorated. Then the hole in the nipple was too small, and I nervously looked through our disheveled baggage to find my Swiss Army knife. The nurse used the little scissors to enlarge the hole, and then the baby's cries were mercifully replaced by sucking sounds as she drained her bottle.

"The nurse then turned her attention to our belongings and began pointing at various pieces of our luggage, tapping her palm and saying *'ya, ya, ya, ya.'* She pointed to our camera, and we thought she wanted us to take a picture, which we quickly did. But the pointing continued, and I suddenly realized that she wanted us to give her a gift. We had gifts; the agency had told us to bring little bits of jewelry and cigarettes. But Yun had instructed us not to give gifts directly to the nurses; they had to be given to the officials. We tried to explain that we didn't have a gift, and she eventually left. I think she was a bit upset.

"Finally we were alone with our baby, Jenna. I took her in my arms. She looked so tiny, just like in her picture. She had just finished eating and was drifting toward sleep when she looked up at me. I was mesmerized. It seemed like she recognized the love and returned my gaze unflinchingly; her dainty fingers touched my face. I felt that God was looking right through those little eyes . . . that this little soul was so pure. I just fell in love. A baby who is drifting toward sleep is so peaceful. As soon as she went under little bubbles formed in her mouth, and her breathing had such a tiny sound that I could hardly stand it. I kept falling deeper and deeper. It was a great moment that I'll never forget."

Rachel said, "When the nurse left, Scott and I were happy to be alone with Jenna. We couldn't stop looking at her. She was so beautiful! I thought, *She's not crying; maybe she will be good-natured.* I felt like a mother right away. It felt very natural, very good. I realized that Jenna hadn't exhibited any separation anxiety, that she probably had not bonded to her nurse. When we put her in her little crib, she started rocking herself. This bothered me because I'd read that babies who weren't used to being held rocked themselves as a way of comforting themselves. Her movements made me realize that Jenna was a real orphanage kid, that she probably had never been close to anyone. I touched her to make her stop rocking herself. I couldn't stand to see it."

That afternoon the parents and babies met in a conference room to sign the adoption papers. Scott recalled, "It was great seeing everyone else's babies. All the parents seemed delighted but in shock. Afterward we went back to our room to resume admiring our little treasure. We could not get over how beautiful she was. She got fussy, so we fed her again and began experimenting with putting her down to sleep. We found that unless we were up on our feet rocking her the crying accelerated. She finally went to sleep about seven o'clock, but that first night she was up crying a lot. She was fairly inconsolable; we had to keep moving and quickly developed techniques that worked.

"It was hard work but not a burden. At some point in the middle of the night I realized it was impossible for a nonparent to understand this feeling of baby love. Rachel and I took turns; there was no conflict. It happened naturally. By morning we were totally exhausted."

The Chinese government required new parents to remain for a week while the paperwork was completed. Rachel remembered, "Yun seemed to be doing a lot of negotiating to get our papers finalized. Her job was to pay people off for services, and that's part of what we paid for. She would come to us and say, 'Okay, I need this much money now for such and such.' I didn't worry about how she did it. I just assumed that was her job and she knew how business was done there. There was never any threat, but I did feel a bit on the spot. I joked, 'What if they think we're not good enough parents?' The idea of getting on the plane and getting Jenna home was a relief."

Scott added, "A group of officials interviewed us in our hotel in order to finalize Jenna's adoption papers. Our notary told us, in halting English, that Chinese law required us to answer some questions. He wrote our answers on a tissue-thin piece of rice paper using a fountain pen. There were times when he couldn't understand us, and he got a lot of things wrong; these had to be corrected with great difficulty. His most astonishing question was: 'Do you plan to abandon the child when you get back to the United States?'

"During that week we took walks around the town and always got good feelings from the Chinese people. They would stop to play with the baby, and many of them said thank you to us. Once in a park an elderly couple approached us and asked where we were from. When we said America the man's face lit up, and he said, in good English, that his daughter was studying medicine in Kansas City. He told us he was a professor at the local university and was delighted that we were adopting Jenna. Then he wished us good luck and said, 'The Chinese love America. We are natural friends.'

"One day Yun took us to visit the orphanage where all the babies had been living. We traveled up a dirt road past a haphazard construction sight. The orphanage was a square, two-story structure enclosing a courtyard. The director explained, through Yun, that they were in the process of building a new orphanage, so most of the children were in temporary foster care. I wondered, *Will our fees be used to finance it?* We saw a roomful of two-year-olds sitting in little chairs at a long table playing with toys.

Nursery music was playing in the background. The children were quiet and concentrated, as though assembling electronic parts.

"The people at the orphanage know babies and take good care of them, given the facilities they have. But the babies are swaddled; their caregivers can't afford diapers. And they're left in the cribs for long periods of time. Babies are fed and held on schedule. Some of the nurses seemed very loving people, but they have too many to care for. It felt awkward to be touring there with our cameras and American banter, but the atmosphere of order and kindness somehow made it okay.

"I was nervous about the paperwork and the money until it was all turned over to the officials. I had brought thousands of dollars in cash with me, which I was carrying in a money belt. It was paid out slowly to various officials and notaries. On our last night there we unloaded our final albatross of cash. We met the orphanage officials in Yun's room. As a token of appreciation for our three-thousand-dollar 'donation,' they gave us a small painting. They also gave us Jenna's adoption papers, which for the first time told us Jenna's [Mei-Mei Chen's] story, or at least a scanty summary of it:

A Certificate of Mei-Mei Chen's Case

Mei-Mei Chen, female, was found at the XiuFong Bridge nearby on November 7, 1993. After much inquiry, we still haven't found her parents. The Children Welfare Institute named the deserted baby Mei-Mei Chen. According to the situation of the child's umbilical cord and eyes, the doctor predicted the baby was born on November 6, 1993."

Scott continued, "Yun explained to us that the bridge was an accepted drop-off point in that city. Since it is illegal to abandon babies in China, the orphanage people are very secretive about how babies end up in their care. They worry that government officials will spy on the mothers and arrest them. Yun added that every once in a while a mother pins a note to a baby protesting the government's policy, providing a little history of the family, and asking that she be placed in a good home. The notes are either kept by the officials or destroyed; they are not shared with adoptive parents. We received no medical records from the orphanage; we don't even know Jenna's birth weight.

"When we got back to our room we vowed to visit Jenna's bridge one day. Rachel couldn't stop crying thinking about our baby spending the first night of her life lying by the side of the road in the cold. I wondered whether the memory of the bridge was stored in Jenna's head and how it might be recalled later on.

"The next morning we left for the airport early. It seemed like a different place, but I realized that I was a different person. Previously the surrounding billboards had seemed ominous and strange; now they seemed like banners of victory. We flew to Guangzhou [Canton], and our arrival there was one of the all-time highs of my life. We'd gotten used to the baby and were confident with her by now. Jenna was part of us; it seemed like she'd been instantly grafted to us. The hotel we checked into was the most beautiful I'd ever seen; our room had a gorgeous view of the river. It was pure joy. Dinner that night was a real celebration. It felt so good. At that point we knew all our trials were over. There was nothing more to it but one grueling flight to go. It was done! We went to the U.S. consulate and got Jenna's visa; then we relaxed and enjoyed ourselves.

"On our last night in China, Rachel and I took Jenna to Yun's room. We paid her for her expenses and offered her a cash gift we'd put aside for her. At first she refused to accept it but later agreed to use it to buy a microwave. Yun gave jade pieces to each of the babies. Yun said, 'I love being with you Americans and watching you get your babies, but the happiest time for me is when you're safely aboard your plane and on your way home.' Then she paid us a compliment: 'You make me smile; no, you make me laugh!'"

Scott said, "On our flight home we sat next to a Chinese doctor who offered this advice: 'Do not have a laissez-faire attitude with your daughter. Do not say "whatever you want is okay with us." Let her know you expect a lot from her and, specifically, that you expect her to take care of you later on. If you don't let her know you need her, you will break her heart. If you do, she will be loyal to you forever.' He also told us that ice cream puts kids to sleep, which a later experiment proved to be absolutely false! We're not sure about saddling Jenna with expectations, but I think there's probably a kernel of truth in what he said."

"My parents were waiting for us at the airport in New York," said Rachel. "My mother stayed for a few days to help us get settled. My sisters all came. Our friends took to Jenna right away; they were incredible.

A week after we got home Scott's father and stepmother had a little family party for Jenna. Scott's grandmother was there; she had always been straightforward with me, so when she told me she thought Jenna was adorable, I knew she meant it. People brought gifts, and it was wonderful to see them welcome our baby."

"When my pediatrician first examined Jenna, she was ten months old and weighed only sixteen pounds," said Rachel. "She couldn't sit up properly, and her legs were completely floppy. Because I was a new mother, I thought this was fine! The doctor wrote on Jenna's chart that her developmental range was between two and six months. For the first ten months of her life, Jenna's diet consisted of a diluted formula mixed with rice cereal. Thank God we got Jenna when we did; another couple of months could have meant she was unplaceable. The doctor didn't tell me this right away, which I appreciated, because it shocked me. She waited until Jenna's weight and size were big enough to put her on the chart. That took just three months from the time we brought her home.

"Complete strangers often ask me if Jenna's father is Chinese. You can see them trying to figure it out. Once a man at a gas station asked me why I went to China to adopt. I told him it was none of his business. I've done that a couple of times. I don't have a hard time doing that. After all, I'm a New Yorker! If someone steps over the line, that's it. But I know I've got to train myself, because now Jenna doesn't know what they're saying, but she will one day. I've got to be prepared for people's questions. I don't ever want my daughter to feel rejected because she's Asian; she has already been rejected because of her sex.

"I'm not too worried about explaining her adoption to Jenna because I don't have any issue with our decision to adopt. It's a different experience, but it's not less of an experience than pregnancy. There's nothing *less* about it. With pregnancy you've got the biology that's carrying you along; with adoption you make a decision and then you have to be the one to keep the ball rolling. The thing that is great about adoption is that both parents are handed the baby. It's not just coming through the mother.

"Recently there's been a lot of negative publicity about Chinese orphanages. People have asked me if I'm clipping the articles about abuses in Chinese orphanages to show Jenna when she's older. Why would I want to show those articles to her? I have mixed feelings about this publicity.

In my mind, when you go to a Third World country it's ridiculous to assume that abuses don't occur. I'm sure the information is true and the writers and filmmakers feel it's important to expose something that's not good, but my point is: what are they jeopardizing? I've dealt with the Chinese government. Their way of doing things has nothing to do with the way we think in the United States. It would be a tragedy if this publicity caused the Chinese officials to close the country to foreigners wishing to adopt. I believe a larger number of children would suffer as a result."

Rachel concludes, "I look back now and realize how silly we were to have dragged our feet for so many years. I mentioned my regret to Scott; he agreed, but he argued, 'If we'd adopted earlier, we wouldn't have Jenna!' I always knew adoption was the right decision. Someday I'm going to tell Jenna that her coming to us was a miracle. . . . Our coming to her was also a miracle. I firmly believe this was a miracle. And it was an adventure. We found her halfway around the world. I love how I had a baby!"

"It's been happily ever after since," said Scott.

6/ Cal and Lee Anne
Foster parenting and adoption

"My kids are the best kids in the world. I'll tell them, 'I just got a phone call, and DSS wants us to take a baby,' and they say hurrah! They love it when a new child comes into the house. They just can't wait for them to get here. They give the new one a lot of attention, make them feel welcome. They say, 'Here is your bed . . . This is my teddy bear, but you can use him; you can sleep with him.'"

THE ILLS that plague our modern society—poverty, drug abuse, and homelessness—have created large numbers of needy children. Although many people advocate that the government should focus on attacking the root causes of these problems, the urgent question of how to care for thousands of vulnerable children requires immediate answers. For economic reasons, institutions and orphanages in this country have given way to a foster care system. It is estimated that the cost of caring for a single child in foster care is five thousand dollars a year, whereas group homes cost about ten thousand, and caring for a child in an institution costs nearly forty thousand dollars. Another major reason for foster care is that most people believe children are better off living in a family rather than in a group home or an institution.

The ultimate goal of foster care is to reunite children with their birth families if the parents can improve the situation that caused the children to be removed in the first place. When parents cannot improve the situation, or when familial ties are irretrievably broken, foster children become available for adoption. Unfortunately, some children spend their entire childhoods in foster care—never completely belonging. But to a large extent, children are absorbed into the foster care community; they are adopted by their own foster parents or by other foster parents interested in adoption.

This is the story of Cal and Lee Anne, a hardworking, devoted black couple who have opened their home and hearts to foster children. Over the years they have adopted four of their foster children and cared for many others who stayed briefly and then moved on. Each child, whether there strictly for foster care or to be adopted, has received love and acceptance. A framed photograph of each foster child is proudly displayed on the living room walls alongside the photographs of the couple's own children.

Lee Anne, a self-assured woman in her mid-thirties, has a girlishly slim figure. Her large, friendly eyes reflect a warm personality and open manner. Cal, who is forty-three, is a trim man of medium height; he exhibits an undisguised love for his children. He is strong yet soft-spoken, with a rich, deep laugh.

Lee Anne grew up in a two-parent family in a suburb of Boston. "I was the middle child of five children and don't remember being asked to help out with the younger kids, but I started baby-sitting for neighbors at the age of ten. When I graduated from high school I got a full-time job taking care of one infant. I also worked in a community center teaching arts and crafts to children. From the time I was a teenager, I decided that I never wanted to be pregnant and have a baby, but I loved kids and knew that I'd find a way to be involved with them. My sister had the same attitude. I'm not sure where it came from. Our mother used to say, 'What's with you two?' My husband went along with my attitude; maybe he thought I'd change my mind after a while, but I never did, and things have worked out just fine for us."

Cal and Lee Anne met in 1987 at his brother and sister-in-law's house; they dated for a year before getting married. Lee Anne narrates, "After our wedding, I wasn't working and I noticed an ad in the newspaper about foster care. I asked Cal if we could check into it. I didn't really know anything about foster care, but I thought it sounded interesting. Cal and I are homebodies; we never go out, so we knew having kids around wasn't going to change our lifestyle. We went to our first DSS [Department of

Social Services] meeting and fell in love with the idea of becoming foster parents."

"I grew up in Boston in a family of seven kids," said Cal. "I'm the oldest boy, and I have two older sisters. My mother and father separated when I was in third grade. I got a paper route to help my mother out. We were poor. My mother died when I was a sophomore, and my father moved back to take care of us. After high school I got a scholarship from the University of Massachusetts, but I passed it up so I could help the family. When my father died in 1979, I wanted to keep the family together, so I did a paper route at four-thirty in the morning; then I'd come home, sleep for a couple of hours, and go to my job at a nursing home. I picked up my sisters from work every day. I was thirty-five when I met Lee Anne.

"After we got married, we baby-sat for my brother's kids and for neighbors' kids once in a while, then Lee Anne came up with this foster parenting idea. At that time I was working for a local public works department collecting rubbish. I was a workaholic. I did overtime whenever I could. At first I wasn't pleased with the idea of foster care. I wanted to see what we could do [about having a baby] ourselves, but Lee Anne had a problem with all that, so I decided to go to the foster parent classes with her and ended up with a diploma!"

Cal and Lee Anne began MAPP [Massachusetts Approach to Partnerships in Parenting] training, which lasted for ten weeks. At the first meeting they learned that foster care is for children whose parents cannot parent them for a while because they might be homeless, in the hospital, or in jail. It is also for children who have been physically or emotionally neglected or abused. They were told that foster care is temporary—a service to keep families together, not to drive them farther apart. Foster parents are seen as substitutes, not as replacements. The social worker explained that problems in a foster child's birth family can cause the child to have feelings of anger, shame, and rejection; sometimes a fear of hunger is seen in these kids, and temper tantrums are not unusual. A lot of these kids believe they are unlovable.

Lee Anne said, "The trainers tried to be honest and not make the picture look too pretty; we were told about bad experiences some children go through. I think they try to give a balanced picture without scaring you away.

"We quickly understood that foster kids don't come on their own;

there are always birth parents, social workers, and lawyers involved. That's why it's called a partnership in parenting. You don't just take a child, like in the old days, and forget about where he came from.

"Cal and I went to three-hour training sessions once a week for ten weeks. One of the things that struck me was learning that foster kids arrive in your home with their things in a trash bag if they have any possessions at all. Later a corporation heard about this and gave DSS a lot of bright yellow zipper bags, so now the kids travel with yellow bags. It's so much better for the kids; it gives them some dignity.

"In other training sessions we learned about ways to reach out to kids who are withdrawn, how to discipline and set limits, how to make your home a safe place, et cetera. A whole session was devoted to losses and gains. Each child goes through losses and gains; he's lost a birth parent but gained a good foster home. They warned us that we might feel a big loss when a foster child leaves, but the best way to look at it is that the child is gaining another chance to work things out with his family or perhaps be adopted into a new family."

During that training period Cal and Lee Anne had to fill out questionnaires, have personal interviews with a social worker, and do a home study and a CORI report (to determine whether they had a police record), just the way adoptive parents do. Initially they went into MAPP training with the intention of being only foster parents, but by the time they had finished they'd decided to adopt, too.

Two days after their training, Cal and Lee Anne met their first foster child, Lewis, an adorable, skinny little black boy with big sad eyes. A social worker brought him over for a visit; he stayed for an hour. "He was a depressed two-year-old," said Lee Anne. "He wasn't eating, he wasn't responding, he wasn't talking. His mother had died when he was eighteen months old; he'd been in one other foster home, which wasn't right for him and he withdrew [emotionally]. Lewis latched on to me the minute he saw me! It was wonderful. It was hard to give him back after an hour. A few days later our CORI came back, and the social worker had Lewis at our house an hour later! This time he stayed for the weekend. They do it gradually when they can; a transition is always best."

Cal continued, "When Lewis came his nose was runny, his face was dirty, and he had a mouthful of crackers that he refused to swallow. It seemed like he was holding on to the food, saving it for later. We found out he'd been spending most of the day strapped in a high chair, and the only food he ever got was take-out. His foster father was on drugs, and his foster mother neglected him. The first day Lewis didn't say anything, but by the end of the weekend he was happy; his face had cleared up. I'll never forget it. We had to send him back to his foster family for a week, and it was Thanksgiving time. That was a lousy Thanksgiving!"

When it was time for Lewis to go back he didn't want to leave. The social worker came to get him on Monday morning; Lee Anne told Lewis he'd be back on Friday. She showed him all his new clothes and said they'd be waiting for him, but he didn't want to go. "I had to chase him to get him dressed," she remembered. "He didn't cry, but I could tell he wasn't happy. When we went to pick him up the next weekend, he stared at us as if to say, 'How could you do this to me?' He looked depressed again. We felt bad."

Cal added, "I could tell he was mad. His nose was running all over his face again, and he wouldn't talk to us. We brought him home and tried to explain to him that he was here to stay. He didn't understand what we were saying. Lewis was a mess. We changed his clothes and gave him some toys to play with. In a few days we could see a change in him."

"Cal and I wondered if we could really do this," said Lee Anne. "We didn't know how it would be to have a child with us for twenty-four hours every day. But it was great; Lewis bonded to us instantly! He started talking right away. He came back to us the day after Thanksgiving. That night Cal was about to eat a plate of Thanksgiving leftovers for dinner. He went into the kitchen to get something, and Lewis hopped up to the table and ate Cal's food. It was so rewarding! He started eating and didn't stop. There was no eating problem after that."

Cal and Lee Anne were told that Lewis was available for adoption; he wasn't legally free yet, but he would be, and they could adopt him if they wanted to. "We knew immediately that we wanted to adopt Lewis," said Lee Anne. "Lewis's father was out of the picture, but we were a little worried because there was an aunt (his mother's sister) who might have wanted him. She could have had legal custody; she loved Lewis and had loved her sister dearly, but she had a child of her own and felt she couldn't handle another one. I was nervous about her wanting him.

"I met her at DSS so I could talk with her about adopting him. It was sad because his mother had died. I brought Lewis along with me. I told her, 'Even though I didn't know Lewis's mother, I think about her a lot and I know she loved him. I will do the best I can for Lewis as if his own mother were looking after him.' We both cried. She gave me a picture of Lewis's mother. That meeting gave her the ability to let go . . . and it gave me the ability to give Lewis some history of his birth family.

"Our first Christmas with Lewis was so nice. We went to my parents' on Christmas Eve, and the whole family was there. Lewis got a little bicycle, Legos, blocks, trucks—all kinds of stuff! I took a thousand pictures. My father had candy in all his pockets to give to the kids. That's what grandpas are for! By the end of the evening Lewis was asleep in Cal's lap.

"Cal and I fell so in love with Lewis. We adopted him a year-and-a-half later on Valentine's Day. Lewis is my heartbeat, even to this day, and he's almost eight years old now."

Four months after Lewis came to them, Cal and Lee Anne got another phone call from DSS. Cal remembered, "I had stopped at home on a lunch break. Lee Anne wasn't home, so I took the call. It was about a little girl. I said, 'Yeah, I'd like to have a little girl.'"

"Cal was so excited," said Lee Anne. "When I came home he said, 'A girl! A girl! We're getting a little girl!' This was an emergency placement; there was no time for a transition. I called DSS and said I'd be right there to pick her up.

"Though I hate to say it, there are some bad foster homes, and Samantha was also in a bad foster home. There are good and bad people everywhere, and not everybody's perfect. Some people do fall through the cracks. That doesn't mean that somebody wasn't doing their job, but sometimes people can fool social workers. Samantha's foster mother was dealing drugs and she was on drugs; the children weren't getting enough attention. Samantha was dirty and emotionally neglected. She'd been in this foster home since birth. She was a drug baby—she'd been exposed to cocaine and heroin in the womb. She had had a bad start and a bad foster home.

"Samantha was twenty-two months old. She was a cute little black girl—short and pudgy but dirty. She didn't smell very nice. We brought her home and threw her in the tub! Lewis recognized her; his former foster mother was a friend of Samantha's foster mother. They were so excited to see each other! I asked Lewis if it was okay for Samantha to live with us. He said, 'Sam, Sam!' and she said, 'Lewis, Lewis!' It was sweet."

Cal said, "We had met Samantha's foster mother at MAPP training; when Lewis came she told us we could borrow her high chair for him. I had called her at noontime to see if it was a good time to pick up the high chair, and she said she was still in bed. When we got there her house was dark. I told Lee Anne I thought there was something wrong with that woman. No matter what time of day we called her it seemed she was always in bed. DSS finally caught on to her and the police were ready to pull a heroin raid at her house; that's why it was an emergency placement. A DSS social worker picked Samantha up from her day-care center and took her to the office, where Lee Anne picked her up."

"Samantha was a different child from Lewis," said Lee Anne. "She wasn't shy or afraid. She'd go to anybody. We had to keep our eyes on her because she would just take off. Cal and I wondered, *When is she going to cry?* She was taken from her day care never to return to her foster home. She acted like she was on vacation! She was talking well, but she wasn't very affectionate. I'm sure her foster mother wasn't handing out too many kisses.

"About two weeks later, Samantha figured out that she wasn't going back home; I took her to see her pediatrician, and it must have triggered something in her: *Hey, I haven't been home in a while!* She had a temper tantrum outside the pediatrician's office. I couldn't get her to go into the car. When we got home we talked about it together. I said, 'Do you miss your home?' She said yes. I said, 'Are you sad because you have a new home?' She nodded. We were sitting together on the floor and both of us were crying. It was sad. But Samantha was okay after that. She got her anger out, and then she was pretty happy. One problem was that her other foster mother had the same name, Lee Anne. Samantha didn't like to hear that name! I told her she could call me Mommy, the way Lewis did."

Cal continued, "Samantha was a hard nut to crack. She had been going to a day-care center, but she was dirty and smelly, and I don't think they wanted to bother with her. They just let her do what she wanted in order to keep her quiet. She couldn't even eat right. After we cleaned her up, the day-care people noticed the difference. They said, 'Oh, we can touch her now!'"

Lee Anne said, "Samantha has bad eyesight, and she's a natural-born klutzy type. I knew something was wrong because she fell a lot as a baby, and she was walking into walls. I had her brain tested, her legs checked, and finally her eyes tested. She got glasses and stopped walking into walls, but she still kept falling. Drug babies have problems; she didn't have birth defects, but she has learning disabilities. She sometimes has trouble remembering and concentrating, but she can learn. I think the environment makes all the difference.

"Samantha wasn't free for adoption when we got her; we took her as a foster child with the possibility of adoption. At first I told myself, *I'm not going to get too close to her. I'm not going to buy her this or that, because she may be leaving.* I tried consciously to hold back, but it didn't work! I couldn't do it. I gave her hugs and kisses. I just had to give her everything. Lewis was always a cuddlebug, because he'd learned from his mother. But Samantha had to learn to kiss on the mouth. Affection is learned, and I think kissing on the cheek is not very nice. Cal and I kiss all the kids on the mouth."

Samantha had family members who wanted her, but DSS rejected them. Her birth mother was still involved with drugs. Samantha knew her birth mother, but she didn't really have a relationship with her. She called her Jeanette. They had seen each other only at irregularly scheduled office visits. Lee Anne met Jeanette after Samantha came to live with them. Jeanette was worried that Samantha might be in another bad foster home. Lee Anne tried to reassure her. "She kept saying, 'You don't know what goes on behind closed doors.' I said to her, 'I promise you that I will look after Samantha as if I'm the one who gave birth to her.'

"Jeanette was in denial; she assumed Samantha would wait for her to get clean [go off drugs] while the years went by."

Cal continued, "We had to go to foster care reviews for Samantha every six months. A whole group of people reviews you: social workers, lawyers, birth parents, everybody who needs to be involved. Samantha's father came to one review. He was on drugs, and he died of AIDS when Samantha was three years old. Before he died, he made his wife promise to try to get Samantha back."

"By the time Samantha was five years old, we were frustrated because she still wasn't legally released for adoption," said Lee Anne. "When she visited with Jeanette off and on at DSS, Samantha always held back. She didn't want Jeanette to like her. I was usually in the next room; Samantha didn't want to go by herself. Jeanette kept moving, so we were bounced around to every DSS office in the state. Jeanette finally got clean and decided to take Samantha back! She had three boys and had custody of them. I took Jeanette to meet our adoption counselor, Joan, who tried to help Jeanette understand that it wouldn't be right to take Samantha out of our home, the only home she could remember. Joan explained to Jeanette that Samantha viewed her as a stranger—and a somewhat threatening one. She said it wouldn't be in Samantha's best interests and suggested an open adoption, where Samantha would be legally adopted by us but could continue regular visits with Jeanette."

Cal said, "Jeanette told us what she wanted; she wanted birthdays, vacations, and holidays. This was the only time I said anything to her. I told her, 'I'm not agreeing to that. That's not the way it's going to be.' All of a sudden the tears started to come, and she said that I was trying to take her daughter away! She wanted everything."

Jeanette went to her own therapist with Joan's open adoption idea, and worked out an agreement with Lee Anne. "She was trying to do the best thing for Samantha but she had to realize that I am not a baby-sitter; I am Samantha's mother!" said Lee Anne. "Judges tend to favor the birth mothers. They look through their papers and say, 'Oh, she's taking her medicine, she's clean, she's going to a therapist. Let her have her kid back.' I think the laws need to be changed. Just because a woman gives birth to a child does not mean that she can be a good parent. If we hadn't worked out an open adoption agreement, the judge would probably have given Samantha back to her birth mother. We would have lost her.

"When we went to court, Cal and I stayed outside in the hallway. We had to come up with an agreement. Samantha's lawyers were with us, and Jeanette had her lawyers. We were all in the hall negotiating. It felt like buying a used car! Jeanette wanted twelve visits a year; I wanted six. We settled on nine.

"A visit is [defined as] three hours in which Samantha and Jeanette do something together, but I am always there. Samantha does not have to be alone with her until she's old enough to decide for herself. I knew Jeanette was going to sign the adoption agreement, but I wanted to get what I wanted for Samantha. I wanted us to be a family, and I didn't want to spend every weekend visiting. Twelve visits is a lot! The lawyers picked days that were not close to holidays and near—but not on—Samantha's birthday. It's complicated. We agreed to keep it going until somebody objects, and then we'll have to go back to court. Jeanette was crying when she came out of the courtroom.

"The visits go well. Usually Jeanette and I sit and talk while Samantha plays with her brothers. She knows they're her brothers. Samantha once asked me if her brothers could come and live with us, but she hasn't really warmed up to Jeanette. The agreement states that if Jeanette misses six visits, it's finished —and she has missed plenty! But we're still doing it. I could be back in court now stopping the whole thing, but I'm not going to. I don't want Samantha to say when she's a teenager that I stopped her from visiting with her birth mother. She's the one who has to make that decision.

"Jeanette is supposed to call me and confirm the visits. I don't call her; she needs to call me. Sometimes she doesn't call, or she'll call the day after. Or I won't hear from her for a month and then she'll call and want to see Samantha the next day. She got mad at me once when I refused, and I said, 'Listen, so far you have missed nine visits! I could be back in court, but I'm not going to do it. I'm trying to help Samantha get close to you so that in a few years, when she's ready, she can come to me and say that she wants to spend more time with you.'"

"It wouldn't be fair to Samantha to cancel the visits with Jeanette," said Cal. "We want to do everything we can for Samantha to know her birth family, even though she considers us her family. We are her family, but she has these other people. I don't want to keep her away from her brothers. One interesting thing happened. Jeanette called Lee Anne once and said, 'If anything ever happens to me, will you take care of my boys?' Lee Anne told her she'd do her best for them."

Tyler, another two-year-old, came to Cal and Lee Anne when Samantha was three and Lewis four. He was severely depressed, he wasn't talking, and he was still in diapers and on the bottle. Tyler wasn't eating and was afraid of everything. He had been neglected and physically and mentally abused at another foster home.

"He was a wreck," said Lee Anne. "We were called because Tyler was legally free for adoption, and DSS knew we wanted to adopt more kids. We went to visit Tyler at his foster home. His foster mother behaved like everything was normal, but none of the kids were smiling. They were all just sitting there, with not a smile on anyone's face."

Cal remembered, "The first time I saw Tyler I knew he was an unhappy child. For some reason, he was the only black child in a foster home with a lot of white and Spanish kids. When we arrived, the kids were just sitting around staring and saying nothing. I knew something was wrong right away. There were no toys there. Lee Anne and I sat at the kitchen table and talked to the foster mother. She knew DSS was taking Tyler away so he could be adopted. The minute we saw Tyler we knew we wanted to adopt him. He was a cute little thing, but he looked terrible because he was depressed. This foster mother had taken care of him for two years but didn't want to adopt him. She had a lot of babies there— too many; there were six kids under the age of three. She also had four teenagers."

"At first Tyler stayed back from us," said Lee Anne. "But the second time we went there he came to us and pressed his hands all over Cal's face. We had a month for Tyler's transition. I went there every morning, picked Tyler up, and brought him home. The kids would go with me to take him back after supper. He was always waiting at the door for me the next morning. I'd call him in the evening and talk to him. He didn't really understand what was going on, but I think you can tell them you're going to adopt them without telling them in so many words. I bought new clothes for him and new shoes; the shoes he was wearing were too small for him.

"Tyler didn't sleep overnight with us until the end of that transition month. We had him for two nights, and then we were supposed to take him back to the foster home so the foster mother could say good-bye; the next morning the social worker would bring him back here. When I took him back, he refused to stay and kicked his foster mother. I gave her a new outfit to put on him the next morning, but he grabbed it away from her and jumped back into my car. There was no one there from DSS, just the foster mother and me standing on the sidewalk. I didn't want to leave him, and it was obvious that he didn't want to stay.

"His foster mother started to cry. She said, 'Don't leave him here.' I asked, 'Are you sure? You haven't had a chance to say good-bye to him.' But she said, 'He's only going to fight me all night. Don't do it to him.' It was a bad situation, but at least she had the heart to do the right thing for him. I told her I'd call the social worker and let her know what happened. We didn't take his clothes or anything else; we just left because he was hysterical. On the way home we bought him a toothbrush. The next day the social worker picked up his belongings and brought them over.

"Tyler's birth mother was severely psychotic. He had lived with her for the first six months of his life. She was into voodoo and did weird things to him. She was a dangerous person. I don't know how DSS caught on to her, but it was probably because Tyler had an older brother who wasn't going to school. He was at home taking care of the baby! The children were removed because she told a social worker she was going to give them bleach to drink.

"We had to break Tyler in because he wasn't doing anything—he just sat there. Lewis and Samantha were great with him. Tyler didn't like them at first. He was very, very withdrawn. He showed no affection, and we knew he was afraid. I held him a lot. Even though he was two-and-a-half, I sang 'Rock-a-Bye Baby' to him while he drank his bottle. I don't have a rocking chair; I just sat on the couch and rocked him back and forth. He'd never been held. He latched on to us immediately. Cal and I like two-year-olds. You can talk to them and have fun with them. I'm not afraid of a two-year-old."

Cal added, "Tyler had to play catch-up with our kids. He was so into himself that he didn't know how to play with other kids. He'd sit outside and cry. Something must have happened to him; he had a lot of trauma and stress. When we took him to the grocery store the bright lights would make him cry. When a motorcycle went by the loud noise would make him cry too. His foster mother said he was dumb and couldn't learn, but that's not true. Tyler is as smart as a whip! He's not good socially, but he's learning.

"Tyler has no family except his brother, Rusty, who lives with a legal guardian. Rusty comes here often; he knows that anytime he calls me I'll come and pick him up. He took care of Tyler when he was a baby. They didn't see each other for a while when Tyler was put in foster care; after that Tyler used to scream whenever Rusty came around. Finally Rusty said he didn't want to see him anymore. Lee Anne and I made it our goal to get Tyler and Rusty back on good terms again. It didn't take long. Now they talk on the phone to each other."

Cal and Lee Anne adopted Samantha and Tyler on the same day. Samantha's adoption had been held up for so long that she was five-and-a-half years old. They didn't want her to have the anxiety of seeing Tyler adopted before she was, because he'd come to them two years after she did. The lawyers and social workers worked everything out so they could be adopted together. Afterward Cal and Lee Anne had a big party at their house. Samantha's lawyer came to the party, and on the first anniversary of her adoption, he gave her a savings bond.

Up to that point Cal and Lee Anne had never had a foster child leave;

they had adopted all three who had come to them! Then Jared arrived. He was a four-year-old black child with a lot of problems. He came from a large dysfunctional family and had been sexually abused. Lee Anne said, "Jared was a total disruption to our family. He caused fights; he didn't interact or play with the other kids. I think there was too much peer pressure for Jared. I had him in therapy, but it wasn't doing any good. Cal and I put one hundred percent effort into Jared. After a few months, Lewis began to feel neglected. That was when we realized we were hurting our own children by trying to help Jared.

"It took me three more months to do it, but finally I called DSS and gave ten days' notice for Jared to be removed. I felt like I was throwing him away. But even our best effort wasn't helping him! I had Lewis, Samantha, and Tyler, plus four day-care kids I was looking after. The environment wasn't right for Jared. He needed to be in a home without other children, so he could focus on himself. Some kids cannot live in a family situation. They don't know what it is; there are too many things going on. Cal and I had many discussions about Jared. It was hard for me to make the call, but the social worker didn't try to talk me out of it. She knew I'd really tried."

"Jared was fun. He could play basketball!" said Cal. "I liked him, but he was always in trouble and disrupted everything. It got to the point where we couldn't let him go outside unless one of us went with him. He had all the kids in the neighborhood fighting. He was the type of kid who needed a man to give constant attention to him. I didn't want to give up on him, because I believe if you keep trying to work with a kid the time will come when you will make a breakthrough. I began to notice that our kids were jealous of the attention we were giving Jared, and we realized that all our attention wasn't doing Jared any good! It was too bad. I felt I could have been a role model for Jared. He called me Daddy. But Lee Anne and I couldn't focus on just one kid."

Lee Anne said, "I explained to Jared that he was going to a home with no brothers or sisters so that he could concentrate on himself. He couldn't wait to get out of here! He said, 'Bye!' The social worker said that was one of Jared's problems: he has trouble bonding and then lets go too easily. He was here for eight months; he shouldn't have been happy to leave, not when nobody else cared for him. But as long as he was able to take his bike with him, that's all he cared about! We had bought him a new bike, and Cal said he could take it with him. He had a big smile on his face when he said good-bye. All our kids were crying! Jared was the first one to leave, and our kids felt horrible. We explained to them that Jared needed to be in a place with no other kids. They understood that; he had driven them crazy! But their crying made me cry. We were all upset. So our first foster child was tough, but it didn't scare me off. I said I'd do it again."

Cal said, "When Jared left I felt really sad, but I didn't want the kids to see me crying, so I got in the car and took off. Actually, I just drove around the corner and shed a few tears for Jared."

"A few weeks later we got our first baby," said Lee Anne. "I got the phone call. Cal didn't want a baby. He said, 'No babies, no babies!' But I wanted to try it; that's how I am. Noah was two weeks old. Cal was so funny: by the end of the first night he was singing to Noah and holding him on his chest. And he got up with him at night. Cal was great!"

Cal continued, "At first I didn't want a baby, and I said I wouldn't change him, but that first night I was drawn to him. I picked him up and changed him. There was nothing wrong with him; he was healthy. I held him on my chest and he latched on to me. I started keeping Noah with me all the time. I carried him around! Sometimes Lee Anne would call me at work complaining that she couldn't get him to sleep, and I'd slip home on my supper break, put him to sleep, and go back to work. I enjoyed taking care of him."

Lee Anne narrated, "Noah's mother was psychotic. I took the baby to DSS for visits with her and she acted as if she hated me; I guess that was because I had Noah and she didn't. I felt that she was a mean and evil person.

"Our kids loved Noah. As he got older they'd push him around in his walker. He loved it. Noah was about five months old when we were given notice that we'd have to give him back. DSS told us that they were going to begin the transition back to his mother. It was a shock, because I felt his visits with her weren't going well. It broke our hearts; we were depressed and upset about it.

"Cal and I thought we were going to be able to adopt Noah; nobody thought this woman was going to pull herself together, because she was severely psychotic. We knew she couldn't even get herself dressed if she didn't take her medication! But she was doing what DSS told her she'd have to do in order to get her baby back. The social workers tried to influence the situation, but she took her medication and went to therapy, so the judge gave Noah back to her. By this time, she was pregnant again and had another baby a short time later! DSS provided a home health aide and a visiting nurse to help her."

Cal admitted, "It was really hard to let Noah go. They had told us he was adoptable, and we were thinking about adopting him. I bonded with Noah and let him bond with me."

"Noah was supposed to leave on December 20," said Lee Anne, "and I wasn't sure how the kids were going to handle it. This was our first baby, and it was Christmas! I bought gifts, and we had an early Christmas with Noah. Cal and I slept with a baby blanket for that month so we could send it with him. I even wore it around my neck during the day. We wanted Noah to feel that we were still with him, so he would be comforted during his transition visits, which went very badly, and when he finally moved back home.

"We made a life book for Noah. A life book is something we learned about in MAPP training. It's a bit like a scrapbook for a foster child with stories, pictures, health and school records, et cetera. Lewis, Samantha, and Tyler each did a page for Noah and said what was special about him and what they would miss most. Since Noah's mother had been hostile to me, I asked DSS to put our life book in Noah's records. I was afraid she might destroy it. He'll have it if he ever looks into his file. That's important.

"All the kids know each other's stories. They're very accepting of them. Sometimes we have family discussions about their stories, and they like to hear them."

Cal added, "I think kids should know something about their background. It's important for them, even at an age when they don't understand. Later on, when they get older they can make their own decisions. But I think it's adoptive parents' responsibility and duty to make sure that their kids know about their birth families, even if it's just pictures. You can't lie to them."

"Noah had one overnight visit with his mother before he left us," said Lee Anne, "which helped our kids get used to the idea that he was leaving. We had a nightly routine where Noah and I would chase the kids to bed. So on his last night with us I said, 'Noah's going to chase you to bed for the last time tonight . . . He's not going to do it again.'"

Cal explained, "I was the one who always held Noah, so when it was time for him to leave, I carried him down to the car. I think he realized he wasn't going to see me again, because when I put him in his car seat and put his pacifier in his mouth, he spit it right out and just looked at me. I had to rub my eyes and walk away. The kids let me mourn Noah for a couple of days. Afterward I didn't know if I was going to be able to take on another baby."

As soon as the baby left, Lee Anne put the crib away and tried to give the kids something to divert their attention. She bought all-new Christmas decorations and decorated the whole house, which she normally didn't do. Lee Anne and Cal decided that the day after Christmas they would take the kids to a nearby hotel for a couple of days; it had a big indoor pool, and they had a great time.

Lee Anne said, "After the holidays I took them to see our social worker to make sure they were handling everything okay. That was the first time I had all of them in her office together. Joan is very easy to talk to, and the kids like her. She assured me they were fine, which made me feel much better.

"My kids are the best kids in the world. I'll tell them, 'I just got a phone call, and DSS wants us to take a baby,' and they say hurrah! They love it when a new child comes into the house. They just can't wait for them to get here. They give the new one a lot of attention, make them feel welcome. They say, 'Here is your bed . . . This is my teddy bear, but you can use him; you can sleep with him.' They just move over! Lewis moved over for Samantha, Samantha and Lewis moved over for Tyler, and they just keep moving over. There's no jealousy. I always ask for their permission.

"My children tell me they want to be foster parents and adopt kids when they grow up. I'm so proud of them!

"After we got Tyler, Cal and I had decided to adopt another girl to round out the family. DSS knew we wanted a girl who was free for adoption, and in March we got a call about Jackie. She was a fifteen-month-old black drug baby. She was in a good foster home, where she'd been since birth. Her birth mother had visited her only once, when she was a month old. Jackie had two foster mothers and was very much loved. The foster mothers were white women, and they told DSS that they'd like to keep her but were willing to see her adopted if she could be placed in a black home. That's how they let her go, under those conditions. Maybe they thought a black home couldn't be found, I don't know. But they loved her a lot."

Lee Anne and Cal's first meeting with Jackie was at her foster home.

"Jackie was shy and didn't want to come to us, so the foster mothers tricked her to get her on my lap," said Lee Anne. "She was so cute, pudgy, and round, with big bright eyes; she sat on my lap while we visited for a while. The second visit was set up so I would pick Jackie up and take her to our house for a couple of hours. Jackie went with me willingly. In the meantime, Cal got the kids dismissed from school early so they could meet her. They were all excited about her and took to her right away. Jackie took to them right away too and kept up with them from the start. After that I picked her up every day, and she had a month of transition. Her transition was easy; she never cried when she said good-bye.

"On the last day she didn't cry, and the foster mothers didn't cry. One of them said to her, 'Go get 'em, Jackie, you're going to be the first woman president!' She may be right. Jackie is smart, she's got a great personality, and everybody who meets her falls in love with her."

Cal said, "At first Jackie wouldn't come to me, because she wasn't used to being around a man. But by the time her transition was over, she was clinging to me. Since then Jackie has always been stuck on Daddy. Every time I went out, she'd cry, so I ended up taking her with me all the time. And for a two-year-old, Jackie can walk a fair distance. At first she wanted to be carried, but now she walks to the corner store with me. Jackie is smart. If the other kids are at the table doing their homework, Jackie wants homework, too. She has a good attention span. She goes to the movie theater with the other kids and she's no trouble. She sits and watches the movie, and afterward she can tell you what she saw."

Lee Anne added, "The kids don't do a thing without Jackie; she'll follow them out in the lake up to her neck! She sits with them and pretends to read when they're reading. Jackie is two going on ten! She watches the kids and keeps up with them.

"We were a little nervous because Jackie's grandmother said she might want her, even though she'd never seen her. But DSS doesn't place a child for adoption if they think she might be removed. Jackie's birth mother was dysfunctional, and her whole family was dysfunctional from one generation to another. She showed up in court a couple of times and said she didn't want Jackie to be adopted; on the other hand, she wasn't interested in her. It's control, I think. Since she had given birth to the child, she wanted to have the right to say what happened to her.

"DSS tries to influence these mothers, but sometimes their minds are so clouded with drugs. The second time Jackie's birth mother came to court she was so high that nobody could figure out how she even got there! DSS took her to court to prove that she was not a fit mother. Now we're just finishing up the paperwork, and her adoption should be completed in the next six months. DSS pays for Jackie's lawyer; Cal and I don't have a lawyer. I feel we have so much support from DSS that we don't need our own lawyer. We're so happy about adopting her! Jackie goes around the house singing, 'I'm adopted now!' But I don't know if she understands it.

"Birth mothers have too many rights, I think. Jackie's mother was allowed to contest her adoption, but she'd visited Jackie only once. She should not have been allowed a choice fourteen months later. If there's obvious interest from the birth mother, that's fine. And if she makes an effort to be a good parent, that's fine too. But when there is no interest or effort and the child is a year old and hasn't been seen since birth, she shouldn't have rights! I think when you give birth to a baby who is addicted to drugs you should lose your rights, too. And the judges keep on giving them [birth mothers] rights. Babies are not property. They don't belong to anybody, and they didn't ask to be here. This is not their choice.

"Jackie has six siblings; two were born after her! Three of them are living with their grandmother, three have been adopted, and we have Jackie. Most of them were born exposed to drugs. When Jackie was born, cocaine was detected in her urine, but the doctors didn't need to treat her. She had no brain damage. She's very intelligent. In fact, she's the queen of this house; she gets what she wants from everybody.

"Cal and I thought adopting two boys and two girls would be just right for us. But now that we have Jackie's adoption sorted out, he's changed his mind. We were riding in the car the other day (with all the kids) and Cal said, 'I think we'll do one more boy and one more girl.' That's fine with me, but we'll need a bigger place to live. Right now we're in a three-bedroom apartment. We'd like to get a house.

"For now, we'll continue with foster kids. Besides our four kids, we've got three foster kids with us right now. Henri is a nine-year-old Haitian boy whose father kidnapped him away from his mother and then abused him. A neighbor called DSS, a twelve-year-old boy who heard Henri crying and crying. They were friends, and Henri had told this boy what was going on."

"We took Henri as a favor to the social worker," said Cal. His first night here I put him in the tub, and that's when I saw burn marks all over his back and on the back of his legs. He told me his father did it to him—he put his cigarettes out on his son! He had a lot of cuts, too, and a hernia—his belly button was sticking out—and I know a hernia when I see one. I didn't tell Henri what to call me, but he started calling me Daddy right away.

"Shortly after he arrived, it was Lewis's birthday, and Lewis was nice enough to say to Henri, 'You can share my birthday with me.' Nobody had ever celebrated Henri's birthday. We took him to a doctor and had his hernia removed. He's thrived with us. His first Christmas here he got more toys than he'd ever had in his life. I got him a bike."

Lee Anne added, "Henri's father is a monster! Henri told us that he would put lemon juice on his skin after he cut him! Henri came to this country on a boat from Haiti; people were dying and being thrown overboard. He's seen a lot of trouble. He has food anxiety and is always hungry. He uses our last name and wants us to adopt him. But Henri will go back to his own mother one day. The poor woman was terrified of Henri's father, and in Haiti you couldn't go to the police. DSS recently located her in New York. Then she came to the DSS office here for a visit with Henri. She can't speak the language, so even though she knew Henri was in Boston with his father, she couldn't do anything about it; she was afraid Henri's father would kill her.

"It was a happy reunion for her; everybody cried. Henri smiled, but he was a bit distant with her. After three years, he still remembered what she looked like, but he'd been taught to hold back. His father had told him that she was an awful woman, that she had given him up, and who knows what else! I told her, 'Henri has happy memories of you, and nice memories.' She cried and said, 'I didn't know he was in foster care.' Now she calls here every Sunday night."

Cal continued, "We don't know how long it's going to take, but Henri is welcome to stay here as long as he wants. We can't adopt him; he belongs with his mother. Anyway, we decided never to adopt anybody older than Lewis; he'll always be the oldest in our family."

It will take a while to sort everything out. There are two states involved, and the New York DSS has to make sure his mother has a safe place for Henri to live where his father won't find him. Lee Anne said, "We've got her address in New York, and Henri has written letters to her. I think he'll be home by Christmas. I can feel good about this one. Henri doesn't want to leave us—he calls us Mommy and Daddy—but we've got him working with a Haitian therapist to get him ready. He refuses to speak French with her because French reminds him of his father, but he understands what she's saying to him.

"We're working hard to prepare Henri to leave here. It's going to be tough on him and hard on our kids. He's fitted in pretty well. He has his problems, but most of them are social. Because he was never allowed to have friends, he doesn't know how to be a friend. But he's learning, and the kids put up with his problems."

A black baby named Evan came after Henri. Evan was addicted to cocaine at birth, had a brain bleed, was premature, and had a chronic lung disease. Evan was in bad shape. Lee Anne had two days of training at the hospital before she could bring him home.

"I fell in love with him the minute I saw him," she said. "A neonatal intensive care nurse named Katie was considering adopting him. She was single and white and had already adopted one child seven years before. Katie's little girl was born with spina bifida and fetal alcohol syndrome; she wasn't supposed to be able to do anything, not even talk. But Katie loved her and worked with her, and now that kid can do almost everything! When I met Katie she said she was wondering if she had the energy to go through all of this again with Evan. She told me she hadn't been his nurse, but she'd been called in to hold him; Evan was so depressed that he'd lost his will to live. He needed to be held, and the hospital had asked for volunteers."

"When Evan came, I didn't want to get close to him," admitted Cal. "But Lee Anne left me alone with him one time and I picked him up, and that was it! They told us Evan was going to be a vegetable, but we started talking to him and playing with him; he always watched what the kids were doing. Once he realized that everybody else was walking and getting around, he wanted to also! We decided he was bored, so we propped him up in the walker so he could get around. He was only going backward, but he was moving! I would sit and hold him, even when he was sleeping.

"DSS sent an early-intervention therapist to work with him, but we were already doing everything the therapist told us to do! He was already thriving! By the time he left to be adopted, Evan was fully alert. He was talking, had gained weight, was off most of his medicine, and was almost ready to walk! I think a lot of love and attention made the difference for him. Lee Anne and I both take credit for turning Evan around!

"I think if you can catch kids when they're young enough and give them that extra bit of attention to show them that they are somebody—that they mean something to somebody—then they will turn around and give you whatever they've got."

Lee Anne said, "We had Evan for almost eight months. He'd just about caught up to his age level, except for being able to sit up on his own. Katie decided to adopt him, and she came here for a month of transition visits.

"After Evan we got Marylou, a white foster child with blond hair and blue eyes. She's going to be two years old next week. Marylou came with a lot of problems; she'd been severely neglected by her mother, who is mildly retarded. Marylou was in day care, and they alerted DSS, who removed her from home. She was filthy. She's a lot of work; she bangs her head, cries constantly, eats dirt, and doesn't sleep for more than three hours at a time. She drives us crazy, but we're not giving up on her. She likes to take a bath now, and when I get her dressed she comes in and turns around so all the kids can tell her how great she looks. She never had clean clothes before. We're getting Marylou involved in the early-intervention program at DSS. She doesn't even know how to play with toys. We're just finding out what her problems are.

"Marylou needs a lot of structure. There's definitely something wrong with her; you can tell by the look in her eyes. Sometimes she seems to black out or have a seizure. Her social worker thinks she may have fetal alcohol syndrome. I'm teaching her to eat with a spoon and a fork and to cover her mouth when she coughs. She's great with the other kids, but she doesn't talk—just 'Mama' and 'hi!' We won't try to adopt Marylou; she's strictly foster care. But we're not giving up on her."

Cal explained, "With Marylou we have to be careful; we have to watch her every second or she'll run out in the street. DSS didn't tell us much about her, except that she was neglected. But she's learning now. She's trying to keep up with the kids. She's learning manners and how to wipe her mouth at the table. Early intervention hasn't started working with her yet, but they can't do anything more than Lee Anne and I can do. Marylou's coming around. Lee Anne has to testify in court this week; we think they'll sever her mother's rights. Then somebody will adopt Marylou—

she's a blue-eyed blonde! But they'll have to have patience. She gets restless; she can't stay in one place for very long!"

Cal acknowledged, "Being a foster parent has been more work than I expected. It's a twenty-four-hour job. And I don't want the kids to look down on me; I want them to look up to me. So they see me taking care of them and also going to work. I work the three-to-eleven shift in the water department, and sometimes I get called in during the night. I tell the kids, 'If I don't work, you don't eat!' Lewis is always telling me he's proud that I have a job and that he can't wait to get a job.

"I think people judge you by the way your kids look. We buy them new clothes because we want them to look nice. The state gives us about fifty dollars [per foster child] every three months for clothes. What can that buy? Tyler has a triple-E foot, and his sneakers cost fifty dollars a pair! If a child comes with no clothes, they give us emergency clothing. And when the kid leaves, we send him with a lot of clothes. Any kid who comes here with nothing leaves with a lot of clothes and toys."

Lee Anne added, "If you want your foster kids to look nice and have a few things to play with, you end up using the money that is supposed to be your reimbursement for taking care of them. DSS gives us about four hundred dollars a month per child. We're not getting rich doing this! We're trying to save money for a house, but it's hard because the kids need things. In one way we are lucky; the kids are on a state health plan and have all the medical help they need. In fact, I think we have more [health care] resources than the average parent who gives birth.

"We have another foster baby now. Toby is four months old; his mother is a sixteen-year-old black girl. She said Toby's father is white and Spanish. This birth mother was living with her mother, who didn't provide much emotional support. She went to live in a foster home with Toby, but after two days she asked DSS to take the baby and went back home. When DSS called me they told me that the birth mother wanted to meet me. I thought she looked about twelve years old! She had no baby skills. The social worker told me this birth mother will be on a strict program if she wants to have Toby back. She needs parenting classes. She'll be on welfare and may need counseling. But she's expressed no interest in having him back. They only thing she told me was that she didn't like to get her fingers dirty when she changed his diapers.

"A new law in Massachusetts gives birth mothers one year to do what they're supposed to do in order to get their kids back. This is better for the kids; it gives them some kind of permanence. She has a year to get herself together, or else Toby will be legally removed from her. Cal and I think we'd like to adopt Toby. He's a great baby; he's happy. All the kids love to play with him. We don't hold back with Toby. We give him all the love that we can. There's no way to keep from getting attached to children, unless you're not taking care of them properly."

"I never planned on getting attached to foster kids," said Cal, "but I can't help it. I even fell for the kids who came here just for day care! I like to line all the kids up and walk down the street to the corner store to get slushes. In the store the kids stand in a straight line, they tell me what kind of slush they want, they wait their turn, and they all say thank you. In every store I take them to they behave like that. I never have any problems with them. When we stay in a hotel people compliment us on their behavior. We've taught them how to behave in public.

"Toby came two-and-a-half weeks before Evan left. Toby wanted my attention, but Evan wouldn't let me get near him! Evan wanted me all to himself. When Evan left, Toby looked at me and smiled; then he lifted up his arms. I've been holding him ever since! The poor baby was so sick with diarrhea when he came here that his bottom was raw. His mother didn't know how to look after him; it's too bad, really, a baby having a baby. This girl says she wants to keep him, but she has no support, and DSS will not let her mother have Toby, because she's dysfunctional.

"I think we'll be able to adopt him. He fits into our family. The social worker says Toby looks like me, but Lee Anne thinks she's just trying to butter me up! Anyone can see that Toby is thriving here. I like to give a kid the chance to reach his full potential. If Toby has to go back to his birth mother, it's going to be a step down for him. It's going to hurt him, but what can we say? It's not in our hands.

"I'm not sorry that Lee Anne and I didn't have a baby together, because after you adopt a child, he's yours. I'm proud of all our kids. God was saving them for us. That's what we think."

7 / Bob and Lilly
The adoption roller coaster

"There's such an intensity to the love you have for an adopted child. Maybe it's because most adoptive parents have come from such despair and anguish that they go totally the other way in terms of their love and the intensity of their happiness."

ADOPTING a child is a complex process that can be frustrating and painful. Bob and Lilly's first adoption experience was particularly difficult, but the couple remain convinced that the joy of adopting a child is worth the struggle.

Lilly is a petite, dark-haired woman who speaks rapidly and enthusiastically, radiating energy. She was the second of three daughters and grew up in a loving, close-knit family in an upper-middle-class northeastern suburb. Her parents were of Armenian heritage and had a strong marriage. Their lives centered on their daughters. "We always did things together as a family," Lilly said.

By the time Lilly was in her mid-twenties, she held a job as a health care administrator and owned a condominium in a fashionable city neighborhood. She was still closely involved with her family, who lived nearby, and was committed to her career. She enjoyed traveling and joined a ski house in Vermont.

Bob is a giant of a man, fair-haired and large-boned; his physical presence is rather daunting, but his manner is thoughtful and charming. He grew up in Westchester County, north of New York City, in a family atmosphere that he likens to the television program, "The Dick Van Dyke Show." While in graduate school Bob also joined a ski house in Vermont, where he met Lilly.

"A friend decided to introduce us because he thought we'd be a perfect pair. She was so small and I was so tall," recalled Bob, "although I was geographically undesirable at the time." Their relationship thrived despite the distance, and after several years of weekend commutes Bob made a career change into sales training to be with Lilly. They lived together for two years and then decided to get married. Bob explained, "When we got married we tried to have a child immediately. Lilly was very anxious to get going on that. But after a few months we became suspicious that there might be a problem."

After trying to become pregnant for more than two years Lilly consulted a fertility specialist. Medical tests revealed that she had extensive endometriosis. She underwent a major surgical procedure in which her lower abdominal cavity was scraped, and she was forced to stay in bed for six weeks to recuperate. "When they told me six weeks, I thought no," Lilly said, "I'm in good shape. But it really was six weeks. I was on my back, in bed. It was very painful." After recuperating Lilly took fertility medications and tried again. A year later when she still hadn't conceived, Lilly returned for a second operation (a laparoscopy), which revealed that the endometriosis had recurred and again was extensive. Her doctor delivered a devastating message: "At this point it's very unlikely that you will conceive."

Bob remembered, "When Lilly had her surgery I spent a lot of time at the hospital. I was there when she came out of surgery. I don't remember it being a 'your fault, my fault' thing at all. I remember being distraught a little bit, but I don't remember it being extended. I think I knew all along that it was unlikely this was going to work. We'd been given a very low chance of success."

Lilly had thought about adoption between her surgeries, but she and Bob had not discussed it seriously. "I wanted a family," Lilly said. "Every month that went by and I was getting my period, I knew it wasn't happening. There was never anything said, but I knew the reason we weren't conceiving a child was that I could not conceive. I felt under such pressure during the time that we tried. It was nothing Bob ever said or did, but it was me."

Lilly began to realize that she'd be just as happy if they adopted a child. "When I brought up the idea to Bob I said, 'If you want to have no children, we're both happy. We have good salaries and a good life. But I'd be very happy to adopt.' He wanted to wait until the last gun was fired; and basically the last gun went off when I had the laparoscopy and the doctor said it was unlikely that I'd conceive. I'll never forget the night we decided to adopt a baby. We were at an outdoor concert, and it was intermission. We hadn't talked about it for a while. I didn't want to force Bob. It was too important for me to push him into it. But that night, out of the blue, he said, 'Let's adopt,' and I remember crying because I was so happy."

Bob explained, "I don't remember the day we decided to adopt. I remember a process. I think she thinks I was very much against it. I think she thinks I was worried about legacy [progeny] or something like that. I think I went through a process; we assumed we would have biological children, and when you hit the point where that's not going to happen, then the decision became easier. It might have been a difficult reality, but the decision wasn't difficult. It was something that I had never considered in my life. I think that Lilly was very, very anxious to have kids, and she came to terms with it quicker than I did. It took a bit of time for me to make the transition. It became a finite choice of no children or children. And if the answer was yes, then the avenue was adoption."

Energized by their decision, Lilly called numerous adoption agencies to obtain as much information as she could. She briefly flirted with the idea of trying to adopt an Armenian baby, but quickly learned that it wasn't possible (this was before the fall of communism in the Soviet Union). "Initially I wanted to adopt an Armenian child because I thought it would be nice if my child looked like me," said Lilly. "We all think that's ideal. But clearly it doesn't make any difference."

Bob and Lilly chose an adoption agency that allowed them some control over the process. "I wanted to get involved and make things happen," said Lilly. "And ironically, by having the involvement we preferred, the price was also a little more affordable." They chose an agency that handled a lot of adoptions, both direct placements and identified adoptions. In a direct placement the agency locates a baby for the parents. An identified adoption is one in which the parents locate a birth mother, and if they decide to work together they inform the agency.

Lilly said, "We felt that this increased the likelihood of a child coming to us. We had heard that the amount of emotional support coming from the agency we chose may not be what we'd like it to be, and we went into it knowing this was going to be the case. And sure enough, it was the case."

Bob continued, "We had to fill out a form for the agency, and it caught us being selfish. We wanted a healthy white infant. The people we were working with said there was nothing wrong with that; this didn't have to be a moment in our lives when we decide to be altruistic and take in a case. Some people do, but it wasn't for us. They asked us if we would accept an infant with epilepsy or with this or that. We were going down a list and checking off no, no, no. In terms of sex we had no preference. I said that I was never going to state a preference, although given a choice I would selfishly prefer a girl. The question was why. And I said that no matter how you slice it, there's nothing like the love I've seen that a daughter has for her father. Most women agree with me when I say that.

"Our agency had an evening introductory session, which was run by their lawyer. He told us, 'If you really want to adopt, prepare yourselves for some heartbreak and a lot of frustration, but ultimately you will be parents.' We also met the agency's director, Bernice. The thing about Bernice is, I have no idea why she is in the job. Nobody comes away from the agency loving her. But when you look back on things, she knows the business, she knows what she's doing. She tries to protect you, but she doesn't take time to be friendly with you. Bernice is very interesting, but her style drove me insane. She and I stood toe to toe and shouted at each other more than once."

Before closing the introductory meeting Bernice warned the group that the agency's statistics showed that about a third of the women who work with couples in the identified adoption process change their minds after the baby's birth. While couples using this process have the benefit of getting to know their child's birth mother before the baby is born, they also risk the pain of the birth mother's possible last-minute decision to keep her baby.

The agency asked Bob and Lilly to write a letter describing their lifestyle, interests, hobbies, and thoughts about parenthood. It also asked them to provide a photograph of themselves. This information was needed for a direct placement adoption and put in the agency's file; later it would be shown to birth mothers who were choosing adoptive parents for their babies. Bob said, "They told us that some people borrow dogs for their family pictures! It's marketing a product, and the product is you."

For an identified adoption, Bob and Lilly provided the same letter and photo as well as a cover letter, which they sent to friends, physicians, close and distant family members, and social workers—in short, anyone who might lead them to a baby. Because Lilly was in the medical field, she had many resources. She asked physicians she knew to pass on copies of their letter to colleagues. She went to the library and made a list of high school principals and guidance counselors who might know unwed pregnant teenagers. Bob and Lilly sent out hundreds of letters; they spent several hundred dollars on postage.

"It was a 'needle in the haystack' approach," said Lilly. "I didn't place a lot of stock in it, but it made me feel better to be doing something. It was a question of covering as many bases as my imagination and our finances would let us do."

Soon after, Bob and Lilly began the home study process with a social worker from the adoption agency. They didn't feel particularly close to the social worker or have a special rapport with her. They admit that they felt nervous when talking to her but believed they were good parent material and didn't anticipate any problems.

"The social worker drove me crazy," said Bob. "We had new couches. I served her a cup of coffee and put it on the coffee table. She took it off the table and put it on the couch. She's rambling back and forth, and I'm watching the cup. At one point I took the cup and put it back on the table. After the next sip, she put it back on the couch! It was completely distracting. I didn't feel we were being tested, because it seemed to me that the only possible gates they could be putting us up against were finances, commitment, and emotional stability. It wasn't going to be if you answer A to column 4 and B to this, it would add up to your typical child beater or anything like that.

"Although I find the concept necessary, I think the home study is foolish," said Bob. "I argued with Bernice because she didn't want to let me see a copy of our home study. After pretending that the copier was broken, she finally agreed to give me a copy but wrote UNOFFICIAL all over it. I think she was afraid I would go to another agency and save ourselves the cost of the home study by bringing it with me. After leaving her office I walked down the street reading it. It was filled with inaccuracies. I was amazed that any of this could lead to a legal decision. Lilly had talked about her grandparents leaving Armenia during the Turkish massacre. Well, somehow the social worker wrote down that Lilly, in her early childhood years, had escaped a massacre! I was standing on the street corner reading this and laughing hysterically. But that document ended up doing the job, so I decided I'm certainly not going to argue with this or do it over again."

A few weeks later Lilly learned that her grandmother's home care worker had an unmarried daughter, Annmarie, who was pregnant. Apparently she had already talked to a Catholic adoption agency in another state; when Annmarie heard that Bob and Lilly were trying to adopt, however, she was eager to consult with them. After several phone conversations Annmarie told Lilly that she very much wanted them to adopt her baby. To complicate matters, she had begun counseling sessions with a nun at the Catholic agency. When the nun was informed about Annmarie's decision to give her baby to Bob and Lilly she categorically stated: "This baby is ours." Unfortunately, Annmarie was too intimidated to oppose her.

"We were heartbroken," said Lilly. "We were about eighty percent sure this was going to happen." Lilly was home alone when Annmarie called to withdraw her offer. Lilly was so upset that she had to leave the house. After a long walk she returned home determined to talk to the nun herself. It was not an easy call, Lilly remembered.

"The nun was very rigid and narrow, and that was it. She wasn't going to do a thing. She had a list of good Catholic families; some had been waiting seven years to adopt. I could see both sides, but it was very painful." Knowing that it might not work out was one thing, but actually experiencing the disappointment was quite another.

"Bernice had done a good job of preparing us for things going south," said Bob. "But this fell through hard on Lilly's surgeries not working. Disappointment becomes something you grow accustomed to. In adoption, disappointment is part of the process."

A few months later another situation presented itself. Lilly had sent a letter to a friend named Elizabeth, a social worker in a hospital in a nearby state. Elizabeth called Lilly one morning to tell her about a baby who had just been born at her hospital. That day was Lilly's mother's birthday, which Lilly felt was a good omen; she started to cry as Elizabeth explained the details to her: The birth mother was only fifteen years old. Her parents, who were wealthy, didn't even know she was pregnant. When she complained of back pains her mother took her to the hospital and was astonished to learn that her daughter was about to give birth.

Elizabeth showed Bob and Lilly's letter to the birth mother's mother, who said it sounded like a good solution to their unexpected dilemma. Lilly talked to the woman on the phone that very day. Lilly was excited and felt that things were going to work out this time. But when the birth mother's father came to the hospital everything fell apart.

"He was a high-powered executive from a New York firm and he took his daughter right out of the hospital immediately," said Lilly. "They put the baby in the nursery without any name on it. He didn't want anyone to connect him with this baby. It just happened too fast. The birth mother would have needed some counseling, or we would have been at risk. It wasn't meant to be. She went home, and her father made sure that the baby was placed very far away, so no one would know."

This second disappointment was harder on Lilly: "The involvement wasn't long in terms of our emotional investment; it happened over a weekend. But it was very intense. And then it just fell apart . . ."

Another strategy in identified adoptions is to place an advertisement in newspapers around the country. Bernice put Bob and Lilly in touch with Hillary, who offered a service to adoptive parents. Hillary lived in Vermont, a few hours away from Bob and Lilly. Because most of their contact would be by phone, distance was irrelevant. The phone number in the ad was Hillary's. This provided twenty-four-hour phone coverage for working couples and ensured that Hillary would be the first person to speak to birth mothers who called. Her training would enable her to screen the calls in a professional way, which was difficult for adoptive parents, who might be caught off-guard by the emotional nature of the calls. If she felt it was appropriate, Hillary could send Bob and Lilly's letter and photograph by overnight mail to the birth mothers so that a connection could be established quickly.

Lilly thought carefully about what to write in the ad. The result was this: "Adoption is kisses for bruises, hugs for tears, and hands to always hold. Considering adoption? Please call Bob & Lilly."

One day Hillary called Lilly to say, "There is this girl; her name is Susan. I've sent her one of your letters, and she's going to call you tomorrow." Bob and Lilly grew excited again. Apparently Susan had read their ad in a Texas newspaper. When she called Lilly, Susan told her that she was seven months pregnant, was living in a motel, and had no money. She said she wanted to be near Bob and Lilly.

Hillary was enthusiastic about the prospect, but Bernice warned them against it. "Bernice tends to go very much by the book," said Lilly. "She talked to Susan and told us she didn't like the situation from the beginning." But since Hillary seemed hopeful, Bob and Lilly decided to proceed.

Lilly remembered: "Susan drove up this way from Texas and got as far as Vermont. We were paying for her to be in a motel up there and went to meet her. Bob didn't respond well to her since she was smoking when we met her. But I said, 'Bob, we're not going to marry this girl. As long as we feel comfortable that she's healthy and everything . . .' She seemed like a health nut except for the smoking, and she promised to cut down on that."

Susan stayed in Vermont for a few days but then told Lilly she wanted to be nearer to them. They met her one night in a restaurant near their home to discuss living arrangements. Bob remembered the encounter very well: "We should have seen a lot of signals up front. There were so many things that in retrospect were obvious signs that something was wrong. When we walked into the restaurant she was sitting at a table. Lilly pointed out the two sodas on the table. 'Oh, I was really thirsty,' Susan said. She told a long story about car trouble and meeting a couple with a nephew who came to fix her car. But it turned out that she had a boyfriend with her. The other soda was his. He probably had seen us meet her.

"We ended up renting her an apartment and he shared it with her for a while. We didn't know how to behave. Are you supposed to be disciplining these kids? They were always smoking cigarettes, but we didn't want to scare them and make them go away."

Bernice had told Bob and Lilly how much money they could spend on Susan and how to document it; they could pay only for health care and living expenses. She said, "You can't make it look like you are paying Susan for her baby." She also told them not to give Susan too much cash but to buy the things she needed whenever possible. Susan seemed unhappy with the small black-and-white television in her apartment and asked Lilly to buy her a VCR. Lilly told her, "That's not possible. We were told that all we can give you, for your safety and ours, is money to meet your expenses." Susan quickly tired of the modest apartment they had provided for her and said she wanted to go back to Vermont. Hillary let Susan and her boyfriend stay in her home and gave them a few odd jobs to do so they could earn some money.

Susan continued to talk to Lilly on the phone. One day she said, "By the way, we haven't talked about the gift." "What gift?" asked Lilly. "I want eighteen thousand dollars," said Susan.

When Lilly turned down her request for money, Susan hung up the phone and turned to Hillary. "I don't want to work with them," she said. "That's just fine," replied Hillary. "That's your choice if you don't want to, but I'm curious—why?" "Well, they refused to give me a gift," Susan said.

Susan and her boyfriend soon left Hillary's home but stole clothes and tools from her. Bob and Lilly were distraught. Later Hillary received a mailing from an attorney in another state warning adoption professionals about Susan and her boyfriend. Apparently they had duped another couple into setting up an apartment for them and then took everything out of the apartment and left. It was like a made-for-TV movie.

Bob said, "I wish we had gotten her license plate number or something. She was a crook. She used being pregnant as a way to rip people off. She just vanished from the face of the earth. As we were going through all these things, I began to think that adoption was the dirtiest industry in the country. It made drug dealers look like reasonable, responsible people."

"The whole episode lasted only about a month," said Lilly. "It probably wasn't even a month, but it seemed like forever. I was heavily invested in it. After Susan left I was crushed, but I was also angry. I wouldn't want to be involved with someone like her. If I am going to know my child's birth mother, I'd like her to be someone I could respect. What an awful person."

Shortly afterward Hillary got another phone call from a birth mother in Texas in response to their ad. "I liked her from the very first phone conversation," said Lilly. "Her name was Maria. She and I had very little in common in terms of background. She was Mexican; just a solid, decent, kind, and caring woman. She already had two children, and her children's father was not with her anymore. The child she was carrying was her boyfriend's child, and he wasn't with her anymore either. She felt that she was doing the best she could for her children. She was working and going to night school. She said she wanted to give her children the best possible life and couldn't parent a third child."

Lilly and Maria had long talks on the phone; it became almost a daily event. They grew very close. Maria confided that her family wanted her to keep the baby, but she was determined to go ahead with her plan. As before, Hillary was enthusiastic, but Bernice cautioned Bob and Lilly. "Her family will never let her do this," she warned them.

Maria sent a letter to Lilly; it was crudely written, but Lilly treasured the sentiment it expressed:

Lilly I hope you will like this photos I am sending you about my kids when they were baby so you will more or less get in idea what this baby that I am caring will look like if he or she make it. To be your baby.

I am also sending you their school papers. so you get an idea how they are doing in schoolwork they are good students. I need to finish my education so I can offer them a better future. Thas why I have to give this baby up.

I hope you will understand. I am sure you do. Plese don't think I am a care less mother.

I am only doing it for the sake of this new baby so it can have a better life and future.

> Thanks,
> Maria

Maria asked Lilly to come to Texas for the birth and Lilly agreed. Maria was going to be induced on a Monday, and Lilly planned to fly down the Friday before. Bob recalled: "We had hotel reservations and airline reservations. Lilly and Maria had developed a relationship to the point where Maria wanted Lilly there to help her. She was getting so much resistance from her family."

Five days before she was due to go to Texas, Lilly took her cat to the veterinarian because he suddenly became very sick. While Lilly was helping the doctor hold him the cat unexpectedly bit her thumb. The bite was severe enough that Lilly ended up in an emergency room. She had been planning to attend a business meeting in Baltimore the next day, but she was told to return to the hospital in the morning for further treatment. She asked a colleague to make the trip instead and met her at the airport the next morning, gave her the plane ticket, and went back to the hospital.

"After my treatment I went to my office, which was just down the street from the hospital," said Lilly. "I sat down at my desk for a minute and the phone rang. It was a high school classmate of mine named Ted; he was calling from Vermont, where he worked as a doctor. I thought he was calling about our high school reunion, which was coming up, but he said, 'Lilly, I have a baby. She was born this morning . . . and she can be yours.'

"Talk about things happening for a reason. I shouldn't have been at my desk; I should have been in Baltimore! I asked Ted a jumble of questions and learned that the birth mother was twenty-five years old and that she had left the hospital immediately after giving birth. Ted said, 'When can you get up here?' I thought, *Oh my God, I'm going to Texas at the end of the week.* I told Ted I'd better coordinate with our adoption agency and find out what we needed to do. I called Bob. He was out of the office. I was beside myself. I thought, *Oh my goodness, what are we going to do about Maria?*"

Bob remembered, "I called my office to see if there were any messages. And there was a message: 'Call Lilly—Emergency!!' I thought it had something to do with Maria, that Maria had fallen through. So I called Lilly, and she told me about this baby in Vermont. After all those letters we sent out to everyone we knew, this was one of those people. As I recall, Ted got a call in the middle of the night from an obstetrician at his hospital telling him about a baby who had just been born. [Ted had passed out copies of Bob and Lilly's letter to all his colleagues at the hospital.] It took Ted several hours to find us because Hillary's number was on our letter, and Ted kept referring to Lilly by her maiden name, but they finally sorted it out and Ted reached Lilly at her office.

"Lilly was all excited," Bob continued. "We always thought we were going to have more than one child, so we said, this is crazy, but we'll go to Vermont on Thursday and take the baby to our ski house, which happened to be fairly near the hospital. I'll stay in Vermont with the baby, and you fly to Texas on Friday to be with Maria. You stay in Texas for two weeks with that baby, and I'll stay in Vermont for two weeks with the first baby. [There was a requirement to stay with a baby in the state where it was born for that length of time in order to complete the adoption.] Then we'll meet back at home as a family of four! That's exactly what we thought we were going to do."

Lilly called Bernice and explained their plan. Bernice said, "You have to tell Maria about the other baby because she might not want this placement now. As far as she's concerned, you are a childless couple, and it may be fine with her, but maybe it isn't. You've got to decide which situation is the main one."

"So I called Bob again," said Lilly, "and before I could call Maria I got a call back from Bernice. She asked, 'Did you call Maria yet?' I said no. 'Well, I just got a call from Maria,' Bernice said, 'and she's changed her mind.' This was within one hour of Ted's call from Vermont! Within an hour we went from having no children to potentially having two children and back to one. It was unbelievable."

Maria's family had finally worn her down. They had put enormous pressure on her and promised to help out with the new baby. "Maria called Bernice because she couldn't tell me herself," said Lilly. "It was so hard for her to do. And you know, after she told Bernice that she was going to keep the baby, the first thing she asked was, 'Is Lilly going to be okay?' which is just the way she was, really sweet. I immediately called her and we both cried. I think Maria probably felt worse than I did. She was a very generous lady."

"By the time I got home from work that day Lilly was sort of shell-shocked," said Bob. Bernice advised them not to go to Vermont until after the birth mother had been counseled. "Bernice tended not to be spontaneous," said Lilly, "but she had a reason. She didn't want us to see the baby and then have the situation fall out from under us."

The birth mother was to receive her counseling and sign the papers at three-thirty on Friday afternoon. Bob and Lilly had not yet purchased a single item for a baby. "I felt it was bad luck to do that," said Lilly.

"We knew which room would be the baby's," said Bob, "but that was it. We had met people who had painted rooms, had bought everything, and had diapers ready. We had not done that. It wasn't that we would tempt fate or anything, but it didn't seem appropriate for us. But I can understand why other people have a different opinion. Fortunately we had friends with kids. On Thursday morning we stopped at our friends' house on our way to Vermont. They had a ton of stuff for us, including a car seat. We hadn't even thought of that! Suddenly it was happening!"

When Bob and Lilly arrived in Vermont, they went to Ted's house. "We had lunch there," said Lilly. "The best meal I ever had in my life. It was just cold cuts, but it was the best meal. They gave us the first toy. We still have it—a little black-and-white cow in a cardboard house. When Ted's daughter handed it to me I started to cry. She was only eight years old and couldn't understand why I was crying, but I was so happy. After lunch we had to see the lawyer. Then we went to a store to buy some T-shirts and diapers."

"We had to see the lawyer twice that day," said Bob. "There were issues to resolve because we were from a different state. We had to sign some papers. Vermont is not too bureaucratic. It became a matter of a simple question: 'Where is this child going?' The lawyer answered: 'We've found adoptive parents.' 'Okay.' It was fortunate that it worked out very cleanly. The lawyers are smart enough to know that in these situations all the i's have to be dotted and all the t's have to be crossed."

Lilly said, "At four o'clock the next day we were sitting in the lobby of the hospital. The birth mother was having her counseling and signing the papers at three-thirty, and we had to meet the attorney there. He was going to let us know if everything was okay. And, you know, because of what had already happened to us, I wanted to be excited, but there was a little part of me that was thinking he could walk in here and say, 'I'm sorry.' But when he walked in he was smiling!

"We went directly upstairs to the nursery. Our baby was the only one there, so we were able to walk right in. She was in a bassinet and had a pink blanket wrapped around her. She was wearing a little pink hat. I'll never forget it. All the nurses knew the situation and were in tears. I reached in and picked her up. She was pink and round . . . so beautiful! She was sleeping. It was wonderful, probably the most wonderful thing I've ever experienced! Bob and I held her, and we were both crying. Hillary was there and she was crying—even the lawyer had tears in his eyes! It was just the happiest thing that I can ever remember."

Bob said, "The baby was tiny, really tiny, and sound asleep. When we were ready to leave we were told that a hospital agent had to carry the child to the door. So we were all walking down the corridor together— this man holding the baby, Hillary, the lawyer, Lilly, and me. It was quite a crowd. When we got to the front door of the hospital the man handed the baby to Lilly. We were standing there with Hillary, and there was a lot of crying going on. Then everybody left, and Lilly and I were standing in the parking lot with this child and I said, 'I can't believe it!' It seemed to happen so fast. There had been such a crowd around us, and then just us . . . the three of us. And that was that."

"We said good-bye to everyone and got into our car," said Lilly. "Bob and I just sat there. It was, here we are . . . It's time to go home . . . We have our baby!"

After their difficulties in adopting their first child, Erin, it would have been understandable if Bob and Lilly had decided to raise an only child. But perhaps those memories are analogous to the pain of childbirth—they fade enough to allow couples to go through it again. Bob and Lilly were thrilled with Erin, and they were eager to adopt another child so she would have a brother or sister to grow up with.

"Our agency required us to wait until our first child was two before adopting a second child," said Lilly. "We weren't in a hurry, but the process had taken so long the first time that we figured we'd better get our paperwork ready, and we put our application in right after Erin's second birthday, which was in early November."

Bob said, "I think we were a lot smarter by then. We wouldn't even have pursued most of those earlier situations. We were very happy with our little one. Two would have been great, but I thought our chances were pretty slim. So we went through this whole rigmarole again, but I thought a very limited number of birth mothers would go for us. They'd come in and say, 'Look at all these people who have no children. Why should I give my child to somebody who already has one?'" But then Bob thought of a likely scenario: "What's going to happen is that some birth mother will have such concern for her child that she's going to want her child to grow up in a house with another child."

"We weren't putting ads in newspapers or anything this time," said Lilly. "We now understood that when it was meant to be it would happen naturally and comfortably, as it finally had with Erin. So this time we were just waiting.

"One thing I'd come to realize after adopting Erin was that there is a little piece of infertility that doesn't go away. I believe that carrying and delivering a child is the smallest part of being a parent. If being a parent is ninety-eight percent loving and raising a child, then 98 percent of my need to be a parent was fulfilled. But that little 2 percent of pain doesn't go away. You don't dwell on it; but it never leaves you.

"There's such an intensity to the love you have for an adopted child. Maybe it's because most adoptive parents have come from such despair and anguish that they go totally the other way in terms of their love and the intensity of their happiness."

That winter Bob's friend Paul came over from England to go skiing with them. He arrived on a Monday, and they planned to drive to Vermont on Thursday morning for a long weekend at their ski house. On Wednesday evening Bob and Paul went out for a drink while Lilly stayed home to prepare for their departure the next morning. She put Erin to bed and was packing when the phone rang. It was Bernice. "Can you come in tomorrow morning to the agency?" Bernice asked. "A birth mother would like to meet you."

"I knew Bob was going to be around because he had taken a couple of days off to go skiing with his friend, so I said, 'Sure, but what's going on?' And she said, 'Well, you'll find out when you get here.' That's typical Bernice!

"The next morning we walked over to the agency (it wasn't far from our condo). Poor Paul, our friend from England—we just had to leave him and go. We took Erin with us. When we walked in Bernice said, 'The birth mother, Mandy, would like to meet you. She's chosen your letter from the file.' I asked if she was meeting other people as well, and Bernice said, 'Well, no, she's chosen you to be her baby's parents.' Bernice thought we knew this, but we hadn't understood what this was all about until that moment. It was so exciting!"

Bernice told Lilly, "Mandy had a baby girl on Tuesday. Ordinarily, in a direct placement, you would not have been called until after the release papers had been signed by the birth mother. But Mandy requested a meeting with you before she signs the papers because she wants to make sure you are the type of people that she understood you to be in your letter."

"It was unlike anything I've ever done in my life," said Lilly. "When we went in Mandy was sitting there. She looked very young to me. She was rather tall and beautiful in a quiet sort of way. She was very nervous, and so were we. She had asked to see Erin, so we brought her in with us for a few minutes, and then Bernice took Erin to a playroom and left us alone with Mandy. It was very touching. She had practically memorized our whole letter. She knew all about us."

"The birth mother was wonderful," said Bob. "She wasn't happy about having to give up her child, but she was going to go to the ends of the earth to make sure she picked the right people. We put in a good amount of time talking to her. She was very concerned about financial stability. Apparently she had come from a financially unstable background, and she felt she understood the ramifications of that. She was very concerned with the will-you-love-my-child type of things."

At the end of the interview Mandy told Bob and Lilly that her baby was being cared for in a foster home. "I'm going there tonight to see her again," she said.

"So we went home knowing that Mandy was going to see the baby that night [with the risk that she might change her mind] and that she wasn't going to sign the papers until four o'clock the next day, Friday," said Lilly. "I think we had a strong positive sense that it would happen, but after what we'd been through with our first adoption we knew nothing is over till it's over.

"That night we went out to dinner to celebrate with Paul. We took Erin with us. I can still picture us walking to the restaurant. Erin was walking on a little stone wall in front of a church. She was happy and carefree, and as I watched her running along I started to cry. Bob couldn't understand why I was crying, but I'd just realized that even though we wanted a second child desperately, Erin's life would never be the same again.

"After we put Erin to bed, I took out some baby clothes. We agonized over the baby's name. We wanted it to have the same number of syllables as Erin, so we finally picked Heather.

"Friday was a long day for us. We just hung around the house and played with Erin. Paul was with us. We tried not to let ourselves get too excited. Finally four o'clock came, and it was time to go to the agency. Bob and I walked over with Erin. I had brought a Snugli with me. When we went in Bernice said, 'The baby is in the other room.'

"We thought the baby would be there with a social worker, but it was Mandy instead. She was holding the baby. She stood up when we walked in. She just stood up, walked over, and handed the baby to me. It was a beautiful gesture. It was such a hard situation for her. I could see her pain; I felt her pain, but on the other hand I was so happy. Mandy and I cried and hugged each other. Erin sat in a little rocking chair, and I put the baby on her lap. Heather was a beautiful baby, just beautiful! We visited for a little while, and then Mandy suddenly said, 'I've got a friend out-side waiting for me, and I really have to go. This is . . . This is just hard for me.'"

Bob later said, "Talk about the emotions you experience in a lifetime—the emotion of watching this poor woman have to hand you . . . She handed the child to Lilly. It was remarkable. Everybody was in tears. The agency's lawyer was running around with a camera copying the moment. And then we walked down the street. It was five o'clock on a Friday after-noon in March—a brilliant day. We've got Erin at our side and we've got this tiny little baby, and I thought, *All these people think this is just a normal family out for a walk—and we've just picked up a baby!*"

8/ Enzo and Eric
Two dads

"Becoming a parent was not what I'd expected. I was astonished by how much my life changed. It was more work than I had ever imagined; it was more exhausting. But it's been a wonderful experience. I don't know what else to say except that it's absolutely the most wonderful thing I've ever done in my life."

THE CHANGING definition of family in our society has influenced the rules and regulations of adoption to allow single, divorced, and handicapped people, as well as those in their forties, fifties, or older, to adopt children. Now gay couples are also turning to adoption as a means of creating a family. This is quite controversial and can be difficult to achieve but, as the following story illustrates, not impossible. Enzo and Eric are devoted to their son, Nicky; they hope that sharing their story will help readers better understand what adoption can mean to a gay couple and what the couple can offer to a child.

Enzo is a charming, middle-aged Italian man who talks with his hands; his gestures range from pounding his fist on the table when describing his frustration with bureaucrats to wiping tears away when speaking of his grandmother's death. Eric is tall, slender, and fair-haired; he is introspective and conscientious, yet witty.

"I was born in the late nineteen-forties and grew up in an Italian neighborhood in New York City," said Enzo. "We played in the street. Everyone on my street and all their parents and grandparents came from the same town in Sicily. I'm first generation. My father is now eighty-five and doesn't speak a word of English. My mother is eighty; she sounds like a Sicilian Gracie Allen! My sister is ten years older than me. She was born in this country but failed first grade because she didn't speak English! That's what finally prompted my mother to start learning English. My brother is seven-and-a-half years older than me; I'm the accident child."

Enzo's family lived on the top floor of a four-story building they owned. His grandparents lived on the first floor, where their three youngest children were still at home. His mother's sister lived on another floor with three kids. "We all ate together," recalled Enzo. "There were about eighteen or nineteen people! We each had our own apartments, but there was one communal apartment with a kitchen, dining room, and living room. We each had a kitchen in our apartments, but it wasn't stocked—no refrigerator, no dishes, nothing. Every morning we went downstairs to eat breakfast, and we used that apartment as a big family playroom. Everyone went home to go to bed, and that was it! It was absolutely wonderful.

"I remember being about three years old and wondering who my father was! My father and grandfather were fishermen and would go out for four or five days and then be home for two days. I finally figured out that the tallest male in the house was my father. That's the way I distinguished him.

"I called my grandparents Nana and Nanoo, and my parents Ma and Pa. Italian families don't use the words 'uncle' and 'aunt.' We just use first names. There were many Vincenzos in the family. By Italian tradition the first son and first daughter are named after the husband's family, and the second son and second daughter after the wife's family. We were living with my mother's side of the family, so there were five or six Vincenzos running around. I am Enzo in the family. At a family get-together I don't respond to Vincenzo or Vinnie. Close friends also call me Enzo.

"When we played on the street the whole street would discipline us. I remember old ladies leaning out the window yelling, 'Don't do that!' We listened to everyone. An Italian boy is treated differently than an Italian girl. When you're thirteen or fourteen you're allowed to go out. But not the girls; they don't go out. They're within eyeshot of someone. I was given a choice to go to parochial school or public school. Girls weren't given a choice. I chose public school. Parochial schools for girls were good because it kept them as virgins. Boys they might make sissies out of, so you had a choice. In an Italian upbringing the Catholic Church is, well . . . very, very un-Irish. Italians had no respect for priests. If you wanted to become a priest or a nun your parents would say, 'Why are you doing this to me? How can you destroy the family? You're going to become one of *them?*'

"I can remember seeing an occasional black kid. At that time (early nineteen-fifties) I don't think there was such hostility between minorities and blacks. For Italians you were an outsider, no matter who you were, except if you were an Italian! Everyone else was lumped together, except for Jews, whom Italians tended to respect. They respected them because they were well educated and because the wives worked with the men. The Irish they didn't know; the blacks they didn't know. These people didn't really have any feelings about race. The term WASP wasn't used."

Enzo spoke English to his family and they spoke Italian to him. He wasn't encouraged to speak Italian and can't speak it now. Enzo admitted, "It's a pity. I can mumble a few words, order a meal in a restaurant, and get a hotel room. And when I'm in Italy, the farther south I go the more I understand."

When he was twelve or thirteen Enzo's family lost their house to urban renewal and moved to the suburbs. "The whole place was demolished. [It was] very, very traumatic for me! I think this is why I went into architecture, specifically renovation. I was already drawing; at the age of four or five I started to draw street layouts.

"I grew up always wanting to go back to Italy, although I had never been there! Because you always heard, 'Go back, go back, go back!' So there was a very strong roots connection there and it was very confusing. I identified with it and realized that when I'm in Italy I don't feel Italian, and when I'm here I don't feel American."

After high school Enzo went to a technical school and got two associate degrees, one in architectural engineering and the other in applied sciences. After that he studied architecture at night for five years. He explained, "I lived at home. Italian boys don't want to move out of their house. There is a saying that Italians treat their mothers as if they were the Virgin Mary; if she's the Virgin Mary, then you're God! We were treated like God.

"I moved out of the house when I was twenty-three. I was the first person [in the family] to ever move out of the house without getting married. I'm talking cousins, uncles, aunts, the whole shooting match. And I moved out only because I knew I was gay; I knew I had to get out of there. It was a big trauma, and I intentionally went to a psychiatrist in order to have an excuse to give to my mother. I said, 'I've been seeing this therapist, and he thinks it would be better if I get out and get my own place.' Now she had an excuse. We're very good at giving each other excuses. I remember thinking, *When everyone moves out they have a celebration of a wedding and all that, and I have nothing."*

Enzo moved back to the city, near his old neighborhood. "I thought, *Let's stay with the roots.* I got a job in an architecture firm, and within a month I met Dennis. [Soon after] it was Thanksgiving. I took him home because the thought of him being alone—he was from Cleveland—freaked me out. That's the Italian in me! I remember my grandfather looking at us at one point, and a voice said to me, 'He knows!' He wasn't judgmental; I was his blood, that's all that mattered to him. You know, they're very much into that. If somebody else is gay they might go 'Pooh, pooh,' but this was your blood.

"My grandfather was adopted. He was a very, very proud man, and he would say, 'I don't know who my parents were, but I know I'm from good stock.' I think this was why he was so interested in his children. He had fourteen—eight survived into adulthood—and there were about twenty-eight grandchildren. And he just beamed; he'd look at you and beam! I still find it hard talking about my grandparents . . .

"He died eighteen years ago; my grandmother died six years ago, and I still miss them. I can't stand it! When my grandmother died it was like it could have been my mother. I was very close to her. The unconditional love, totally unconditional love . . .

"There's different levels of speaking in the family. You can tell me something and say, 'This is a secret; don't tell anyone.' And I know I can tell the following twelve people: I can tell my brother, I can tell my younger aunts because they're in our generation, but not the older ones because that's another stratosphere, and then that goes to a whole new level. So there's this little manipulation going on constantly."

Dennis and Enzo had an open relationship for about four or five years. Enzo explained, "I mean really open! I'm talking about the height of gay culture in this country—mid-sixties, early seventies—with lots of running around. Gay liberation had just started. [Gays] were starting to come out of the closet in a big way.

"The Vietnam War was on. I went to a therapist so I could stay out of Vietnam. I told him I was gay. *I thought, If they want to shoot each other, let them. I don't care!* It was just my attitude—my Italian upbringing again. Your family comes first, your religion comes second, and your country comes in a distant third. There's no real sense of being part of the country. You take care of yourself. Authority is not to be trusted. I ran around for six years. I tended to have relationships with people but didn't let them go, like Dennis. I was literally building a family around me, an extended family.

"I always liked having kids around me. I'm the type of person who sits on a plane, and if there's a kid next to me, I don't think, *Oh, my God!* It's part of life! I'll talk to them, give them crayons, play with them. I got involved with my cousins when I was a kid. My aunts lived across the street from us and they were having babies. I baby-sat all the time. I baby-sat my cousin, Joey, and I have a cousin, Lucille, who's my age. She took care of our cousin, Frannie. She had the girl baby; I had the boy baby! I'm given credit for teaching Joey to walk and everything. I was very, very used to kids. It wasn't unusual in our background for boys to take care of other kids; it wasn't wimpy at all. It was okay to look after younger kids and to protect them and all that stuff. It was encouraged.

"I was in high school when I figured out I was gay, and I remember thinking, *You know, you could get married and pretend you're straight and have kids.* And then I thought, *It wouldn't be fair to her or to the kids.* I figured that out in ten seconds. So I gave up on kids quite young. I just said I wouldn't have them. I got very attached to my brother's kids instead.

"I also figured out other things in high school. Other people who were obviously gay were very wishy-washy, and I remember thinking, *There have to be other people*—I didn't know the word gay—*like me who are not into this feminine stuff. Where are they, and how do I find them?*

"My brother and I are very, very close. He was the first one in the family I told that I was gay. I was in my mid-twenties. About ten years later I told my mother. She said, 'I know.'

"'How did you find out?'

"'Nana told me.'

"'Who told her?'

"'Your grandfather did, but I didn't want to believe him.'"

Eric, third child of five, was born while his father was a neurology resident in New York in the late fifties. His parents had five kids in six years—two boys and three girls. "It was great growing up. We never had a shortage of friends to play with."

After Eric's father finished his studies, his parents relocated to Ohio, where he lived for ten years. "My father bought a cute, sensible home across the street from an elementary school," he said. "It was an idyllic childhood. My family was very conventional. My mom was president of the PTA. She just wanted everyone to get along and not worry about the big problems. We lived in a very white neighborhood, and all the years that we lived there there were only one or two black children in my school.

"My father had a very progressive political orientation. He fashioned himself as a progressive states' rights Democrat. But I've always thought of him as a socialist. He was very supportive of all kinds of things; we lived in a household where respect for different races was very important. He didn't have any bigotries as far as I could tell. He was Protestant and my mother was Catholic. He had high standards for people. He wanted everybody to work, and if you worked hard, it didn't matter what you did with the rest of your life, as long as you excelled professionally. He was an early embodiment of 'don't ask, don't tell.' At least you knew where he stood.

"My mother was into babies. She thought babies were amazing. She was the perfect mom—she had all the credentials. When I was in sixth grade, she took me to visit a friend involved in a foster care program. I thought this was amazing, just wonderful. I loved holding the babies. It seemed that a really nice thing was going on there.

"My mother subsequently became a foster mother. When my youngest sibling was seven, my mother brought in a foster baby, a newborn black boy. He lived with us for six months. I remember it as being very exciting. We had a bassinet, and it was all decorated. We were so happy to have a baby in the house. It was wonderful watching the little fingers and the clothes. I remember the five of us competing for time with this baby. We were fascinated watching my mother make the formula and sterilize the bottles. It was incredibly painful for all of us when he left. I can remember weeping. I think that's why he was the only foster child she ever had."

When Eric was thirteen his family moved to southern California. This was a period of big opportunity in California, and his father quickly was promoted to dean of medicine at a university there. Moving was hard on the family.

"It was okay for me," remembered Eric, "but I think middle and younger children are a little sheltered. I spent a lot of time learning from my older siblings' mistakes, which was very beneficial. I went to junior high and high school in southern California. The weather and the beach were wonderful. And being outside in the winter, after Ohio! It was a period in my life when I was more interested in sports, being outdoors, and getting away from the family, so that was great.

"It was a transitional time for the country and a transitional time for southern California. The schools were on double and triple session. There were a lot of problems with drugs and other upsetting things. My father had to devote a lot of attention to his career, and my mother was struggling with five kids, changing hormones, and drugs.

"Both of my parents were very much into family. They struggled for years to get the relatives together, and we spent our childhood traipsing across the country to visit them. Even when things were painful and frustrating, my father would say, 'Family is it. You never know how important family is.'"

After graduating from high school Eric went to a small college in rural Pennsylvania. "It ended up being a little too monastic for me," he admitted. "I was in the process of defining myself as an individual, and part of it was coming out as a homosexual. That was very difficult to do in rural Pennsylvania! I felt isolated there, so I took a year off after my sophomore year. My parents had a heart attack! I came to New York with a friend from college. I met Enzo in August of that year, and we've been together ever since.

"When I met Enzo I was only twenty years old. He was thirty-one and in a different place [from me]. He thought a relationship was moving in, spending the rest of your life together, and having kids! I had never taken a relationship very seriously. I wanted to be irresponsible, run around, and finish school (I had two years of college to finish). We struggled because he was interested in a very heavy commitment, and I was reluctant to make a big commitment. So we fought around that issue for three or four years, and I spent some time away from him. I experimented with dating other men. It was a rough period of deciding what I wanted to do with my life.

"I finished my degree in English and went to France to teach for six months. That was a turning point in terms of my relationship with Enzo.

When I came back I moved in with him and really felt we were going to make it. We were going to have a relationship. I was twenty-five then.

"We did what people did in the late seventies and into the eighties—making a lot of money, going to fine restaurants, traveling to Europe extensively, and having a great life. Enzo was restoring old houses, and I started my own business, a temporary agency for word processors and computer operators. In the late eighties we went through transitions and began to rethink a lot of things. We'd spent a lot of money, bought a second home [on Cape Cod], and had all the delights of the worldly life. That was a lot of fun. But we were looking for something more and beginning to look forward to the rest of our lives. We were confident in our relationship and wanted to see if we could take that a step further.

"Enzo had talked about babies forever. The first day that I moved into the house he wanted kids! I was horrified by the idea—I was only twenty years old and he wanted babies! But by the late eighties I was thirty-one, the age Enzo was when I first met him, and I started to turn. I thought, *We have something really nice here. We have this beautiful home, and we've lived in the same neighborhood, the same house for a long time, and I'm beginning to feel that I want something more in my life.* We'd spent a lot of time thinking about what gay relationships were and how we fitted into the gay community. We were never politically active, which was fine for me. We were more interested in domestic issues and in our own relationship.

"A lot of gay people are frozen in whatever personality archetypes there are in the gay community. One of them is the promiscuous male or the Peter Pan, the perennial young adult who does not form family relationships. That was very unsatisfying for us. We saw our friends go through tumultuous relationship changes, break up, date, and break up; it was completely uninteresting for us. I can't think of one relationship that has lasted as long as ours has. We've buried seven or eight people from AIDS in the last four years. It takes a tremendous toll. I often say that if I hadn't been in this relationship, I would be dead!"

When Eric came out to his parents in 1982, they had a hard time with it. He said, "I think in the beginning, before my parents were confident that Enzo and I were in a monogamous relationship and would stay together, they worried about AIDS. My father loves his children and wants them to excel, and if they do something that he's not too excited about or too proud of, then that's disappointing, but he's ultimately concerned about what they do with their lives. It took [my parents] a long time to feel comfortable with my homosexuality and my relationship with Enzo. But as we persisted as a relationship and didn't show any symptoms of illness, they felt that maybe it was better that we stay in the relationship, because otherwise I'd be exposed to all these horrible things."

Enzo narrated, "I'd always assumed I could never have a child. Then I heard about Mia, a lesbian psychiatrist we knew, who had adopted. I immediately called her, and she put us in touch with our social worker, Winifred. Winifred is a straight woman in her late seventies whose family spent their lives forming unions—real left-wing. She's a down-to-earth person. She said jokingly, 'I assume you're single, because you came through Mia. There's a joke around the office that I take only single people.'

"Winifred never asked Mia whether she was a lesbian. She did ask me at one point whether I was gay, so I told Winifred about Eric. I got the feeling that she decided whether you were suitable in the first five minutes and then went from there. From her point of view it was not a deception but a mission. 'So we do a home study,' she said. 'So we don't mention Eric. You had a girlfriend at one time?' She took this tack.

"Winifred is a licensed social worker, but I was never in her office. Our meetings took place in her apartment. She was chain-smoking and had a funny wig on, and she gave me coffee and cookies. She'd chitchat with you and was very loose. I have no idea what was going on in her office. They let do her own thing because she'd been doing it for years. I told my family nothing. It was a typical pattern in my family."

Eric admitted, "During my first meeting with Winifred I was very nervous and babbling. I was trying not to be nervous. I'd made sure that we had juice and cookies and milk. I felt like I was on trial. Enzo had met with her several times and we had to make a decision. As a gay couple you make a decision that one of you is going to do the adoption and the other one is not. Legally it can be only a single-parent adoption. I had been very busy with my work and had sold my company in the late eighties. Part of the sale contract was to work with the company for two more years. So I was downtown from eight to six, and I had enough money to finance an adoption, but I didn't have the time to go through the process and the paperwork.

"For that reason and other reasons, Enzo was a better candidate. His work had tapered off; the architecture world was experiencing a recession. Everything dried up and blew away with the desert wind. We were lucky not to have lost more. Enzo had some foreclosures, and it was a difficult period for him, but we made it through.

"I think Winifred just wanted to meet me. I never made it into the paperwork! She said, 'I won't take people who are political.' I don't know what that meant to her, but we felt she didn't want people who would publicize what she was doing or what we wanted to do. I think she thought that what she was doing was wonderful, and she wanted to work with people who thought the same way. She didn't want to work with people who were just trying to make a point and to use the child to meet some political criterion or agenda."

Winifred told Enzo to write a story about how he had been involved in a long-term relationship with a woman, that that union had been childless, and that he had left that relationship wanting a child but couldn't get a child because he no longer had a relationship.

"I think we trusted her and she trusted us," said Eric. "But I was very nervous through the whole process that something horrible would happen. While Enzo did the paperwork, I sat on the sidelines and nagged, 'Did you send that in? Did you get this done?'"

The home study took a couple of months, but Enzo was already working with an adoption agency in another state before it was finished. He never met with them. It was all done over the phone. Sonia, the woman Enzo worked with, didn't know he was gay. He told her the home study was being done, and she said, "Fine."

"I told her I wanted a newborn, a boy," said Enzo. "First she suggested Colombia. A pregnant woman who was expecting a boy was picked out for us, but then the Colombians said, 'No single-male adoptions.' It was like having a miscarriage. It was . . . disturbing. Sonia said, 'Countries open and close. Maybe we can go here, maybe we can go there. They accept only single women, but you're a man. How old are you?' Talking to her drove me crazy! Sonia dealt only in South America. We didn't want an adoption in this country, because we were afraid of a birth mother showing up."

"We got very excited," said Eric. "Winifred and the agency had warned us not to get too excited and that mishaps and changes occur, but it's a horrible period, because you don't know what's going to happen. We had a guest room that we planned to use for the baby, but we didn't want to set anything up. We thought it would be like a ghost. So that was very frustrating.

"We put some thought into our choice of gender and we felt that as men we'd be more comfortable raising a boy. We thought it would be easier to explain to the child about potty training and other things."

The disappointment with Colombia's apparent policy of discouraging single men from adoption soon gave way to hope. Eric explained, "We heard from the agency that single people seemed to be having a lot of success in Peru."

Enzo continued, "Sonia knew people in Peru. She could set you up with a lawyer and an interpreter. She had done many adoptions there and had been there frequently. But she was very flighty; she was infuriating! She kept saying, 'I have a three-year-old,' and I would say, 'No, every kid has his own problems; let me give my son my problems, which I'll know how to deal with.' Sonia was a mess, but I never thought of giving up on her. For some reason, I'm entrenched once I start something. I'll start a book and hate it, but I'll finish it. The phone bills with Sonia were astronomical—we talked two or three times a week for a few months.

"Finally Sonia called and said, 'They have a four-month old baby' (*they* being Peru). 'You can go down in a couple of weeks.' I reacted the way I always react to big things. I got very quiet, my stomach went on its own little trip by itself, and I thought, *Don't get too carried away—you lost one already, you know.* I take it really low key. It wasn't a big celebration when I got the phone call. I just said quietly to Eric, 'They've located a baby for us, and I'll probably be leaving in a couple of weeks.'

"I think then it started to hit us that we had a lot to do. I immediately painted the guest bedroom yellow. I hate blue. I enjoyed painting it. Holly, a friend of Eric's, took us out shopping for diapers and stuff. She knew where the best bargains were—she saved us a fortune! We went everywhere with this woman. It was fun but overwhelming to buy everything at once for a kid you haven't seen. She calculated how many diapers, how many wipes, how much formula we needed based on a six-week stay in Peru. I remember shopping at one point by myself and feeling really awkward. I felt very strange, very shy, very out of place. I thought, *What are you doing? You don't really know. Do you need this? Do you need that? I don't want pink and I don't want blue. I'm an architect! I want clean lines. I don't want any of this gaudy stuff.*

"We didn't tell the neighbors. Holly was one of the people who had written me a letter of recommendation for the home study. We told those people. But it was kept relatively quiet. A few of our close gay friends knew we were looking for a baby. In the gay community ten percent have rejected the family in everything. They want nothing to do with it. Friends told us they knew someone who adopted and who then couldn't go out much. And we said, 'We don't go out to dinner so much, we have dinner at home.' We were already into this settled married life, and we weren't socializing and partying. We had our own businesses, our winter and summer homes; we had the whole routine. All that was missing was the kid!"

When he heard that a baby had been chosen for him, Enzo told his mother: "By the way, I'm leaving soon for South America; I'm adopting a baby." She pretended not to hear him. "I'm adopting a baby," he repeated.

Enzo remembered, "She went off the wall! 'Why are you doing this to me? I know you're like *this*'—she gestured with her head up to the left, which meant gay—'I've accepted you like *this*. Why are you doing this to me?' The upshot was, 'I can sort of hide the fact that you're gay, you're not married, but now you have a baby. What am I supposed to tell people? Why don't you get married if you want a baby? What am I going to tell your father? I don't want to talk to you again!' And I thought, *Thank you, God. I won't have to deal with her anymore!* One of my aunts was ecstatic. She kept saying, 'This is going to be the luckiest kid in the world.'"

At that time, Eric and Enzo had been together more than a decade. "We had never spent a night apart," explained Enzo. "I had never been on a plane by myself. Someone said I'm becoming an old Italian male—you turn everything over to another person. I had never been in another country where I wasn't with someone who could speak the language. So what did I do? I took my cousin Lucille with me! The last thing my mother said to me before I left was, 'Get a young one; the older ones know too much.'

"My cousin and I flew down together. It was a mess when we arrived. We get down there like immigrants, with ten large duffel bags full of diapers! We had about ten thousand dollars cash on us, because they want everything in cash. It was in my shoes, my cousin's bra—all in hundreds. This man comes up to me and starts helping, and [I knew] this was not done out of kindness. But I had all these suitcases, and there was a line for days. It's one o'clock in the morning and I'm thinking, *Oh, well, I don't know where my interpreter is; I don't know what she looks like. I can't get to her, and she can't get to me. What am I going to do with this man? He's really nice, he's helping us out with the luggage.* He said, 'Are you here for a baby? Don't worry.' He went up to the immigration person, and we skipped two hundred people and went through!

"Then my interpreter came up and I offered the man ten or fifteen dollars for helping with the luggage. He was really upset; he wanted a lot more. But I know the value of a dollar down there, and it was more than enough! My interpreter got into a fight with him, and he was very angry. What a great way to arrive! It's now two o'clock in the morning.

"The interpreter was a con artist. She had a driver and a van, and the first thing she said was, 'I need forty-five dollars for the van.' I said to myself, *The guidebook said five to ten dollars, but you're in a bind here. She's your interpreter, and it's two o'clock in the morning. Just give her the money, just go along with this.* On the way to the hotel the interpreter told me I wasn't getting the four-month-old baby they had told us about. They had decided that since that baby was from a small village, the local authorities would freak out if a single man came to adopt him. (You had to go back to the child's city of birth for the adoption.) They had found another baby for me, in Lima. We got to the hotel at three o'clock in the morning. It was a residential hotel; we had a one-bedroom apartment with two baths—really nice. Before she left, the interpreter told us, 'The baby will be here at three o'clock tomorrow afternoon.'

"My cousin and I stayed in the apartment the next day. We didn't know the neighborhood, and we could speak only English. The television was all in Spanish. We saw "Zorro!" I thought to myself, *This was the way your parents lived when they came to the United States. They watched television and didn't understand the programs. They could figure out certain programs because of black hats/white hats.* It was an interesting feeling. My cousin and I played cards. The hotel was full of people adopting kids; people came and went. It was nice, the people were wonderful, and it was worth the money. The interpreter got us a good rate. The rent was posted at sixty dollars a day, but we got it for twenty-eight. I think she was skimming off the top on that too.

"Three o'clock arrived: no kid! The interpreter called, 'We'll be late.' This was the only time I got nervous. I thought, *I don't want a kid!* It really hit me. The baby came in around five o'clock. My cousin opened the door.

She was bright enough not to reach for the kid! The lawyer was holding him, a female lawyer who was dressed up as though she was going out to a disco! When I saw Nicky I said, 'He looks perfect!' He was asleep. The lawyer handed him to me and the interpreter said, 'Now your life is changed forever.' I sat down in the living room with Nicky. He was small. We called him chicken legs after we changed his diaper; he was underfed. He had weighed eight pounds at birth, and now, at eighteen days, he weighed five-and-a-half pounds."

The lawyer and the interpreter told Enzo that Nicky had been in the hospital since birth; the birth mother had left him there. She couldn't take him home. They told him he was a fussy eater, which is why he had lost weight. Enzo said, "It took him forty-five minutes to eat two ounces. He woke up and stared at me intently. It felt very strange."

Eric narrated, "The first time Enzo called he said, 'I have this baby and he's absolutely beautiful! And he's only eighteen days old.' I asked, 'What do you mean you have this baby?' I was totally disoriented. I thought we were getting a four-month-old baby, and now he has this other baby! But it was a great relief that he was holding a baby! Once they'd given him a baby we were okay! I was very excited. We had talked about using Enzo's father's name. There's a tradition in Enzo's family of naming the first son after your father. His father's name is Domenico and it's almost the same in Spanish so we thought that would be a good name for a Spanish baby. I wasn't comfortable calling the baby Domenico so we thought of truncating it and calling him Nicky. We thought that would give him an easy name—easy to spell, easy to pronounce, easy to understand, and it would be part of a larger name that he could use later. My Dutch grandfather's name is Joseph (Judokas in Dutch), so we gave him Judokas as his middle name. We both have part of his name. Poor child—international potpourri!"

Enzo continued, "Lucille and I were sleeping in the same room in twin beds, and Nicky was in an adjacent room (the hotel had provided a crib). We had gone to sleep early—we had gotten only about three hours of sleep the night before and were exhausted. He started to cry in the night, and I remember waking up. I didn't know where I was. I was totally disoriented. I thought, *You're not in your own bed because your head's going the wrong way. Where are you? Your head's in the wrong direction and there's a baby crying!* Then it hit me: *You're in Peru—and this is your baby!* That was the only time I lost it. He was fine. I fed him, and he stared at me all the time. It was so strange. It felt as though he knew I was coming.

"I didn't let my cousin feed him or hold him. She never changed his diaper, because I wanted to do it. She was there for two weeks, and I think I let her feed him the last two days she was there. He always slept, always ate nicely. He was a very, very easy baby. He never spat up—I hate kids who spit up! When we ate dinner I would hold him in my lap and he would sleep. We often went out to dinner with a dozen other parents, all the other kids were screaming. We started to call Nicky 'the Prince' because he was always so good."

Enzo kept asking his interpreter, "Where does the money go?" She didn't tell him. He compared notes with other parents in the hotel who used her and decided that she was charging outrageous prices for everything and pocketing the money. She finally told him, "The lawyer gets four thousand, I get five hundred, the judge gets two thousand, the prosecutor gets five hundred, the therapist gets two hundred, and the social worker gets twenty dollars. She comes to your room and you have to have coffee and nice cookies for her, okay?"

The other parents gave about the same amount of money, so Enzo knew his spending was on a par. He explained, "The birth mother gets nothing. You cannot give the birth mother money. It's illegal. It would give the impression that you were buying a baby!

"I found out that I could understand a bit of what people were saying, because Sicily was conquered by Spain for four hundred years, and there's a bit of Spanish in Sicilian. But I didn't let them know. I played the total macho sexist pig while I was there. I heard someone say to my interpreter, 'He's good-looking, you shouldn't let him get away.' And I understood it! So I flirted. I found it very natural—I grew up Italian! I had the whole thing down pat. I could flirt, I could look into the eyes. The interpreter knew the whole story about how my girlfriend had left and didn't want to have children. She said to my cousin, 'I think he was hurt very badly by that woman.' My cousin had to keep a straight face."

Nicky's birth mother was from a small town outside Lima and had gone to a secretarial school in Lima; she had not been home in a year. When she got pregnant her family didn't know about it. She never told them. She said she was still going out with the guy, and they wanted to get married eventually but not at that point. This was her only child, her first child. Enzo elaborated, "She was twenty, and part Indian. She had a strong nose and long black hair; she was short like most people there. She was very quiet.

"When you go to court you have to say that the birth mother gave you the baby. You cannot say you've had the baby for two weeks. I was to give the baby to the lawyer, and then she was going to give the baby to the birth mother, and the birth mother was going to hand the baby back to me—within seconds. I didn't even want to hand the baby to the lawyer! I was thinking, *Who is this woman? I don't trust my translator, and I have this conchita for a lawyer with the long nails and gold jewelry—it's so bizarre!*

"I didn't like the idea at all. The kid was going to be out of my sight for about two minutes. I handed the baby to the lawyer, and they went into another room. When they came back the birth mother handed the baby to me. Her face was expressionless. I think she intentionally closed down. I thought, *Thank God I've got my baby back!*

"We did go out to lunch a couple of times during court procedures, and the birth mother was very, very shy. I think she was intimidated by my lawyer and interpreter, who were white and made derogatory remarks about Indians and the dark kids. Both of them were obviously from well-off families and here was this poor peasant girl from a little village. She asked the lawyer to order for her in the restaurant. She ate very meekly and shyly. I was holding Nicky. At one point she looked at Nicky and apparently she thought he should have another blanket on him. I thought, *Fine, she's showing some interest. I'm not going to go into battle with this woman. I'll cover him up!* That was the only time she showed any interest in him."

The last time Enzo met with the birth mother, his interpreter asked if he would like to say something to her.

Enzo explained, "I thought, *Oh, God, I have to come up with something profound!* I took the Italian stance: 'Tell her that no matter what Nicky does, he will always be my son. He will most likely go to college, but if he doesn't he'll still be my son. He will most likely get a good job, but if he doesn't he'll still be my son. If he grows up to be a thief and lands in jail, he will still be my son. He will always be my son. And tell her that I think she was God's way of getting a baby to me.' I was very sincere, but I'd always taken this macho pig stance to everything and my interpreter was surprised. I thought she was going to cry! She said, 'That's the nicest thing anyone's ever said [to a birth mother].' The interpreter translated what I said to the birth mother and she just sat there and nodded.

"The birth mother was right in doing what she did in that she didn't abandon Nicky. Apparently she even knew how to go about this, because a lot of mothers go to the hospital, give a false name and run away, which makes adoption very complicated. She had to identify a father; she did this. He has to deny it. Now, if he doesn't deny it, that's a whole new can of worms. If he claims to be the father, he can get in trouble for getting her pregnant, he has legal responsibilities, and he has to give up the baby. So she says, 'He's the father.' He says, 'No, I'm not.' The court says, 'Okay.' He was never in court, but it was done symbolically somehow. She got good advice and she knew: *This is how I get my child adopted.* So somehow she went through this process and, you know, in that way I respect her— she was taking care of her kid.

"I screamed at my interpreter at one point. I began to realize that everything down there takes one week, from beginning to end. They drag it out, no matter what it is. Apparently there had been a television program accusing Peru of various adoption scandals. The Peruvian government's response was to make the adoption process long. There was nothing to do. I became friends with Nancy, an adoptive mother at the hotel, but she went home before me. I went crazy after Nancy left. I was afraid to leave the capital because they might call me to court."

"Enzo was in Peru for six weeks!" said Eric. "I got letters, phone calls and pictures. I immediately rushed the pictures off to my parents and Enzo's parents, and we actively celebrated. There were three baby showers. My company held a shower for me, and then our friends held showers before Enzo came back. The house started to fill up with toys and baby carriages, and I set up the crib. I had bought it myself. It was a lot of fun.

"But all of this was tinged with my general fear that Enzo still had to get out of the country and the legal process had to be completed. It was frustrating waiting for that to happen. Six weeks is a long time. We talked almost every day and had a monstrous phone bill. We never ran into a firm obstacle; it was just general anxiety.

"Enzo made sure that his paperwork was absolutely complete before he went down. He had found out that a lot of other people's problems had to do with the paperwork. For us there was all the excitement of the original giving of the child and then we entered no-man's-land, the doldrums, which is just like the period we had left, where we got information, but the adoption is incomplete. You don't know whether it's definitely going to happen tomorrow or the next day. Day dragged into day.

"Enzo talked about going to court and not understanding what was going on. He felt it was his job to make these women [the lawyer and interpreter] love him so that they would want to help him. He flirted with them mercilessly, took them out to lunch, and told them all the wonderful things he would do for them, that he knew other Americans who wanted to adopt and would connect them with these people. They fell for it! He told me that a lot of people whose processes got stalled were people who didn't manage it well, didn't ingratiate themselves. Some of them would say, 'This child is kind of dark,' or 'I didn't expect an Indian baby.'"

Enzo continued, "Interesting things happened in court. My judge turned out to be married to a Sicilian. She wanted to hold the baby, and I said to my lawyer, 'Are her hands clean?' My lawyer blushed and said, 'Don't say that! Don't say that!' I said it in English, and the judge asked what I was saying. Then I said it in Italian, and my interpreter almost fell to the floor! But the judge just smiled. Of course I let her hold him, and while she was holding him I said something. Nicky immediately turned his head toward me. She said, 'Look at that. The baby is used to his voice!' Every time I said anything Nicky turned toward me. It was very cute, and she was touched by that.

"Down there they all kiss each other, even when they don't know each other. In Italian culture you give people a peck on the cheek, but they are people you know! So I couldn't figure out what was going on. My lawyer kissed the judge, the judge kissed my interpreter, my interpreter kissed my lawyer. I kept saying, 'Do I get a kiss?' Finally my judge said, 'Well, I'll give you one kiss. Sicilians are too jealous!' I endeared myself to her in that way.

"I had the same judge each time, a young woman judge dressed up like a conchita. She didn't wear a robe; she wore a party dress! The lawyer and the interpreter dressed the same way; they were all overdressed, with lots of jewelry and long fingernails. We were in a little room in a big old courthouse with long corridors. Most of the lights were out because the government hadn't paid its electric bill that month!

"The only time we did anything on time in Peru was when we went to court. You had to be on time or early, but the judge was late! Once I had to take Nicky for a physical. We had a two o'clock appointment, but my interpreter didn't pick me up until three. We got there at four, and the doctor was another half-hour late! Nobody thought anything of this!

"When we went in the courthouse we walked down a long corridor toward the juvenile section where they do adoptions. I saw candles flickering; what more could a good Catholic boy want but a statue of the Virgin Mary with all the candles around her! I'm thinking, *This isn't too bad, this isn't too bad! This is from God, from God! I love it! We've got the Madonna here . . . the candles . . . this isn't too bad!*

"The prosecutor—the only other man there—represents the child. He's the devil's advocate. He gets paid three or four hundred dollars. I played up the idea of the Italian family, the extended family, and he bought into that. The judge and prosecutor loved the fact that I named the baby after my father. Because I gave him my father's name, they knew I wasn't ashamed of having a brown-skinned baby. I mentioned that my grandfather was adopted, and they loved that too. I was playing everything right to the hilt. They were moved by it all. I didn't think decisions were being made; I felt we were just going through the motions. I was trying to cut down on the amount of time I'd have to spend there. I was out one day shy of six weeks. My friend Nancy had been there for only four weeks. But I met people who had spent three months, four months! Our paperwork was done up front. Sonia did get the paperwork right.

"I was supposed to leave after two weeks. You get the kid, you go to court, and then you're supposed to go home and come back to pick up the kid [after everything is processed]. Meanwhile you have to pay to board the kid while you're away. And where does the kid stay? With my interpreter's sister! As soon as they gave Nicky to me I said, 'I'm not leaving!' 'Well, your paperwork has to be done. Why don't you go home?' I said, 'No way!' and my interpreter was a little miffed. The judge asked me why I was staying and I answered, 'I'm in construction and it's winter up there, so there's nothing going on. And I don't want to leave him.' They were touched by that, too.

"The most frightening thing was meeting the psychiatrist in a dingy part of the courthouse that had cubicles with doctors in them. We came into a room where about five dozen people were sitting. I came in with Nicky, who looked so clean, and these people were grungy and bleeding! It looked like the *Rocky Horror Show!* I asked my interpreter, 'What is this?'

"'Oh, these are people who have had accidents, or they've been abused or been in a fight. They come here for a claim, so they get medical treatment in the courthouse.'

"I thought, *Oh, wonderful!* The birth mother was with us, and immediately my interpreter disappeared, came back, pointed at me, and disappeared again. The next thing I knew we're in the doctor's office in five minutes! This was what her five hundred dollars were for! The psychiatrist wanted to give me a physical! She asked me to strip down to my underwear, went in the back room with me, sort of looked at me, and seemed a bit embarrassed. She said, 'Ummh, ummmh . . . ' and left! This was the physical! I don't know if she wanted to see whether I had bruises! The interpreter was holding the baby for me. Then they made the birth mother go through the same thing! My interpreter got into a little tiff with the psychiatrist because she wanted to give me two hours of therapy.

"We had to go back the next day. First we went to her office. Oh, I love offices in Peru! We went up a flight of stairs. The building looked abandoned—it was dusty, dirty, and the door was off the hinges. The psychiatrist immediately said, 'Let's go to my house.' Her house was in a middle-class neighborhood, not bad. It had very little furniture. It reminded me of Sicily—a terrazzo floor, not a lot of personal stuff on the walls. We sat at a table. She had an assistant. She said, 'This is my niece, who's studying to be a therapist.' My lawyer went into another room with the psychiatrist. They came back, they went away again; they were negotiating the price! It turned out that the assistant was not the psychiatrist's niece. She said, 'I don't know why, but she always says that. However, I am studying psychiatry.' I think, *Okay, what next?*"

The psychiatrist showed Enzo a series of pictures—not ink blots—and asked him to identify what he saw. She also asked him a couple of times if he'd ever had an affair with a man, when was the last time he had slept with a woman, et cetera. Then she gave him a piece of paper and said, "Write who you are in one word." Enzo wrote "I am Vincenzo." Then he wrote "I am a man." "What do you love?" He wrote the interpreter's name! She blushed, and the psychiatrist grinned and said to her in Spanish, "He's a good catch! Why don't you marry him?"

Enzo's lawyer argued with the psychiatrist because he had had a psychiatric report done in the U.S. He said, "She insisted it had to be done again. She was looking for her two hundred dollars. Also it was a holiday, so that was extra. And it was at her house.

"She showed me picture cards and one of them was of an androgynous man. There was a body on the table with doctors around it, and the androgynous man was in front of it. I said, 'This is an angel. Catholics know angels have no sex, so this is neither a man nor a woman. This is the spirit of the man on the table, and the spirit doesn't know if it should go to Heaven now or go back into the body.' She just looked at me and said, 'Okaaaaaaaaay.' Then she showed me a picture of a beautiful boy in a log cabin. I went into the architecture. 'You don't see log cabins very much anymore in America.'

"I kept doing this with everything. She'd show me a picture of a woman and I'd say, 'See that refrigerator? This is from the nineteen-forties.' She kept saying to the interpreter, 'Would you tell him to talk about the people? This guy is always into architecture. I need the other stuff!' She said, 'What about the boy?' I said, 'Well, the boy has no shoes on, and he's not wearing a shirt, but he's well cared for. You can see that he's clean, his hair is combed. Even though he's small he's going to be big, because his hands and feet are big. Did you ever see Michaelangelo's *David?*' She said, 'Excellent!'

"In another picture, of a mother and daughter on a staircase, the daughter was crying. I said, 'Really nice staircase.' I kept a straight face, and she went on to the next card. We were there for three or four hours. At one point the interpreter, who was holding Nicky, gave him a kiss and got lipstick on his cheek. The therapist screamed at her, 'Wipe that off his face!' I don't think her report was shown to anybody. I have no idea what happened to it, but I didn't try to get out of this. I tried to get out of nothing."

There was a small earthquake the last week Enzo was in Lima. "All of Nicky's paperwork was on a table and the room was shaking," explained Enzo. "We were on the seventh floor. I thought, *Which do you go for first, the paperwork or the kid?* The hotel would never admit to the earthquakes. I said, 'Was that a bad earthquake last night?'

"'Well, it was far away.'

"'I felt it!'

"'Well, this one was closer.'

"I heard gunfire sometimes at night, but I felt very safe there. The people were really nice. It was the only time in my life that I was totally confused about money—there were 462,000 intas to the dollar! In restaurants and supermarkets I would just throw money at them. I would calculate when I got back to the hotel. They always gave me the correct change! The drivers were crazy. When you were crossing the street, they would drive around you; they wouldn't stop! I started to shake my fist and kicked a few cars as they drove by. They looked at me as though I had two heads.

"I had trouble with the U.S. consulate down there. The interpreter took me to get Nicky's visa. There was a line that goes out of sight, and she said, 'Just wave your passport.' So I waved my passport, and everything stopped! They were going through someone's luggage, and I thought they'd put me behind her, but they just pushed her aside! I'm a citizen! I went upstairs and waited and waited. The baby was with me. This kid was with me the whole time for six weeks! I had him in a Snugli. They started calling off numbers in Spanish! I think, *Great! Everyone speaks English here, but they call off the numbers in Spanish! Thank God it's almost like Italian. My number's twenty-two; just watch for twenty and twenty-one.* I finally got my turn. There was a black guy behind the bulletproof glass, and I knew he was gay! He said in an effeminate voice, 'Oh, you're a single-male adoption . . . Oh! I need your passport and other things. Oh, you're from New York! Are you into sports up there?'

"'No, I can't stand sports. What do you do down here?' He wasn't going to get any information from me!

"'Oh, I just like the culture and I speak Spanish and I'm very friendly.'"

Enzo elaborated, "I'm making eye contact as though the guy's at a bar, and he was getting very embarrassed. According to this wonderful book called *Queer in America*, the biggest problem gays have is other gays who don't want to be detected. I thought, *Great! I have to put up with this, too!* He said, 'There's a mistake in the baby's passport. They put his mother down and you down. You have to get this straightened out so that he does not have a mother.' I started screaming at him, 'Do you know what it's going to take me to get this straightened out? I'm trying to get out of the country tonight!' He said, 'There's nothing I can do about it. When you get it straightened out you don't have to wait in line. Just bang on the window.'

"I went outside to find my interpreter, who immediately called the lawyer. Then she put me in a cab. She said, 'I'll meet you at the passport office; I have to meet somebody else first.' She sent me to a place that looked like a major league baseball park. You walk through a gate and there are five thousand people milling around in lines for passports! As soon as I got there twelve people were on top of me, screaming in Spanish, 'Do you need a passport for your baby?' I brushed them aside—my Italian upbringing again. I said, 'Get out of here. Move! I don't need you!' I got very mean. They just parted. Most Americans were very timid. All of a sudden a woman came up to me and said, 'I am here to get the passport for your son.' She went in a back door and came right out with a new passport—with a fingerprint on it! I said, 'Where did the fingerprint come from?' She laughed. 'Oh, yeah—fingerprint! I used my little finger and smudged it a bit.' I thought, *Great! I've got a kid who already has false fingerprints! He's Sicilian, he's definitely Sicilian! We'll get him out of the country illegally!*

"I went back to the U.S. consulate but it was now closed! I started shaking the gate. Machine guns came out! They saw that I was an American. I said, 'Open up! Open up!' They opened up! They knew nothing. They're all Peruvian guards paid by the U.S. consulate. Then I went upstairs, and the screen was down over the window where I had met the guy before. I bang on the window, *boom! boom! boom!* And they opened up! There was a different person this time. But he acted as though this was the most normal thing in the world! All the Peruvian people were sitting there quietly. They didn't dare make a fuss. I finally got my paperwork done, but it was now too late to leave. I thought, *Oh, God . . . I'm going to shoot myself!* So I said to my interpreter, 'Let's go to a good restaurant.'"

When Enzo got to Miami the next day he felt at home and relieved. Someone had told him not to go through customs but to go up to an agent and say he had an adopted baby. He took this advice and three customs agents came over and took his luggage. Enzo said, "I've got the kid, and they're carrying all my luggage for me! They brought me into a special room where they process adopted kids! They said, 'Do you have a sealed envelope?' This was from the U.S. consulate in Lima. They took it and I never saw that again. One agent was Italian. He said, 'Heh! The kid's name is Domenico. Is your father's name Domenico?' Yeah.

"It was about eight o'clock in the morning. I called Eric and then waited two hours for our flight. When I heard the wheels hit the pavement in New York I thought, *I'm going to burst into tears. I'm home! I'm home! There's New York!* First I thought I'd wait for everyone to leave the plane, but then I went charging down the aisle with the baby in hand like a football, pushing people! I was the first person off that plane, and I'd been sitting at the back! I had bought Nicky a Peruvian hat and decided to put it on him before we landed. I ran up the jetway and a woman came rushing past me. She looked at Nicky and did a U-turn. She said, 'A Peruvian baby! Wow! I'm from Peru; I recognize the hat! You just adopted him, didn't you? Oh, this is wonderful. I see your family down there. Go. Go. God bless you!'"

There were about thirty people waiting with Eric at Kennedy Airport. He admitted, "I can't tell you what it was like when I first saw the baby— I can't tell you without crying! It's embarrassing. Parts of it are tender and parts of it are horrible. You don't want to be in a crowd, you don't want to be at an airport [when you meet your child for the first time], and you don't want to be hiding. You want it to be open and wonderful. I felt that I had to hide it. There were all these people with balloons, and strangers asked, 'What are you doing?' I said I was adopting a baby from Peru. I had a feeling they were expecting a mom and a dad to be there, and there weren't! I felt that I could tell eighty percent of the story. I don't feel compelled to come out to absolutely everybody in the world. So it was a combination of a public and a private event, and that's hard to do.

"I saw Enzo walking down the jetway holding the baby. Nicky was all wrapped up and had a Peruvian cap on. I started to cry. Enzo handed the baby to me. I think he was sixty-one days old. He'd been really good on the flight, but now he was wailing!"

"When Eric first saw the baby I just stared at him," said Enzo. "Nicky was staring at him and staring at me. Nothing was said. We were just embraced in this little circle. It's a good thing it was mostly the American side of the family there, because the Italians would have been on top of us, taking the kid from us and holding him! These people were restraining themselves a little bit. It was really funny; Eric was so awkward with the baby. I said, 'Did you bring a snowsuit?' He said yes and tried putting it on Nicky. I looked at him and said, 'What are you doing?' I ripped the snowsuit from his hands, threw it on the floor, put the kid on top, and said, 'That's how you do it!'

"Eric was in awe of the baby. He had no idea what to do. My brother and his whole family, Eric's sister, and lots of friends were there, which was sweet. But I wanted us to be alone. I remember sitting in the back seat of my brother's car with Eric and Nicky on our way home. We held the baby together.

"We went out to a dinner party with the baby the night I got home. It had been planned months in advance. Nicky was only about eight weeks old, so he slept through everything. I remember lasting until about ten-thirty and then saying to Eric, 'Let's go home.'

"After that we had the whole neighborhood to contend with. We heard that one of our neighbors was shocked when she learned about Nicky. Apparently she said, 'How dare they adopt a baby? This is not a toy. This is serious.' Another neighbor said to her, 'I don't think they're doing it as a joke. It took them two years, so I think it's been planned.' She was miffed at this. Then her husband said to me, 'Uh . . . Uh, I didn't know you liked kids. Ha! Ha!' He didn't know what to say.

"I was wheeling Nicky in the stroller one day and I ran into a realtor I know. She said, 'Is business so bad that you're baby-sitting now?'

"'No, it's my son.'

"'Oh, no.'

"'This kid is my son.'

"'No.'

"'I adopted.'

"'Well, bundle him up then; he's going to catch cold!' It was hilarious.

"One straight guy—I was always curious to know if he was closeted, but he never admitted it—said, 'Do you think it's right, a gay person adopting? Are you going to raise him gay? What are you going to do?'

"I answered, 'I don't know how to raise a kid gay.' It seemed like he was dealing with a gay issue himself. He wasn't hostile, he just seemed really puzzled.

"When my mother first saw the baby she was all goo-goo over him. She actually got my brother to drive her to my house. I think she's been to my house only four times in twenty-six years! She took it as though it were the most natural thing in the world. The Italians' typical reaction is to fight something, but once they know they can't change it they accept it. Nicky calls her Grandma and my father Grandpa. I won't let him call them Nana and Nanoo, because that's what I called my grandparents, and there's no other Nana and Nanoo.

"When we wanted to christen the baby we had trouble with the church. I went to the church I went to as a kid and said, 'I'm a single man and I want to baptize my baby.'

"'Whoa! What do you mean you're single?'

"'I adopted a baby.'

"'Well, we can't just christen anyone—you have to come here and go to classes. What's your name again?'

"He called the cardinal! 'I think we have a gay person trying to make a stance in the church by trying to get a kid baptized.' Then he called a nearby church. The priest there told me, 'Yeah, he already called us, and he's called the cardinal and informed him.' This really ticked me off! But the priest at the second church said, 'Come to church for a few weeks and let the people see you and develop a rapport.' I decided their feeling was, *Baptize the kid—who cares what 'they' think? Keep it quiet if we have to.*

"Within three weeks everyone in the church knew us because we were two guys with a baby! We chose a private baptism. We ended up with seventy guests—all family, except for six close friends. My whole family and Eric's family from New Hampshire and California, all my uncles and aunts, everyone came! [Before the service] the priest was up front and all our relatives were buzzing around the church. He looked at me and said, 'I'm glad you decided to do a private one. Do you think you can get them to sit down now?' He was a little bit nervous. He said, 'I don't know what to say—do you think I should say that they shouldn't talk to their parish priests about this?' I said, 'Listen, they're Italian . . . You think they're going to tell a priest?' He said, 'Yeah, you're right. God bless the Italians—they're so unlike the Irish!'

"After the service we went to Eric's sister's house, a big Victorian house in the suburbs. There was Eric's WASP family, all blond and blue-eyed; my family came in with bowls of food. Eric's sister said to me, 'You can tell they're Italian, because they all brought the food, and when everything was done they all ran to the kitchen and cleaned it—and their names were on the bottoms of all the pots and pans!'

"It's been good ever since. Now the family asks for Eric. We have now bonded in their eyes. Before, Eric was 'Enzo's friend.' But now people call and ask, 'How's the baby? How's Eric?' If I take Nicky to their house, they say, 'Where's Eric?'"

Eric added, "My parents get along great with Nicky. He calls them Grandpa and Grandma. They come out from California four or five times a year. It's nice for Nicky to know he has a family and that they love him. In fact, they dote on him! He gets along really well with my father because my father plays with him; he's good at interacting with kids. When we take him out to California, my mother buys him books and clothes. It's nice that we have those families in addition to what we have here. You can't raise a baby in isolation. This has definitely been a process that has gotten us very close together and fixated on being a family."

Eric added, "Nicky calls me Daddy and calls Enzo Pappa. Enzo feels comfortable with Pappa because of his Italian background, so this works for us. But I wouldn't feel comfortable, because it's not in my culture. As Nicky has gotten older he's figured out that we weren't calling each other Daddy and Pappa so he asked us our names. For a while he was calling me Eric, which bothered me very much! I know progressive couples want their children to call them by name, but I want to be Daddy. That's what he calls me now, unless he wants to get my goat."

Enzo said, "When we applied to nursery school we were very open. We said, 'We're gay parents. That's the way it's going to be—Pappa and Daddy. Can you deal with it?' They did! It's interesting, I find that everyone at the school knows us automatically. If we introduce ourselves to people, they know us. At the playground a father asked Eric one day, 'Where's your wife?' Eric answered, 'I'm with Enzo.' The father said, 'Oh! You're the ones my wife told me about. You're Enzo and Eric!'"

Eric continued, "I read several books on adoption. They offered general scenarios on how to tell that story. We put together a book. I thought it was important for Nicky to know his story. I feel that my job is to give him information so that he can answer questions that are asked of him if he wants to. Nicky gets asked not only, 'Why don't you look like your daddy and pappa?' but, 'Where is your mommy?' On the very first day of preschool a three-year-old girl asked me in the playground, 'Where is Nicky's mommy?' I was not prepared for that question! I answered, 'Nicky has two daddies.'

"When Nicky had been in preschool for three months he started talking about his mother. What happened at school that wasn't happening at home was mothers! It was Christmastime and the stairs were decorated with twigs and berries. He sat on the stairs and picked the berries off and said, 'I'm going to take these red berries and give them to my mommy. I want to see my mommy. I'm going to visit my mommy. You can leave me at my mommy's house. I'll stay there for a little while, and then you can come back and get me.' I felt very upset. But I just said to him, 'That sounds great.' I let it ride. I tried to probe a little bit, but you can't probe a three-year-old. He didn't really want to be asked. He wasn't going to think imaginatively and respond to questions. He was just going to tell his own story.

"Well, Mom was ever present for about eight months! He talked about Mom all the time. He said he had toys that his mommy had given him, books that his mommy was going to read to him. He wanted his mommy to visit him at school, he wanted to call his mommy on the phone, and he wanted to go on a plane and visit his mommy. I worried but Enzo said, 'He'll be fine.'"

Enzo added, "Nicky came home from school one day and said, 'I wish I didn't have brown skin.' I thought, *Who said something to this kid about that?* I said, 'Pappa has dark skin and dark eyes and dark hair.' Eric said, 'I wish I had brown skin.' So Nicky said to Eric, 'Can we swap?'

"The neighbors I mentioned earlier who were initially critical of our adopting Nicky have seen us with him for four years now. They've seen us taking care of him, and they get the big picture. They know this isn't a joke. The husband asked me about our school plans for Nicky. I told him we'd send him to private schools, because the public schools are too dangerous. He mentioned a school and I said, 'That's too experimental. I don't feel like experimenting with my son.' I could see that he approved. Now both he and his wife write letters of recommendation for us to use when applying to private schools.

"Every once in a while I'll hear Nicky playing and think to myself, *There's a kid running around this house!* I still can't quite believe it. What worries me is that it's never going to end. So I say to Eric, 'We've only got fifteen more years, and then he's out of the house.' I think, *You're always going to be wondering what he's doing. Is he going to come and visit you?* I don't want him to feel obligated to visit us, and if he doesn't, I'll kill him! I'm laughing, but all that goes through my mind. I worry very much about who he'll marry! I think, *Fine, we'll get him through the schools and all that. Who is he going to marry? I hope she's going to be nice. I wonder how they're going to raise their kids.* Then I think, *Would you stop already?* For some reason the next fifteen to eighteen years don't bother me. It's after that. What if he moves away? These Americans—they're always moving across the country."

Eric concluded, "Nicky is four now, but I still have sleep loss. He has always slept well and was always very healthy. We were tremendously fortunate that he didn't bring a health problem with him, but even so, he's a child! He wants to get up at six or seven every morning, whereas I was used to staying in bed until at least eight. I spent the first year checking to see if he was still breathing! I'm sure it's a normal process, but the first year I was horrified that harm would come to him. I was very surprised that I felt so protective. I was very concerned about Enzo already having spent all this time with him and that the baby would be linked to Enzo, so it was my turn! I spent a tremendous amount of time with him.

"Becoming a parent was not what I'd expected. I was astonished by how much my life changed. It was more work than I had ever imagined; it was more exhausting. But it's been a wonderful experience. I don't know what else to say except that it's absolutely the most wonderful thing I've ever done in my life."

9/ Maureen
Transracial adoptions

"My kids are going to have to deal with black children not wanting to acknowledge them as really black because their mother is white. I think I have to arm them with information so they can respond to these comments. I tell Roberta to say that there are different kinds of families, and this is the way our family is. I've told her that it isn't always going to be easy that our family has no daddy, that our family has different colors."

ALTHOUGH our society is becoming increasingly diverse, transracial adoption remains a controversial topic. Many white people are eager to adopt minority children, but the black and Native American communities put obstacles in their way, with the result that transracial adoption has become an emotionally charged issue. Many black and Native American social workers believe adoption into white families denies minority children their cultural heritage.

Opponents of this view believe that insisting on racial matching in adoption defies common sense. Statistics reveal, they argue, that there are not enough minority parents to adopt all the minority children who are waiting. Therefore, racial matching policies force large numbers of minority children to languish in foster homes for years; some spend their entire childhood without permanence. Critics of racial matching policies also point to several research studies which conclude that transracial adoptions satisfy the "best interest of the child" argument and that transracially adopted children can grow up to be well adjusted and comfortable with their racial identities. While the arguments continue about race and culture, children's lives hang in the balance.

This story is about a single white woman who concluded that adopting transracially in the United States was the best decision for her. Maureen, a fair-haired woman with a dynamic personality, spent her early childhood years in a Chicago suburb, in a neighborhood she describes as a classic fifties development: "It was a long street with a rotary at the end and three varieties of ranch houses that were endlessly repeated. The neighborhood was packed with kids." Maureen has two older siblings and one younger one. When she was nine, her family moved to an affluent suburb in Connecticut; her father, a car rental company executive, had been transferred to New York City.

"After graduating from a private high school in our town, I went away to college," said Maureen, "but I dropped out before I got a degree, came back home, and worked in a flower shop. I wasn't making much money, and I had to keep getting progressively more revolting apartments because the rents kept going up. When I was twenty-seven, I looked around one day and realized I was bored. I knew every road, every person, every shopkeeper; I liked the town, but it was frightfully expensive, and there was no way to meet people. I was still single and felt I'd never meet anybody if I stayed there."

Maureen decided to relocate to Denver, where a friend lived. Within a short time, she landed a job in a flower shop and enrolled in an evening course to qualify as a travel agent. She remembered, "It's hard to believe that I had so much energy then. I worked all day, went to school at night, went out on dates, had a million friends. If I had to do it now, I'd be a lunatic!"

Shortly after completing the course, she was hired by a travel agency. "I started traveling right away," said Maureen. "It was 1979. I went first to Ireland and then all over Europe; I had the high life for several years. It was great! But I woke up one day and thought, *I'm thirty-four, I'm not married, I want to have a family . . . I'd better get moving!* I was sick of waiting for a husband. I wanted a baby."

In July 1986, Maureen started her journey toward adoption. The first thing she did was to look in the Yellow Pages for adoption agencies. "I started gathering information," she said. "First I decided I was going to adopt and then I told people. I didn't ask them what they thought about my decision. People were largely positive, except one friend, who said, 'I think it's too much. You're single, you don't have the resources.' It annoyed me, made me mad, because I think friends should be supportive. My parents, who already had several grandchildren, were less than enthusiastic also, particularly when I told them that it was most likely going to be a child who didn't look like me or them. At that time I was thinking about trying to adopt in South America. I assumed it was impossible for a single woman with limited resources to adopt a white infant."

Maureen was friendly with a couple who were in the process of adopting a child; they recommended their adoption agency to her. She trusted their judgment and in August attended an information session given by the agency. The meeting was crowded, and there was no opportunity to speak personally with anyone from the agency, so Maureen picked up an application form and mailed it back a few days later.

"This agency was huge and had several programs for single people who wanted to adopt. They were obviously a rich source of children, so I assumed that one way or another I'd get a kid," said Maureen. "I was overwhelmed with the price they were asking, but at this point I was dauntless. I got a letter from the agency which acknowledged my application and informed me that I'd be contacted within the next several months to start my home study. That time frame seemed a bit outrageous, but I thought, *I've got the rest of my life; I'm going to end up with the right kid. I've just got to be patient.* I was embarking on something that had no timeline. I figured it would happen when it was supposed to happen."

Maureen's home study began in December 1986. When her social worker, Glenda, arrived at her home, it was the first personal contact Maureen had with someone from the adoption agency. The home study was planned for five sessions over several weeks. "Glenda was nice," said Maureen. "She wasn't loaded with personality, but I wasn't looking to make a new friend. She didn't look in the closets or under the bed. Of course, the apartment was spotless because I thought she might!

"I enjoyed the home study. I like to talk, and I was trying to run through, for myself, what I wanted. I was also trying to get information from her. She asked me what kind of child I wanted. I said, 'I want an infant. I want one that's healthy.' I had a rosy picture of a perfect baby who was going to come to me. Because I was so forthcoming in the interviews, Glenda needed only two sessions with me. The second one took place in her office."

Glenda told Maureen that El Salvador was a good country for her to consider, given her requirements as a single woman. Maureen liked the idea and prepared the necessary documents, applied for a visa for the child, arranged for papers to be translated, and so on. Glenda could not submit the home study until after Maureen had completed a four-week course that the agency held for adoptive parents. But because the agency was so busy, Maureen couldn't get into a group until June. By that time, nearly a year had passed since she'd decided to adopt; Maureen was beginning to feel annoyed.

"I finally got my home study in August. I was horrified that it took from December to August to produce it. I had been reading about El Salvador; I was primed! One reason I particularly liked El Salvador was that they would escort the children to this country. I didn't want to go there because of the political situation. Also, I was going to take only eight weeks off from work, and I didn't want to spend four of those weeks in a hotel room in a foreign country. I wanted all of my baby leave to be spent at home. I had a lot of naive expectations about the way my life was going to go, how easy everything was going to be, and what I was going to do to make that happen.

"In September I got a call from Glenda: 'I'm sorry; the agency has just been informed that El Salvador is closed.' I was horrified at this news; it was terribly disturbing. My head was in El Salvador. I didn't know what to do. I thought, *Why am I going through this?* Out of the blue I asked her, 'What about a domestic transracial adoption?' Glenda said, 'You don't really want that, do you?' I said, 'I don't know. What do I want?'"

That afternoon Maureen learned from someone else at the adoption agency that Glenda was leaving. She called Glenda back. Maureen remembered, "After she confirmed it, I asked her why I had to hear about it through the grapevine. She replied, 'The grapevine shouldn't do that.' By now I was furious. It had been a year and three months since I had started the adoption process, and everything was falling apart. I said to her, 'Don't even call me. I don't want anything more to do with this until after Christmas.'"

Glenda insisted on introducing her replacement, Janice, to Maureen before leaving the agency. "Janice was nice," said Maureen. "I felt her heart was in the right place. But I was completely frustrated with the adoption process. I got through the holidays and realized I still wasn't ready. Every time I'd think about it, I'd say to myself, *Not now!* It wasn't that I'd never adopt; I just pushed the thoughts back down."

By the end of April, Maureen had made a decision. She called Janice and arranged a meeting with her. "I want to adopt a child in this country," Maureen told her. "I want to go somewhere where I can read the laws, where there's a paper trail, where I can see the child. I want to help somebody in this country."

Janice said, "That's fine. Here's a list of domestic agencies that place kids with single people. The paperwork still comes through our agency. Go and find a baby and let us know how it goes."

Maureen felt annoyed. She realized her adoption agency didn't care about domestic adoptions; they'd been clear about that. "It's because they don't make any money on domestic adoptions," explained Maureen. "They don't say that, of course. They say they've gone to these other countries and developed programs there, that they specialize in international adoptions. They were willing to do the paperwork for me on a domestic adoption, but they wouldn't help me find a baby."

Janice gave Maureen the names of two single women who had recently adopted. One of them, a white woman who'd adopted a black child, recommended her agency in Texas. "She told me she'd had a great experience," said Maureen. "She said, 'It's wonderful doing it yourself. The people at the agency are fabulous. You can be in control; they'll keep in touch with you. I highly recommend them.' So I decided right then and there to toss everything else aside and call them. My first conversation with them was fabulous; I talked with the woman in charge of interstate placements. Her name was Anita. She told me she'd placed babies through my agency before. 'Tell them to send your home study down,' she said. 'We're having babies all the time.' I told Anita I wanted a healthy infant and that I'd prefer a girl. She told me I'd be in a pool of applicants and asked me to send photographs of myself, my house, my cats, et cetera, which would be shown to birth mothers. But I didn't have to write a 'Dear Birth Mother' letter."

A couple of months later, at the end of June, Janice called Maureen and told her she had a Brazilian baby for her. She said, "I know you were thinking of a domestic adoption, but we have a seven-month-old black girl who is healthy and available. Brazilian courts are closed in July, but you can go the first week in August. You only have to stay for a week, and the adoption will be finalized before you come home."

Maureen said, "I was worried about my father's reaction, but when I told him I was going to adopt a black child he said, 'Maureen, she will be your child and I will love her.' When I told my mother that I hoped she would love my child as much as she did her other grandchildren, she said, 'I hope I can, dear.' I thought, *You weren't supposed to say that, Mom!* But a friend said to me, 'Maureen, face the fact that your mother is in her seventies. She didn't mean to be unkind, but you're changing her family photograph. You can't expect her to be jumping up and down. Give her time. She'll figure it out.'

"I called my friend Roberta: 'Would you like to go to Brazil with me?' She said, 'Absolutely!' Because I'm a travel agent, I quickly arranged everything for us to fly there the first week in August. My friends came over and painted a room for the baby. They gave me a huge shower. My mother and sister, Eve, came to the shower. They bought me a bureau for the baby's room. I also got a car seat, a stroller, and baby clothes. Everyone was excited.

"Five days before I was supposed to leave, I got a phone call from Janice. 'You can't go the first week in August, because the courts are backed up, but you can go the second week.' Later they changed it again and said I could go on August 20. The day before my flight Janice called again and said, 'Don't go. The baby is no longer available. The adoption has officially failed; her birth father has come back to claim her. But don't worry about it—we'll get you another kid.' I was devastated! The call came on a Saturday morning; I spent the entire weekend in bed sobbing. I woke up with my heart broken in pieces. I couldn't go in the baby's room. I was too embarrassed to look at all the baby gifts I'd been given. It was awful! People kept saying things like, 'It wasn't meant to be.' I just wanted to tell them to drop dead.

"It's funny, I still look back on the day that the Brazilian adoption fell through as the saddest day of my life. Despite all the sorrows I've been through with boyfriends, deaths in my family, et cetera, that day was the most devastating. It was hideous.

"With me stress provokes action; anger motivates me. I woke up Monday morning feeling furious! I called Janice and said, 'Now I am your top priority. You will get no peace until I have a child.' Then I called Anita in Texas and asked her, 'Why haven't I heard from you? It's August, and I last talked to you in May.' She said, 'You're the travel agent, right? We wondered why your agency never sent your home study to us. We've placed five babies this summer. How quickly can you get your home study to us?' I told her I could get it to her overnight. Then I called Janice back. I was livid. She said, 'That agency in Texas has lost a lot of our home studies.' I didn't believe her! I told her I wanted my home study sent by overnight carrier. She agreed.

"Half an hour later, Janice called back and said, 'There's a little problem. Your home study expired yesterday. They're only good for a year, and an update will cost three hundred fifty dollars.' I replied slowly and calmly, 'No, it isn't going to cost three hundred fifty dollars. An update will be free. And it will take place in your office this afternoon!' She said okay."

The next day Anita called Maureen and said, "I've got your home study in my hands. The reason I wanted you to send it so quickly was that yesterday, five minutes before you called, a baby girl was cleared for adoption. She was born in June weighing only four pounds; she was in the hospital until the end of July and has been in foster care since. She weighs eight pounds now, and the doctor said her lungs are strong enough for her to fly. All we have to do is go through your paperwork here."

Maureen was thrilled yet cautious. She pleaded with Anita, "Please don't tell me that I can have this baby unless you're sure that I can have this baby."

Anita reassured her, "We have put this baby on hold for you. I'm going to send you her picture, her medical history, and an interview with her birth mother. I don't anticipate any glitches."

On a Friday afternoon before Labor Day weekend, Maureen was sitting at her desk at work thinking about the long weekend ahead, which she was planning to spend at a cottage with friends. She felt restless and decided to leave early. As she was walking out the door, someone called her back to take a phone call. "Tell them I'm already gone," she said. "Well, it's Anita . . ." [Everyone in the office knew who Anita was.] Maureen rushed back to her desk and picked up the phone.

Anita said, "We've got all your paperwork back. It just came through the door this second. Can you fly down Monday and take the baby home on Tuesday?"

"I told her yes—definitely!" said Maureen. "I was so excited. But I knew I couldn't just sit around all weekend, so I went away with my friends anyway. Everything was ready to go. I came home Sunday night and flew to Texas Monday afternoon."

Maureen arrived at the adoption agency early Tuesday morning. She met Anita, who asked her to sign all the paperwork first, because, she said with a smile, "Once you lay eyes on your baby I won't be able to say anything to you!" Anita gave her several travel-size bottles of formula and some diapers. "I kept telling myself to calm down," said Maureen. "I said to myself, *You have the rest of your life. Just enjoy every moment.*

"Anita left the room and then came back holding the baby. She put her on my lap. I looked down at her and sobbed. I said, 'Oh, my baby! My baby!' She was beautiful—a tiny little thing with tons of hair. I ran my fingers through her soft curls. At the roots I could feel wiry hair coming in. She fretted a bit for a minute or two but was easily comforted. Anita said, 'I'll give you ten minutes alone with her.' After Anita left, I unwrapped the baby's blanket so I could look at her. She had on a sleeveless dress with matching pants underneath. Her eyes were huge, and her eyelashes looked like window shades. She was just adorable. I held her up to look at her from other angles. Then I hugged her closely to me.

"When Anita came back I still had tears running down my face. She asked me what I was going to name her. I said, 'Roberta, after my good friend.' Anita gave me medications and explained how to administer them. Because Roberta was premature, she was on iron and vitamins. The instructions were easy; I wasn't frightened.

"After a few more minutes Anita said good-bye, and we took a taxi to the airport. We flew on a small plane to Dallas. I was frightened that flying would hurt Roberta's ears, and I held her tightly in my arms. She was working away at her pacifier and didn't cry at all. I was supposed to have forty-five minutes between flights, but unfortunately a four-hour delay was announced when I got to Dallas. I thought, *Great, I've got only two diapers and two bottles left. What am I going to do? What if she's hungry?* I started talking to a woman sitting next to me and waiting for the same flight. She asked about the baby: 'What's she like?' I said, 'I don't know. I've only had her for three hours!' I confided that I needed to go to the bathroom, and since I didn't have a stroller with me, I didn't know how I'd manage with the baby. She took out her wallet and said, 'Look inside— I have seven hundred and fifty dollars in cash here. I'll walk to the bathroom with you. You can take my wallet into the stall while I hold your baby. That way you won't have to worry.' She was wonderful.

"While we waited for our flight, a few other people came over to peek at Roberta. She was so tiny, and people like to look when you're holding a tiny baby. I guess we made a striking presence—I'm so fair and she's so dark. Some people were clearly taken aback—after all, this was Texas! But most people were wonderful.

"When we got home friends were waiting for us at the airport. As I walked off the plane, all ten of them burst out crying. I was crying, too, but the baby wasn't crying! Someone threw a sweater over my shoulders—the weather was unexpectedly cool—and we all went back to my house. One of my friends had cooked dinner, which was waiting for us when we arrived. It turned out to be a very late night; no one wanted to leave. Everyone was mesmerized by Roberta. One friend stayed with me overnight.

"The baby was in a crib next to my bed. The next morning when I woke up I sat bolt upright in bed and looked over at Roberta. I thought, *Oh my God. She really is black! Can I do this?* I wasn't horrified that she was black; I was worried that I might not be able to do right by her.

"My parents came two days later. They went nuts over the baby, completely nuts. My father—who was dark-skinned—took a look at Roberta and said, 'You told me she wouldn't look like us, but she looks exactly like me.' That was a huge breakthrough! They were wonderful. I knew my mother would be because she loves babies. She was funny. When we went for a walk to the store every neighbor we passed said, 'Oh, the baby finally came!' And my mother quickly said, 'Yes, she's adopted.' She was very welcoming, but she wanted to make sure that everybody knew that I had not done the unspeakable!

"I stayed home for eight weeks. The only thing that surprised me about being a mother was that it was much better than I'd expected. Roberta was the easiest baby you could possibly imagine. In the beginning she was up only once a night. She was a happy baby. She babbled all the time.

"None of my friends made any hurtful comments—only people on the periphery. When I went to get new glasses, the receptionist at my optometrist's office said, 'Whose baby is that?' When I answered that she was mine, the woman said, 'You never had a baby. Did you adopt her?'

Yes. 'Was it hard?' No. 'But you're single,' she added. 'Didn't you care what kind you got?' I replied, 'I wanted a girl.' She said, 'No, you know what I mean: the color.' I wasn't going to let myself meet her at her level, but that last comment prompted me to say, 'I just gave you the opportunity not to make a total fool of yourself, and you blew it!' I was furious. She didn't even bother to apologize."

Shortly after adopting Roberta, Maureen met a casual acquaintance at a Halloween party, who made a strident racial comment. Maureen remembered, "I was sitting in a rocking chair holding Roberta. At first I ignored what the woman said; I tried to pretend I hadn't heard it. I looked down at Roberta and thought, *How could anyone say that? You're beautiful. . . . You're gorgeous!* The woman raised her voice and repeated what she'd said. That's when I left the room. I was crying. A friend followed me into another room and tried to comfort me. I never spoke to that woman again. I couldn't even look at her. I'm not shocked to hear someone on the street scream a racial epithet, but a derogatory remark directed at an infant? I had waited so long for this baby, and I was so proud to have her. I'll never get over that."

Maureen lost her job when Roberta was two years old. She explained, "After I got Roberta, I was no longer interested in working until eight o'clock every night and on weekends. My boss's attitude toward me had changed completely. He told me he could hire someone for less money, and that was that. I got a job at another travel agency, but had to take a big pay cut. I no longer had a company car.

"When Roberta was three it drove me crazy when people talked about her as if she weren't there. Once we were standing in line and a woman said, 'Is that your daughter?' Yes. 'She's beautiful.' Thank you. 'Is she adopted?' Yes. 'Oh, so she knows?' I looked straight at this woman and said, 'Well, she knows now, doesn't she?'

"Twice in the grocery store I've had comments from strangers, but they were so stupid that I had to laugh. One old lady said to me, 'Is that your daughter?' I said yes. I've never minded being stared at or asked that question, because it is unusual to see a white woman with a black baby. The questions are not necessarily negative. Then she said, 'Her father must be very dark.' I said, 'I don't know; I've never met the man!'

"For years I was happy having a family consisting of just Roberta and me. I couldn't afford another child, therefore I didn't let myself consider the idea of adopting again. But my father's death changed my thinking. He was sick for a year, and my brother, two sisters, and I leaned on each other to get through it. We made difficult decisions together, and one of us could be weak while the others were strong. It was wonderful to feel our strength as a group. I had a vision of Roberta growing up and having to cope with my death all by herself. I didn't want her to be alone to make all those decisions with no one to comfort her and give her strength.

"When I decided to adopt another child, I knew I didn't want another baby. I don't have unlimited time off from work and didn't want to go through the one- and two-year-old things again with a cold every other week, ear infections, et cetera. I told the social worker I wanted a girl, aged three to five. I thought kids over five might need a lot of therapy. I also said I wanted a full African American child, not a biracial one. I wanted what Roberta was. I didn't want her, in her adolescence, to think that the other child was favored because she looked more like me. I wanted Roberta to have an ally. I don't think Roberta and I will have huge race problems between us, but there will be racial issues that we'll have to deal with.

"I met a black social worker who told me she wouldn't place a black child with me even though I had already adopted Roberta. She said it flat out when I met her: 'No, I want to place them with black families.' Everybody knows there aren't enough black families to adopt all the black kids waiting for homes. Her attitude made me angry, particularly when she added: 'White people don't know how to care for our hair.' She had the nerve to say that to me even though her own hair had been straightened! What is the big deal? Of course, it's important for a black child's hair to be cared for properly; I've learned how to do it. Anyone can learn how to do it if they make the effort."

A friend of Maureen's named Betsy was president of a single-parent adoption support group and had access to information about foster children available for adoption through a state agency. The information was in a manual, which was updated each month. A photograph of each child was shown along with a fact sheet including the age, how long the child had been in foster care, and the reason the child was placed in foster care.

Maureen said, "Most foster kids are older or are considered harder to place. Betsy would call me and say, 'The new pages are in. Why don't you come over and have a look?' One time she handed me the pages and I saw the picture of a child and thought, *I need that child.* I don't understand it—it was strange. There was something about her face. She was a four-year-old black girl—just gorgeous. But it wasn't because she was pretty that I was captivated. Kids don't appeal to me just because they're attractive. There was something in this girl's face that said, Please help me! She didn't look sad; many of the children in those photographs looked dead behind the eyes. But this child looked friendly and animated.

"I felt I couldn't even commit to investigating another child without discussing the idea with Roberta. She was a huge part of the decision. I prepared her for the fact that the girl whose picture we'd seen might not work out. She cried and said, 'Well, if it doesn't work, will you still get me a sister?' What could I say? I sat her down and tried to help her understand that some things would be better with a little sister and other things would be harder. We made a list together. She couldn't think of anything that was going to be harder, so I had to help her."

When Maureen called the state agency to inquire about this child, she was given disappointing news. The child had already been chosen by another family. But a social worker told her, "We have many other children, and you sound like just the kind of family we need." At her urging Maureen updated her home study report and filled out various forms needed by the state.

"By now I was a loose cannon," said Maureen. "I thought, *I will not be stopped until I have another child in my home.* When my paperwork was finished, I went in to talk to the social worker again. She said, 'This morning a colleague called to tell me he has a three-year-old black girl who's available for adoption. Her name is Rose and she's healthy and happy. Are you interested?' Of course I was!

"She continued: 'I will inform my colleague right away. He'll call you back to set up a meeting. What his phone call will mean is that the child has been placed on hold for you—because you seem to be an appropriate family—but he's not allowed to say that. You'll go in for an interview with him and with the child's case worker. We'll see what happens.'"

During the interview, Maureen learned that Rose had been placed in foster care at birth because she had been born exposed to cocaine. She had gone home with her birth mother when she was a month old, but was removed again a short time later and had been living in the same foster home since. Rose's development was age-appropriate, and she was progressing nicely. "They told me to go home and think about it," remembered Maureen. "But I felt frustrated. During the meeting the child's social worker was completely noncommittal. I couldn't read her; she seemed detached. I knew right away that I wanted to adopt Rose. I wasn't worried about her exposure to cocaine. I'd met children who were born exposed to drugs and knew that the problem can be overcome. I didn't need a week to think about it. Two days later I called them back and told them I didn't need to wait; I was ready to go ahead with the adoption."

Then Maureen received photographs of Rose in the mail. "When I looked at the photos I couldn't feel anything for her," said Maureen. "In one of them, she was sitting on Santa's lap, and I thought she looked really sad. That picture bothered me. I thought, *The poor little thing . . . She looks scared.*"

A few days later the first meeting between Maureen and Rose took place. Maureen took Roberta along to meet Rose at her foster home. "When we walked up to the front door, Rose and her foster mother, Shirley, opened it together. Rose was adorable. She looked happy and eager to meet us. She was beautifully dressed, and her hair was perfect. Roberta said, 'Oh, Mommy . . . She's so cute!'

"Rose's social worker was there, too. I knew Rose had been told that she was going to meet her new mommy, but I'm not sure how much she understood. As soon as we sat down Rose jumped up on my lap and threw her arms around me. I thought it was a bit weird. I worried that it meant she had no attachment to her foster mother. Within a few minutes, Roberta and Rose were rolling around on the floor together like bear cubs. It was such a wonderful sight that I started to cry. I realized that Roberta was going to be the bridge that got Rose to come with us. I knew that if I had just shown up and had tried to take her, she probably wouldn't have wanted me. Shirley, who was black, seemed a bit nervous but gave me a lot of information about Rose and her routine."

The next day Maureen picked Rose up and took her to a party at Roberta's school. "She had no problem going with me," said Maureen. "She talked constantly during the drive. When we got to Roberta's school, the kids were all over her carrying her and playing with her. Rose had a great time." Two days later Maureen and Roberta took Rose out for the whole day. They stopped by their home to show Rose where she would live and took her swimming. Everything was going well.

Maureen continued, "For the next five days Roberta and I went to see Rose every night after work. It was a forty-five-minute drive to the small town, and there was nothing to do there, so we just sat around her foster mother's apartment talking and playing. By the third night it was like a nightmare. We were exhausted and Rose was exhausted. Fortunately the transition only lasted for a week. It was time to start living our lives together. We couldn't keep up these visits for a month.

"On Saturday morning we went to pick Rose up. Everybody was crying—the foster mother, her other kids, and I. Rose was not crying. We got in the car and I said, 'This is it! This is the deal—you're moving to your new house today.' Rose was fine all day, but bedtime was hard. She seemed really sad. She was lying in her new bed, and she looked at me and said, 'I don't like this . . . It's too different!' I was kneeling down beside her bed. She put her arms around my neck and cried hard. It was awful. The saving grace was Roberta. She was terrific. After listening to Rose cry for a couple of minutes, she crawled into bed with Rose and held her. She said, 'It's okay, Rosey, it's okay. You're going to like it here.' It was adorable.

"Without Roberta I think Rose and I would have had a very difficult time. Roberta has been very protective and kind. Rose trusted her from the beginning. After two nights, Rose stopped crying at bedtime. The transition was too smooth, really. After three months we had some regression, actually a complete meltdown at day care. It was so bad that I had to rush over there from work. After I calmed her down, I said, 'Rose, can you please tell Mommy what's bothering you?' She said, 'Well, I just wanted you.' I think she was testing her day care teacher.

"Rose has been with us for five months now, and things have been going pretty well. But just recently she started acting out. This seemed to come out of nowhere. After days and days of asking her, 'What's bothering you? Please tell Mommy.' I finally got her to sit in a chair and talk to me. She said, 'Somebody's going to come in a car and take me away from you.' I said, 'No, Rose, they won't. Nobody's going to do that.' She said, 'You put me in a car. You took me away from Shirley. That hurt my feelings!' Then I realized what had happened. I had taken the kids to visit Shirley the previous week; that must have stirred everything up inside Rose. I hugged her and said, 'Nobody can ever take you away from me, Rosey. I am your mother.'

"I've just had a psychological evaluation done. The doctor said Rose has no attachment problems, and he foresees no emotional difficulties. That was a huge relief for me.

"Once at a playground a black child asked Roberta, 'Is that your mother?' She said yes. 'But she's white!' 'Well, I'm adopted,' Roberta replied. End of conversation. My kids are going to have to deal with black children not wanting to acknowledge them as really black because their mother is white. I think I have to arm them with information so they can respond to these comments. I tell Roberta to say that there are different kinds of families, and this is the way our family is. I've told her that it isn't always going to be easy that our family has no daddy, that our family has different colors."

"Bringing Rose into our family has been great for all three of us. It certainly seems to be improving Rose's life, and I know, in the long run, Roberta's life is going to be enriched a hundredfold. And I can't even say what it's done for me, or I'll start to cry. I can't believe what she's brought in. I never thought anything was missing in my life with Roberta. I adore Roberta; I worship the ground she walks on. I think she's the most terrific human being I've ever met. And I bring in this other little creature thinking, *Am I ever going to be able to attach to this child the way I attached to Roberta?* We are so tight.

"I will be perfectly honest and admit that for the first three months it wasn't easy. My attachment to Rose has gone through several levels. It's very complicated. Before I brought Rose home, I committed to her on paper and in my head for her lifetime, but it's only in the last few weeks that I realized I am also committed to her in my heart. I think I'm finally inside Rose's heart, too. She's always said, 'Roberta, I love you.' But now she tells me, too. Sometimes I hear her in her room singing, 'I love Roberta. I love Mommy.' It's gratifying to hear her say it, because I think it means that she knows that I love her. It's a huge breakthrough and things are very different around here now. With Rose I've learned what it means to fall in love with a child. We're a family now."

10/ Tessa and David
An international family

"Talking about adoption was constant with our kids. We never knew when they'd understand what it meant, so we talked about it from day one. We'd tell them how much we wanted to have a child and that we'd fallen in love with them, that we were thrilled to give them a home, and that we'd chosen them. Tessa put together a photo album for each child. It's been of great value to our kids. They pored over them—they still do! We've also given each child artwork for his or her bedroom, traditional costumes, and books to help them appreciate their heritage."

THE FAMILY that Tessa and David created is unique. One child is Peruvian, two are Colombian, and one is Vietnamese American. Tessa and David have blended their children's cultures with their own to create a warm and loving household, a stimulating environment in which their children have learned to respect, understand, and appreciate diversity.

Tessa is a fair-skinned redhead who exudes a no-nonsense, down-to-earth manner which is accompanied by a warm and generous spirit. She grew up with her twin sister, Libby, in Maine. Although fraternal twins, Tessa and Libby were very close. "I went away to college in Chicago because I needed to separate from my twin," recalled Tessa. "Libby chose a school closer to home.

"I was working as a social worker in Chicago when I met David, and within nine months we were married. It was a whirlwind romance. We talked about the fact that we wanted to have children; that was resolved before we got married. And we also knew that we wanted to be married for a while before having children."

David said, "I was the second of nine children. We lived in a big old house with lots of land in a Chicago suburb. We were the biggest family in the neighborhood. My parents had a wonderful marriage, and all my memories are of a happy childhood. There were always babies around. I can remember changing diapers since I was very young."

Although of small stature, David has a commanding presence and a forceful personality. His confident mien softens engagingly when he speaks of his wife and children. As a child, he went to boarding school and then to an Ivy League college. After graduation, his draft status exempted him from the Vietnam War; he spent two years in the Peace Corps in the Philippines and then returned home to attend business school.

"After business school some friends and I went on a camping trip in Yosemite National Park," recalled David. "There I had a wonderful epiphany about my place in the world. I decided it was time to find a wife and have a family. On the way back I stopped in Colorado to see a classmate and met other old friends at his house. One of them had had a very attractive girlfriend I had met a couple of times. 'Where's Tessa?' I asked him. He explained that she was no longer his girlfriend and said I ought to call her when I returned to Chicago. He wrote down her number on a matchbook, which I still have. The first thing I did when I got back was to call Tessa. We went out to dinner and there I made up my mind. This was the woman I was going to marry. We started to date and I was very aggressive; once she said, 'You're going too fast!' and tried to break off the relationship. My first date with Tessa was on August 15, and by September 15, I had persuaded her to abandon her apartment and to live with me. It took us a month to sort things out; we had to find a new roommate for her roommate, et cetera, but by October 15 she had moved in, and in mid-December we decided to get married the next June. I was completely smitten with her."

After their wedding, Tessa pursued a master's degree in education, and David started a business with several friends. "Tessa and I were just full of ourselves and our young life together. We had a great time, whether traveling or just going out to dinner." After four years of working long hours David decided to disengage himself from the business but was uncertain about what to do next. Tessa, who had just read the book *Zen and the Art of Motorcycle Maintenance,* persuaded David to go on a six-week motorcycle camping trip through Eastern Canada. "We had a wonderful time," said David, "and on that trip we made up our minds that we were ready for kids; we really wanted to have a family."

"We camped and thought," elaborated Tessa. "David was trying to decide whether to go back to school and become a doctor, which had been his dream. We talked about the direction of our lives. It was 1975; we developed a plan which we've basically followed since. David decided to start another business and not attempt to go back to school. That was probably the first time he'd ever shelved a fantasy. I think he knew that a family is a very time-consuming undertaking and, therefore, medical school and being a doctor would mean much less freedom."

David recalled, "We were somewhere in the Northumberland Strait when Tessa stopped taking her birth control pills. I thought, *Great! We'll conceive a child in Nova Scotia!* Of course, it didn't work out that way."

"I was quite astonished when the first month went by and I wasn't pregnant," said Tessa. "And, as the months wore on I began to think, *Well, maybe this isn't so easy.*"

David remembered, "It was very frustrating. I thought, *The more you try, the harder it gets! So just relax; forget about it! Let's go somewhere and get her mind on something else.*"

Tessa and Libby knew they may have problems with infertility because their mother had taken diethylstilbestrol (DES), a fertility drug commonly prescribed in the mid-1940s. It has been found to cause fertility problems in the children of the women who took it. Tessa discussed with her gynecologist her difficulty in getting pregnant. "He said I had a very odd cervix," explained Tessa, "and that it appeared to be partly eroded. He thought that was due to DES and questioned whether my cervix was capable of holding a fetus. He said he could do a laparoscopy to determine whether endometriosis might also be a problem. But David wanted to have medical tests first. As a result, he found out that he had a low sperm count. His doctor prescribed a fertility drug."

"While David was going through his fertility treatment, I had a laparoscopy because I felt that I should do my part. I wanted to make sure that I had investigated this for myself, and I think it's necessary for couples to share the investigation and the guilt that goes along with infertility.

The laparoscopy revealed that I had a moderate amount of endometriosis."

"I got up to a normal, respectable sperm count, but that didn't do any good," continued David. "Tessa's doctor suggested surgery to remove the endometriosis, but we didn't seriously consider it. At that point I went through a brief but intense period of mourning. I remember sitting at our kitchen table with Tessa and crying. I was throwing away my dream of having kids who were little Tessas and little Davids. Tessa didn't cry; she sat on my lap and comforted me. It was a release. But it would have been madness to subject Tessa to surgery when having children wasn't the important thing for us. We just wanted to raise a family. So we said, 'Let's take action; let's adopt.'

"Tessa's parents were quicker to accept the notion of our adopting than mine," said David. "I'm sure it was very difficult for my mother to get comfortable with the idea. I think I suspected Mother of every possible feeling, from her thinking that I married the wrong woman to I don't know what. I guess adoption was something new for her; it had never been an issue before."

Tessa remembered, "When we visited my parents in Maine, they advised me to talk to their neighbor, Jackie, who had adopted three children. David and I went together, and when I saw her family in action it became clear to me that this family was exactly like any other family. Jackie was so positive and so in love with her children. I remember thinking, *I could do this.* Before that there had been a little doubt in me: *Could I really love adopted children?* When we left Jackie's house David and I turned to each other and said, 'Let's start!' As we began investigating, our resolve became even firmer."

Tessa and David talked to a Catholic adoption agency and were given very discouraging information. The agency had compiled a list of people who were waiting to adopt. It was ninety-nine pages long (with four names to a page). David recalled, "I said to them, 'Well, there are lots of poor black kids who need homes; can't we adopt one?' Then we learned all about racism in adoption and the black social workers and the white social workers who don't want to help each other. We looked at several different agencies and quickly realized that adoption was commercial. Anyone could legally adopt a white infant as long as they had influence, sophistication, and money—that's all that was required. And the more money you had, the faster you could do it and the choosier you could be about the child. You could have anything you wanted. We talked endlessly about this because there was a political dimension that we didn't like. First, because we were white and affluent, there was a clubbiness to it; second, there was an implicit racism in the whole thing that we didn't like; and third, matching a child to our looks allowed the fantasy that we gave birth to the child.

"I was also intrigued by what I was learning about private-placement adoptions. I became convinced that adoption was a business, and the consumers were so desperate at times that children were created solely for the business. I came to believe that some women will get pregnant intentionally in order to be supported by adoptive parents and to sell their babies. We decided not to have anything to do with private adoptions or to get involved in anything illegal. I said to Tessa, 'This is crazy! There are kids all over the world who need homes. Let's just put our wits together and try to find some way to adopt a foreign child.'

"Then I heard about a fifty-three-year-old woman in my company who had just adopted a child from Peru. I talked to her and was quite enchanted with her story; I asked her to put me in touch with the lawyer she had worked with in Peru, which she did, and I started to correspond with the lawyer, whose name was Isabel. We developed a correspondence friendship and then began talking on the phone. Isabel asked for a lot of background information on us, and we wrote long essays. She told us we'd need a home study from a local agency who would also administer the adoption."

Tessa continued, "We already knew that we didn't care what race the child was, but we wanted an infant. The other issue was what disabilities we would accept, and we decided they had to be medically correctable and the child had to have at least average intellectual capacities. We knew that was important to us, and I think every parent has to [decide], much as our heartstrings were pulled. The Catholic agency told us about a couple who had adopted two Down's syndrome children. I thought, as the waves of guilt flooded over me, *But that's not me! It's one thing if it just happens to you; you accept it. But I can't choose it.* I knew what I had to have."

Tessa and David signed up with a local agency and attended information meetings and seminars with other adoptive parents. They had a terrific social worker, Alexandra, with whom they felt very comfortable. Tessa said, "We had to give the agency pictures of our house, pictures of our families, and a letter from a priest (suddenly we had a priest!); references had to be on fancy stationery. We knew somebody who was working at the White House then, so that was lucky because that letter of recommendation was written on White House letterhead. We knew this was a game and we played it. We learned that all the signatures had to be the same, that people got into trouble if they signed their name one way one time and another way another time. So we made sure that they always matched. The social worker told us that the picky details were important, so we were sticklers for detail. I think that helped."

"We were blessed with a very capable social worker," said David. "Alexandra was sensitive and very smart; we learned a lot from her. I would periodically laugh with her and say, 'Any fifteen-year-old can conceive, and she doesn't have to answer all these questions! So please forgive me if I don't take this conversation too seriously.'

"We went to slide shows and read books about Peru. All my concepts of Peru came from my fifth-grade social studies class! We managed to internalize quite successfully the notion of having a beautiful little Indian child."

Tessa added, "I could see myself as the mother of an Indian child. I was so charged up thinking of this that I wouldn't have considered going back to the idea of adopting a white infant."

David said, "I felt sorry for some of the people we met in the adoption support group; they were unsophisticated, desperate for a child, but frightened of foreign travel. They didn't know what they were getting into. They looked at the staff of this adoption agency—who were bozos—both as their salvation and as experts. I just viewed it as a necessary bureaucratic licensing procedure that we had to go through and tried to learn from it. I thought the director and the staff were incompetent; it was a wonder to me that Alexandra had the patience to deal with them. The staff tried to appear more expert than they were and clearly loved the control they had over people's lives. They really abused their position with these people. It was hard to watch. Maybe I'm being too hard on them, but I know that several of them were later fired.

"We also discovered that not all pediatricians are helpful. We had a conversation with a well-known pediatrician, who said he would never advise adopting a child unless we were able to control the prenatal care from day one! Tessa and I just looked at each other. We couldn't believe that he was saying this to us. We knew we were taking potluck; that's the given. That doctor had nothing helpful to say. Later we found another doctor, who was wonderful."

David continued, "The Peruvian government had a series of requirements, and you have to understand them in context. First, it is a very bureaucratic society and government. You need something like eighty licenses to start a business there, which is why their economy is so sick! And everything has to be notarized with stamps and translated, et cetera. It was clear that the bureaucracy was trying to be certain they were dealing with a bona fide family unit and not just a name that was a front for a syndicate that imported children as servants, or worse, prostitutes. They had a particular interest in making sure that you were who you said you were. Therefore, you had to go to your local police department and get evidence that you were a family unit, to prove that your house was your house. All these things clearly didn't make sense to an American.

"There was also another, seamy side to the Peruvian demands. More pieces of paper, notarizations, and translations meant more opportunities to find something wrong and ask for money. In fact, a lot of what goes on (what we would call corruption) is what Peruvians view as a privilege of the office. People get those jobs and are expected to earn a significant portion of their income from 'sharing in the license.' I don't think Americans know how to handle that. Most Americans would say, 'Absolutely not. Not me! I'll just wait them out,' or 'I don't want to know anything about it; just help me!' Most of them said they relied on their lawyers to tell them what to do. The whole process was confusing. It was clear that there was money to be made in adoption, and people were making a lot of it and not spreading it around to take care of the kids. The kids were just the products.

"We were very fortunate, because Isabel was a true patrician, very honorable and dedicated. She refused to charge us for her services. I had to force money on Isabel. I'd say to her, 'Look, help out the little nunnery you're dealing with on the other side of the jungle.' I'm pretty confident there were two occasions on which Isabel probably had to grease the wheels to break deadlocks, but I saw her go to heroic efforts not to. It was very impressive."

Tessa added, "Isabel was a true humanitarian, and she saw her legal gifts as something she should give back to her country because she'd had the great good fortune of being born into a wealthy family.

"Then it happened. We had been working with Isabel for about three months; it was Saturday, January 27, and I was home by myself working on report cards for my fifth-grade class. David was out sightseeing with weekend guests. Isabel called and said, 'I have a baby boy for you; can you come in a week?' I thought, *Oh, my goodness. I have all these report cards to do!* I was so excited that I had to tell someone. Since David was unreachable, I called a friend who had been adopted as a three-year-old. She was thrilled. She said, 'Oh, Tessa, you're just going to love this! It's so exciting—I can't wait to see the baby!'"

David recalled, "When I got back home with our guests at about one o'clock in the afternoon Tessa was extremely excited. I immediately called Isabel back, and she said, 'David, I have a beautiful baby for you!' But there was a complication. The birth mother had given the baby to Isabel about three weeks earlier, and Isabel had placed him with a foster family, thinking of us as potential parents. At that point Isabel was planning to go abroad, but just before she left, the birth mother asked to have her baby returned. So, of course, Isabel gave him back to her. While Isabel was abroad, the birth mother brought the baby to Isabel's house and told Isabel's mother that she couldn't care for the baby the way adoptive parents could. She was working as a maid and trying to save enough money to go to nursing school. A few days later the baby was returned to foster care and soon became quite sick with diarrhea. The foster mother called Isabel's mother, who placed him in an upper-class clinic and so saved the baby.

"When Isabel returned from her trip, she visited the baby in the clinic and called us immediately. She said to me, 'I really think he's okay; he's going to be fine. They think he got dehydrated. Will you pay for his hospital care? Do you want me to assign this baby to you?'

"Now immediately a funny thing went on, for both Tessa and me. The mere announcement that you have a baby makes a bond. It's unbelievable. Just the statement 'We've got a baby for you' and boom! You've got a child! She said the magic words 'I have a baby for you' and I heard a voice inside me say, 'Now I have a son!' *Of course I'm going to pay the hospital bill! I'll buy the hospital! What do you want?* My mind was operating at a couple of levels here; I knew intellectually that this was something I should be concerned about. This was what they had warned us about, kids who might have had a severe medical trauma. But because she said the glorious words, 'I have a baby for you,' I was gone emotionally, totally gone! What got me through was my confidence in Isabel. It may have been misplaced, but that's the risk you take. I believed that if there was a tough decision to make, she'd help us make it; she'd understand. I guess I had confidence that I could always assume the best. My feeling is you're always going to be confronted with tough decisions, but life is a lot happier if you assume the best of people until proven wrong. So I abandoned myself to this notion that I now had a son.

"Of course we wanted to go there as quickly as possible. Isabel said, 'Come as soon as you can,' and nine days later we were in Peru. Tessa had what she called her nine-day pregnancy! We went through a wild week of getting ready. I had recently started a new company and had to get the business ready to function without me for a month or more."

Tessa related, "I went in and told the principal of the school where I was teaching that David and I were adopting a child and I wouldn't be there after February 6. It was overwhelming trying to get all my report cards done before we left. My next-door neighbor gave us a crib, a stroller, and a pram. I was thrilled. Another friend gave us hand-me-down clothes. She said she was planning to have just one child and I could keep everything. They were expensive French baby clothes, just beautiful. I didn't have to buy a thing!

"It's a long flight from Chicago to Lima," continued Tessa. "I had Dr. Spock's book with me and read the section on diarrhea several times during the flight. We got there at about nine o'clock at night."

David added, "We were told to bring down lots of diapers; after all, our baby's got diarrhea! Isabel asked us to bring extra diapers (for the foster mothers) because they were expensive in Peru. We went down with two gigantic cardboard boxes full of disposable diapers. One of the most horrible moments of the trip was when the customs agent wanted to know the contents of the big boxes; since I couldn't explain it to him (I couldn't speak Spanish), he took out a knife and started jabbing at the boxes. I guess he thought we had guns or something. I shouted, 'No! no!'"

Tessa said, "I remember thinking each time he stabbed the boxes, *Oh no, there's three more diapers I can't use!* We finally got him to understand."

"The airport was kind of crazy," remembered David. "I had worked out with Isabel that she would meet us. We didn't know what to expect, and the diaper thing had been unsettling. We found ourselves out at the curb, and there was no one there except for several unemployed men who wanted to carry our bags. I was getting very concerned; we didn't have hotel reservations or anything. Then out of the corner of my eye I saw an extraordinarily self-confident woman wearing a pink dress and a big smile. I said to Tessa, 'That's got to be Isabel!'"

Tessa continued, "She said, 'I'm sorry I'm late, but I had to get the baby.' I thought, *Baby? Now? I'm not ready!* Isabel directed us to her car, and an elderly lady in the back seat was holding a baby. There was little Richard!" David said, "I will never forget looking through that car window and seeing the baby looking up at me with big dark brown eyes; he was a bundle of smiles. It was love at first sight! Tessa got into the car and gathered the baby up in her arms. She was enthralled and concentrated on soaking up impressions of her long-awaited baby. There was mutual cooing, smiling, and waving of arms. It was great!"

"I was pleased to see that he looked fairly healthy," said Tessa. "He had a round face and lots of dark hair. I thought, *My goodness, this is happening so fast!*"

Isabel took them to a beautiful apartment she had rented for them in a wealthy section of Lima, near a park and lovely shops. The first night with Richard was both exciting and frightening. David remembered, "I spent most of the night with the baby—just watching him and making sure he was breathing! He was three-and-a-half months old but was pretty skinny and had a big head. I remember experiencing an undercurrent of insecurity: *Do we have what we need? If he gets sick in the night, what do we do? What happens tomorrow?*"

Tessa continued, "The first time I undressed him he had many layers of clothes on, even though it was summer and ninety degrees! I thought, *This poor child is sweating. Even I know that babies aren't supposed to be sweating like this!* That first night I kept waiting for the baby to wake up. I was afraid that I wouldn't wake up, but I was pretty tired and slept blissfully. At seven-thirty the next morning I got up and went to see if Richard was all right, and there he was smiling and gurgling in his crib! I thought, *Gosh, what do people mean about babies waking up? What's this?*

"Then began the era of keeping very careful notes of what he ate, what color the poops were, et cetera—the fascinations of a new mother.

I spent hours just staring at Richard—and feeling so lucky! This was a new adventure, a new chapter. I was much worse than David. He'd changed so many diapers in his life that he'd say, 'Oh, Tessa, he's fine, he's very happy.' Richard was weak physically and couldn't hold his head up. I think he weighed twelve pounds, but he quickly gained weight. I probably overfed him!"

David added, "Tessa and I noticed right away that this baby would change our relationship. How are we going to react? How is our life different? How are our roles different? Who does what? Who's in charge here? Our time in Peru was interesting. We established a lot of patterns in our relationship. Tessa had a siege mentality about this. She became extraordinarily protective of the baby, introspective; he was mine only at night. I did the eleven p.m. feedings and enjoyed wonderful periods of bonding alone with my baby late at night."

"In the beginning I had a fear about going out by myself," admitted Tessa. "Lima was so foreign to me. The expensive houses had German shepherds walking along the roofs, and there were layers of broken glass to discourage prowlers. And right next to that would be a hovel up against a wall where some poor family was squatting! We walked around with the baby in a Snugli, which the Peruvians thought was very odd.

"A court workers' strike had begun in Lima immediately after we arrived. We worried that we'd be languishing in Peru for months. Every day we'd ask Isabel, 'What about the strike?' and she would tell us it wasn't settled yet. A social worker came and did a quick home study, which consisted of a couple of questions for David and me and then a fifteen-minute chat with Isabel in Spanish! We were so lucky to have Isabel. I think couples seldom think that they need to investigate the source, that they should never get involved with anything at all that's illegal. She took care of everything. She knew the ropes entirely.

"Isabel thought that Americans would feel uncomfortable if they didn't have a little entertainment now and then, so she got couples together. Two other couples were from the United States. She had a whole group of translators and helpers. She charged nothing but asked us to make a donation to an orphanage."

David added, "I spent a lot of time with Isabel in the court system walking our papers through. Only one parent had to be there, so Tessa stayed in the apartment with Richard. A whole series of papers had to be executed, and the court workers' strike made everything quite difficult for us. Isabel had to establish that she was the legal guardian of the child. The judge then needed to sign the adoption decree. Isabel knew the judge personally and took all our papers, the social worker's report, et cetera, to his home for his signature."

Tessa elaborated, "Isabel's family was completely above reproach, and she had much evidence that we were an upstanding couple. The judge signed the papers, but we still needed an exit visa for Richard and had to wait for the strike to end in order to get that last piece of paper. Then we went to the U.S. embassy for Richard's visa, and there were no complications there. We got the Peruvian visa and the U.S. visa on the same day and left that night on a late flight!"

David's mother met them at the airport in Chicago. It was a rainy March day, but Tessa and David were so happy to be home that it didn't matter. David said, "My mother is magical with babies, and she went right for Richard."

"It was fairly calm the first day," remembered Tessa, "but the next day all our friends and relatives came over—endless congratulations. Our social worker, Alexandra, came to visit once or twice after we got home. She thought the baby was wonderful, and, of course, I thought he was wonderful! I was very comfortable with her. I didn't ever think I had to dust under the beds or anything like that before Alexandra came over. I felt fairly confident that I could do this. We had a huge party when Richard was christened; a hundred and fifty people came."

David added, "Midway through the party a business school professor, a mentor of mine, came in with his wife. I hadn't expected them to come and thought it was wonderful that they did. By this time, Richard was napping in his crib. I took them upstairs and they peeked into his room. I was moved to see that they both had tears in their eyes at the sight of our baby."

"I'm one of these people who are not particularly sensitive to the way people word things," said Tessa. "I know people mainly have positive feelings about adoption, so when they don't express things exactly as I would I don't get upset. Maybe it's that they don't have enough experience with adoption.

"Initially my mother-in-law kept introducing Richard as her Peruvian grandson. I realized that made me uncomfortable, and I had to think about why it did. I decided it was because she didn't say anything about the birthplace of her first two grandchildren. She didn't say, 'These are my Georgian granddaughters.' I didn't like Richard's being singled out. So I said, 'You know, Elinor, it really makes me uncomfortable when you say that Richard is from Peru, because you don't introduce Louisa and Pauline as being from a particular place; so I'd rather you didn't with Richard.' She said, 'That's all right, Tessa, that's fine. I'm so glad you told me.' So that was easy."

Tessa continued, "Almost as soon as we got home with Richard we knew we wanted more [children]. We had talked about four children; that was our fantasy. One day I got a phone call from the principal of the school where I'd been teaching. He asked, 'Are you coming back?' I hadn't even made that decision yet, but it seemed right to say that I wouldn't, because I knew that we would soon start the next adoption. I was almost thirty-three; I had been a social worker for three years and a teacher for almost eight. I was ready for something different.

"All of a sudden offers of children started to pour in; they were from odd sources. For example, a woman I used to teach with called and said, 'There's a cousin of a family in the school; the parents were just killed in a plane crash and left three children. Do you want me to investigate them?' But my fantasy was babies; I loved having this baby, and I couldn't get off the baby track. Then the translator we'd met at the Peruvian consulate called to tell me about twins from El Salvador. But El Salvador was involved in a terrible war then, and it looked very tricky. I guess I just had a radar for situations that were going to give us trouble.

"When Richard was thirteen months old, Isabel called and said, 'I have two boys—half brothers. Patrick is four and Vincent is two months.' David instantly wanted these children! He already saw them as his. He said, 'Three boys, Tessa, that's just what you want! Let's go! Let's go!' I said, 'I'm not ready for nursery school.' Isabel told us she would place them in separate families in Sweden if we didn't take them. We talked about it, agonized over it. Night after night we were awake. I remember staring at the two children's bedrooms in our house and thinking about where I could put these two kids. After a week of hashing it over, I knew I couldn't do it."

David said, "That was very hard for me; Tessa and I had talked and talked about it, and I was under the impression that she was saying she'd do it, although she didn't want to adopt someone older than Richard. My attitude was that Richard wouldn't know; he wasn't old enough to be aware of that. The reason I felt so bad about it was that I had already begun the bonding. I felt very remorseful about that."

Tessa added, "To this day David considers it a great loss that we didn't adopt Patrick and Vincent. But David and I know the major things that we must agree on. It can't be one person holding out. He knew that I was going to have to do the work, and because these offers started rolling in like this we thought we could adopt anytime we felt like it. We were quite overconfident. So we said no to Patrick and Vincent. It was mixed, but we believed other opportunities would come. It's like getting married. We couldn't have doubts about adopting."

Shortly after this incident, a friend of David's, who had been actively supporting a local adoption agency for many years, invited them to meet a social worker named Sarah and learn about their program. The agency had a small domestic program, but its main focus was facilitating American adoptions of Colombian children. "I was favorably impressed with all that Sarah said about the agency and the orphanage in Bogota; so after much encouragement from them we decided to apply," said David.

"We were told that every child in this orphanage was held while being fed," said Tessa. "There was no bottle propping. We talked with other parents who had adopted there and felt confident that this could work for us."

Then a phone call came from Isabel in Peru: "I've got a baby boy who was born on March 19. A brand-new baby. Do you want him? I'm going to help three more families, and then I'm not going to do any more adoptions. The red tape is too much. It's heartbreaking to see what the parents have to go through. There's anti-U.S. feeling here that I can't change." Tessa told Isabel that they were just starting a Colombian adoption and she didn't know what to do. Isabel gave her the names of three couples who had recently adopted in Peru and suggested that Tessa and David talk to them.

"They all said it was stressful," said Tessa. "They never knew if they were going to get out of there; one couple stayed three months, another three-and-a-half months. At this point David's business was starting to take off, and he couldn't afford so much time away. I would have had to stay there alone! Also, what would I do with Richard? He was already a

U.S. citizen, but there was an issue about dual citizenship, and the Peruvian government can be completely capricious. I was concerned; again, I think I had a radar for sticky situations. So we called Isabel back and told her, 'We're not going to do it. It sounds too tricky, too dangerous.' She had lots of other people she could call, and she ended up helping a single mother adopt that baby.

"Two months later we received a phone call from Sarah. 'We have a baby boy born on June 4 in Bogota,' she said. 'He weighed nine pounds and four ounces. Your papers should clear and in a few weeks you can go down!'"

David said, "I was at the office, and we had just gotten a big piece of business. Then the call from Tessa came. I was elated!"

Tessa added, "We got a picture of Andrew and I showed it to everyone. His eyes were closed, and he had a sweet smile on his face. I thought, *Oh, he'll be just like Richard!* They told us we'd have to stay for only one week; we wouldn't be languishing in a foreign country. We waited five weeks from the time Andrew was identified for us and then were given about two days' notice to travel!

"I vividly remember preparing Richard for Andrew. I would hold a little boy doll and say, 'This is going to be your brother.' Richard was twenty months old. We'd put the doll in a bassinet and pretend the baby was crying; then I'd show Richard how to comfort him. Richard was totally uninterested in the whole proposition! He would grab a blanket, stuff it on top of the doll's face, and say, 'All done!' I think preparing the first child for the second is the hardest."

Libby stayed with Richard while Tessa and David flew to Colombia. In Bogota they were met at the airport by a man named Pablo, who ran the pension where they'd be staying. "He looked like a character from a Graham Greene novel to me," said David. "He loaded us into a 1930s Mercedes and drove us to the pension. It was full of families who were adopting children. It was clear we were in a reasonably affluent part of the city."

Tessa said, "We went to the orphanage the next morning. People in white nurse's uniforms were bustling around. It was spotless. We were told to sit in a little reception area; it was very crowded, like a dentist's office."

David recalled, "The irony was that while we were waiting two women came in with babies. We admired the babies, not realizing that one of them was our new son! A few minutes later we went into the presentation room and there was Andrew! It was great; I remember Tessa's tremendous bonding; you could see it happening in front of your eyes."

Tessa said, "I looked at Andrew and thought, *Yes, they were right about his birth weight. This kid is gigantic!* He was five weeks old and weighed twelve pounds!

"The first night we were perplexed by the baby; he woke up every twenty minutes and couldn't be calmed. That night was awful, but I told myself, *You can get through anything once, and by tomorrow night he'll adjust.* But it was the same every night. He seemed a little distant. I remember sitting on the bed and rocking him back and forth.

"It was great to have the camaraderie of the other couples in the pension; it was different from our experience in Peru. People developed intense relationships very quickly. I still have the gold diaper pins that one woman gave me.

"We didn't have to go to court; it was all done. They had the system down to a science. We'd get in Pablo's Mercedes and travel around Bogota. I'd say, 'Where are we going now?' 'Oh, we're just going to get a picture taken.' Two minutes later we'd be back in the car and he'd tell us where we were going next. It was like a whirlwind."

David said, "We went on a tour of the orphanage. I was favorably impressed. One section was for older kids, who were harder to place and who therefore stayed longer; the other part was an infant factory—babies were quickly adopted unless they had medical problems. The orphanage was clean and orderly, but the equipment was a little primitive. The older kids had nothing to play with outside—just a broken-down basketball hoop and a dirt field where they played soccer. So I got someone to take us to a place that manufactured wooden toys that were brightly painted and lacquered. We bought quite a few toys and the kids were greatly appreciative."

Tessa said, "Andrew had to be examined by the U.S. embassy doctor, who was famous for denying people exit visas. He was fierce. I've never seen an exam quite like the one he gave Andrew. There was not one fingernail that he didn't look at! His job was to make sure that children did not become wards of the state. One of the couples we met had a problem with him. He was convinced that their baby was retarded, and he would not let them leave."

Andrew passed his physical and Tessa and David were allowed to bring him home. "It was interesting to come back home to Richard and say, 'Here's your baby brother!'" said Tessa. "He was quite fascinated with the baby initially. Three days later Richard stared at me at the breakfast table and said, 'Baby go!' I said, 'What?' 'Baby go back. Baby go back home!' I realized that all the role-playing I did with him didn't make it clear that this was going to be permanent! Richard was quite young to take all this in, but his reaction wasn't as bad as that of my friend's son, who screamed at his mother to come quickly with baby John because the garbage truck was outside and it was time to get rid of him!"

David said, "Andrew was a difficult baby, and it was very hard on Tessa. I think she had a sense that she couldn't provide for this child. We tried various baby formulas, but he kept throwing everything up. I continued to do the late-night feedings. I finally took an old shower curtain and cut a hole in it so I could wear it like a serape; I would put it on and give Andrew his bottle. He would throw up all over me, and I'd rinse the shower curtain off and put him into bed. I'd do this every night!

"I'll never forget this," continued David. "One night Tessa was at her wit's end; she was upset, angry, and tearful. She lamented, 'I just can't take it; I can't do it. I don't understand...' I think she felt that the baby was taking control, and that she was losing control. This was one of the few times I've ever spoken sharply to Tessa. I said, 'Now shut up! I don't ever want to hear that again. This is your child. You'd just better get used to it; for good or bad, this is your child, and you're just going to have to learn. Let's figure out what we can do differently.'

"In retrospect that turned out to be the right thing to say to her. She began to think positively. The next morning she put Andrew in a Snugli and wore him all day! Over time that made all the difference. Tessa confirmed her belief that affection and closeness would solve all difficulties."

"Andrew grew extremely attached to me," said Tessa. "All that time in the Snugli made him more loving and had the effect that only I would do. I think this was hard on Richard. He was like a little vampire; he would come running over, out of nowhere, deliver a huge bite, and leave! Then he'd say, 'Baby's crying!'"

As Andrew adjusted and their life became easier, Tessa and David began to consider their next adoption. Tessa said, "I loved my two little boys and thought, *Oh, why not get a third boy?* I had always done well teaching boys, fifth-grade boys. I had a reputation for being able to take obstreperous boys and make them love to learn. But Sarah talked me out of it. She said, 'I think you'll regret it that you didn't have a daughter. Since you have a choice, you should choose a girl, or you should at least think very carefully about why you might not want a girl.' I decided that I really did want a daughter, and now I'm so glad I reconsidered."

"It was clear to me," said David, "that Tessa had residual issues from her childhood about being a girl. Her father had always wanted a son. Tessa, the dominant twin, was constantly made to act like a boy in many respects. She was confused about being a girl. We worked on it and thought about it. I was concerned that Tessa would discover too late in life what she had missed by not having daughters. I tried to convince her. I don't know what broke the logjam, but she finally got excited about the idea of having daughters."

Shortly before Andrew's second birthday, Tessa and David told Sarah they were ready to adopt a girl from Colombia. This adoption took the longest; it was close to Andrew's third birthday when Sarah called to say that a baby girl had been identified for them. Tessa said, "Before we left for Bogota, two other couples had gone down and taken pictures of Lydia. Those pictures were essential; we just stared at them. I remember showing them to the boys. Every time someone came over I'd show them the pictures."

David added, "I'll never forget seeing the first picture of Lydia. I immediately bonded with that child! That was my daughter. Her picture communicated tremendous personality. I thought, *That's a girl I can't wait to meet! What a firecracker! She'll be the perfect daughter for Tessa.*"

"It was fun picking out clothes for a baby girl for the first time," said Tessa. "Everyone had told me that you must bring a bonnet and booties because in Colombia all little girls wear them. In fact, all little girls wear dresses there, even newborns; they never wear pants!

"Lydia had weighed seven pounds at birth, but since she had been quite sick with pneumonia she had gained only one pound and eight ounces in her six weeks of life. We met her in the same room at the orphanage where we had met Andrew. A nun brought her to us; she was dressed in clothes we had brought for her. It was frightening seeing her for the first time because she was extremely thin. She was so tiny compared with Andrew! When we took her back to the pension she stared at me with a very complex look that seemed to say, *Who are you? Where am*

I? She hardly ate; I was a little worried about that. She was my first child who didn't finish bottles. I thought, *She's a very tiny baby; she's not going to finish these bottles, but she's perfectly happy.* I trusted her more. I was more relaxed. She didn't do any of the things Andrew did—no throwing up, no crying—she went right to sleep.

"This adoption was very similar to Andrew's: now it's time to go to the passport office, now it's time to go to the doctor. We hardly paid any attention to it. Lydia passed the physical exam—given by the same doctor—with no problems."

David added, "This second trip to Bogota was less eventful. Tessa took to Lydia right away; she was an easier baby than Andrew. She was tiny and her big eyes were constantly appraising us. She looked exactly like her picture. She was strong and had a good grip. She was tirelessly arching her back in her crib, exercising. Tessa was worried that she'd be a thumb sucker, but I was surreptitiously guiding Lydia's thumb into her mouth!"

Tessa said, "We have cute pictures of the boys holding Lydia when we came home. They didn't perceive her as a threat. She was both peaceful and active—very alert. Lydia was always very sure about what she wanted and always seemed to get it. She turned out to be a great addition, a very amusing personality, which helped her get along with the boys. She was so funny; we called her good-time Lydia. Even when she was very little she would throw back her head and laugh a belly laugh.

"When Lydia was nineteen months old, I got a call from Sarah offering us a biracial baby. We were intrigued by the idea of a domestic adoption, because it would mean we wouldn't have to travel anywhere; we wouldn't have to leave our children, which was always rather wrenching."

Tessa and David, however, had a lot of misgivings about the baby they'd been offered. For one thing, the birth mother was only thirteen and claimed to have been raped. "David and I stayed up several nights talking about this baby," remembered Tessa. "I didn't like the fact that she said she'd been raped. The interesting thing is there's no guarantee that the birth mothers of our other children weren't raped, but it seemed to me so violent. I'd never had these scruples before, and I wondered whether it was the baby's biracialism. I looked into my heart of hearts and tried to admit, *Am I really, down at the bottom, racially prejudiced?* But I think the issue was this violent act. The other concern was that I felt Lydia was still too young."

David added, "Tessa wasn't ready. Lydia was still a baby, and she didn't want to crowd her. She suspected that Lydia needed more time."

They rejected Sarah's offer, telling her they would be ready in six month's time. Sarah told them that another Colombian adoption would not be possible. The policy was only two children per family from Colombia, unless they agreed to adopt a child with handicaps. "After my conversations with Sarah I was quite confident that she would come up with another girl within the time frame that Tessa had given her," said David.

But Tessa and David went back to their first adoption agency and began the paperwork for a Brazilian adoption. One of the reasons that they looked to Brazil was that a stay of only five days was required. They rewrote all their essays, and were about to start interviews with the social worker.

Tessa said, "It seems to me, when I look back on it, that twice we were offered a baby out of the blue, and that stimulated us to get going on the next adoption. The Vincent and Patrick offer got us started on Andrew's adoption, and this biracial baby got us started on our fourth adoption. Then one of those things that everyone dreams about happened. It was May 29. David and I had passed papers on a new house that morning. We were feeling a little overburdened because the new house was much bigger, and it was a little scary. When I got home the baby-sitter said there was a message to call Sarah! I just knew she had a baby for us! When I called her back my hand was shaking.

"'Here I am. Do you have a baby for me?'

"'Yes, I do. A little Vietnamese girl.'

"'This is so funny, because we're already filling out papers for a Brazilian adoption.'

"'Well, you can tell them no. That's okay. Do you want to call David?'

"'I know he'll say yes!'

"'Do you want to think about it?'

"'No, I've thought about it! I know it's okay—it's fine. It's a great time!'"

When Tessa called David at work he said, "Yes, of course! Can we get her today?" Tessa called Sarah back, but she said, "Can't you wait until tomorrow?" Tessa remembered, "I said, 'All right ...' But that night, of course, we didn't sleep at all. We were too excited."

The baby's birth parents were Vietnamese-American teenagers. The birth mother's parents had insisted that the baby be put up for adoption so that the birth mother could attend college.

"David and I discussed names while driving to pick her up. Somehow it hadn't occurred to us the night before to choose her name! We were too excited. Now we had only twenty minutes in which to decide! I remembered a letter we had received from an old family friend, Petty, who died when Lydia was a baby. It was her last letter to me. She wrote, 'I have a name for your new baby (meaning Lydia). It's Jessica Anne. That's all. You can think about it. Love, Petty.' I didn't take her suggestion then because I couldn't give up the name Lydia, which I had always loved. But her suggestion stuck with me. I said to David, 'Petty liked the name Jessica. Do you?' He said, 'Yes, I really do!'

"At the agency we walked into the reception area and were greeted by the secretary; we knew her quite well by now! She said, 'You can go right into Sarah's office. The baby's here.' And there was Sarah holding the baby! She handed her to me. I looked down and saw a round, healthy-looking baby. She was all prettied up in a cute little blue dress."

David added, "I thought Jessica seemed dreamy; she was asleep when she was given to Tessa. She had a beautiful round face, like a china doll—a really gorgeous little baby."

Tessa said, "The foster mother had done a great job with Jessica; she'd weighed six pounds at birth, and now, at ten weeks, she weighed twelve pounds. Sarah handed us a book with wonderful pictures that the foster mother had taken every few days . . . absolutely adorable. We asked Sarah if we had to give her a name right away and she said, 'Yes, and by the way, fill out this application!' So we didn't have to do all the paperwork again, thank heavens!

"When we brought Jessica home, the boys thought she was great. For Richard it was just one more kid to boss! We were planning to move in two weeks, and I didn't want to change everybody's bedrooms around, so Jessica was the only baby who ever slept in our room. Babies are so noisy! I found it almost intolerable, even though she was angelic. She slept twelve hours every night! I don't know what that foster mother did, but this baby was on a rigid schedule. She stayed on that schedule for weeks and weeks. I'd have to wake her up every morning after I'd fed everyone else. It was heaven."

David said, "We called Jessica the Zen baby! She was calm and tranquil, very self-assured. There's something about infants that communicates personality. It was quite striking. She was adaptable and easy. I think Lydia was tremendously excited to have a baby sister. By that time Lydia had bonded to Tessa, but Tessa was careful always to have Lydia with her while she took care of Jessica. And she was careful to give Lydia special time alone; Tessa was very sensitive to Lydia's needs.

"We felt that we'd reached the point we'd agreed on when we adopted Jessica. We had formed our family. Any decision to go beyond would have meant a major reappraisal. We talked about it a lot. Our feeling was that unless I was willing to change my work style, it wouldn't be fair; it would be too much of a burden on Tessa. We didn't want to hire full-time staff; we wanted to raise the kids ourselves. There were a number of times when Tessa or I would see an infant and wistfully say that we should adopt again, but then we'd agree that we have two matched sets; we'll leave it at that."

"If I had gotten pregnant in the middle of bringing this family into being, I would have welcomed it," said Tessa. "But because we had these children I was more able to accept the fact that I wasn't going to get pregnant. There's a feeling of loss, but there are lots of losses in life, and this is just one of them. I believe acknowledging that loss is important. It took me a long time to realize that part of me grieved for the fact that I never got pregnant. Here's how I knew: every time I got my period I always thought, *Well, I'm not pregnant.* The fact that I would even think of that—this was a complete fantasy! How could I keep that fantasy going for so long? I think it's important to realize that there is grieving, that there is always part of you that doesn't get over infertility. I'm pretty much finished with menopause now, so it finally puts that to rest, because getting pregnant is truly impossible now!"

David continued, "Talking about adoption was constant with our kids. We never knew when they'd understand what it meant, so we talked about it from day one. We repeated stories and took every opportunity to confirm them. We tried to tell each child the circumstances of their adoption, but the whole point was to stress to them that their birth mothers loved them enough to find them a good home. We'd tell them how much we wanted to have a child and that we'd fallen in love with them, that we were thrilled to give them a home, and that we'd chosen them. Tessa put together a photo album for each child. It's been of great value to our kids. They pored over them—they still do! We've also given each child artwork for his or her bedroom, traditional costumes, and books to help them appreciate their heritage. We've read lots of books about adoption with them and have tried to give them answers they can use when people ask questions.

"When the kids ask me, 'Do you think I should look for my first mother?' I say, 'It's up to you. What do you think?' I try to make certain they understand that there are two sides to the issue of meeting their birth mothers. They have to remember that their birth mother may have strong feelings about this too. I tell them, 'You shouldn't fantasize about the feelings of your birth mother; the separation was probably so painful for her that she may not want to encounter that memory. She might have her own fantasy that she wants to live with—that you went on to become a prince or a princess! Or that you just don't exist for her. How do you think she'd feel if you found her? What do you think her world would be like? She might be very poor and appear much older than she actually is. She may have a lot of other kids. What do you think you would learn?' Now, what is the question that the child wants answered? I think the child wants to know that he or she was loved and to have a beautiful, Cinderella-type mother say, 'Oh, I'm so happy. Now you can be mine again. I never wanted to give you up and I love you dearly.' That's the fantasy. I try to help the kids think through the implications of that, to demystify it.

"I think searching for birth mothers is an activity for an adult. A teenager in distress might want to do it, but it will cause all sorts of complexities. It should be approached with great respect and care and maybe some skepticism."

Tessa related, "Lydia has a tremendous fascination with young, unwed mothers or teenage moms. She also concludes, erroneously, that most of them hit their children, based on watching them in shopping malls. It may be her subtle way of rationalizing her adoption. She'll say, 'It's a good thing I don't have one of those teenage mothers!' I think this is very comforting to her, and she feels a little bit rescued.

"Sometimes my children say they're not going to do something 'because you're not my real mother!' So I agree with them, and this shocks them! I say, 'Look, you know this is a family that we made—like lots of other families. In fact, my feeling is that children who were adopted are just a little bit more loved because their parents have to go through so much more to get them! So think about that, kid!' Sometimes that's what it takes, more honesty. I think it's wrong to make it pleasant and sweet when it isn't pleasant and sweet; there are a lot of things in life that aren't so nice. But that's tough! Think about people who have lost their parents.

"At family reunions I look around at my parents and relatives and see an incredible resemblance. It's all biology. There are no missing pieces. But for our children there are missing pieces, and it's tough for them. That's what they face as they get older and realize they can't have that history. That part is not there. It is as if someone has died.

"Lydia finds it the hardest to accept that she didn't grow inside me. She's twelve and this is still an issue for her. She's the one who calls me 'fake mommy' and then laughs, which I think is a wonderful, forthright way of dealing with the situation. Sometimes her joking is very serious, but because she's so up front about it we can discuss it right then and there. We don't have to probe and pry and wait for the right moment. I think that's good. She's very clear about who she is.

"We've told our children that they got a deck of cards and they have to play with what they've got and not spend a lot of time thinking about what might have been. *What might have been* could have been a lot worse than what they've got! That's what Lydia truly appreciates; she sees that *what might have been* would have been a very different life. They might not have curfews and job charts! But they might have been out begging in the street. They might have been one of the lucky ones, but probably not. Richard once wrote a poignant essay about his adoption; that when he sees homeless people he thinks, *There, but for fortune, go I.*

"Andrew has been the least talkative about adoption. 'Why are you always bringing this up?' he asks. But Andrew is also the one who looks the most North American; you might think he was Italian. When he recently applied for boarding school, he had to write an essay about himself, and he wrote about adoption. It was an interesting essay; in it he said he was glad he's not in a family in which a child was born into the family. He feels he would always have wondered if that child were favored or loved more. I found his essay very touching. I'm really glad things turned out as they did and that our kids are all different shades of brown. I think these things happen for a reason."

11/ Carrie and Alex
A baby boy from Lebanon

"I think being a parent is surprising. It feels very natural. You get the baby, and then all of a sudden you realize you've forgotten when you didn't have the baby. In the beginning you're so caught up in taking care of the baby and all of a sudden being a parent that the surprise is how immediately you bond with the child. You look at this little creature and you think, *Is this mine? Mine to care for all of my life?*"

WHEN planning a family, people don't always view adoption as a last resort. Some grow up with the idea that they'd like to adopt a child one day. They may have been personally touched by an adoption in their family or community, or they may have been inspired by a book. "I don't know why," said Carrie, "but as a child I was always interested in adopting. I think it came from the *Anne of Green Gables* books that I read when I was little. I loved them, devoured them. From the beginning [of our marriage] I had talked to Alex about hoping to adopt, even if we had our own children."

Carrie is a slim woman of medium height with short, dark hair and engaging eyes; she exhibits a quiet and gentle manner. Her childhood, in a middle-class community outside Washington, D.C., was idyllic. "My mother was born in Germany and met my father (an American soldier of German heritage) when his troop cleared out a schoolhouse during the Second World War. Her home had been bombed, and that's why her family was living in the school. The Americans knew that German officers were hiding in the school's basement, and since my mother was the only one there who could speak English, she had to accompany my father and other American soldiers into the basement to facilitate the surrender of the German officers. At the end of the war, my father returned home. Several years later my mother came to the States and married him.

"My mother came from a difficult family background, and she compensated for it by giving us an absolutely wonderful childhood—both my parents did. When I was eight years old my mother's brother came to live with us. We called him Bruncle (for brother/uncle). We lived in the same house all of my life; the school was up the street. My parents never had a lot of money, so I was on scholarship at university and lived at home."

After her freshman year in college, Carrie traveled to Germany for the first time and met her mother's family. "I loved it so much that I vowed to go back for a year when I finished college. I ended up staying for seven years!" At the university in Munich, Carrie designed and taught a course on the impact of Western television on the development of Third World countries.

"In Munich there was a group of 'forever students,' and we had a wonderful time. It was very exciting. I fell in love with a Palestinian doctor [who was studying there] and developed a strong interest in the Middle East. We had some Palestinian friends who had grown up in Lebanon, and during the civil war we were concerned about the heinous atrocities going on. We gathered sixty tons of medications and asked the honorary consul to Beirut to provide a plane. We unloaded the medications into cars and traveled up and down the coast to the refugee camps. In Beirut I went through several orphanages, and that experience has never left me. I still have a picture of those children on my desk. It was so heartrending. The buildings were rubble, there were mortar holes in the walls, and very few people had running water. Many of the children had been traumatized by seeing their parents killed in front of their eyes.

"I found the Arabic children hauntingly beautiful. One little boy would not speak. He had blond hair and blue eyes; he had seen his parents being murdered. Another little girl brought her puppy up to me and said, 'Take a picture of my puppy.' I could speak Arabic at about kindergarten level then; I was just learning the language. It was 1974 and I was twenty-two. Certain things stay in your heart and mind. It was very difficult to walk away from those children."

After several years in Munich, Carrie received word that her father had suffered a heart attack, which prompted her to go home. "When I came home I decided my relationship with this Palestinian was not going to work, but I had developed such a strong interest in the Middle East that I did a master's in Middle Eastern studies at the School for Advanced International Studies. That's how I met my husband. We both demonstrated in Washington, D.C., against the invasion of Lebanon in 1982."

Alex, a slender man whose soft-spoken demeanor is occasionally punctuated by infectious laughter, was born in Madison, Wisconsin, in the early 1950s. When his father joined the foreign service he lived in Turkey and Jordan. He said, "In Amman, Jordan, there was no American school, so my brother and I were sent to Lebanon. The kids were primarily American oil company kids; there was a day student population and a boarding student population. I started learning Arabic in high school. I had a strong desire to learn it. I did not succeed the way I wanted to, but I did learn rudimentary spoken Arabic. In 1970, when the Black September war broke out in Jordan, we were evacuated out of Beirut. My father was trapped in the embassy for twenty-nine days but eventually joined my mother, my brothers, and me in Athens. That was the end of my junior year. My parents moved back to Washington, but they took pity on me and sent me back to Beirut so I could graduate with my class."

Afterward Alex enrolled in the foreign service school at Georgetown. He remembered: "I had a tremendous culture shock after nine years of living abroad. My attitude about the Arab-Israeli conflict was completely out of sync with the attitude here. I expected that a university would be a forum for open-mindedness and free discussion. Absolutely not! That repelled me from my career plans. I took a year off and went to Spain. When I came back I went to law school at Georgetown."

After three years in New York City as a prosecutor, Alex returned to Washington to work as a trial attorney for a government agency. "It was 1982, and on TV I saw Israeli tanks running over the Lebanese countryside and Phantom jets flying over Beirut and dropping cluster bombs. It was enough to draw me back into the problem. A van was driving through the streets of Washington with a big Palestinian flag. It sparked so many memories. I thought maybe there was some organization about Palestinian rights; I found in the phone book the Palestine Human Rights Campaign and called them. This led me to volunteering for the Arab-American Antidiscrimination Committee.

"People who had lived in Lebanon were coming out of the woodwork, reaching out for any organization to grab onto to try to lobby Congress, to get the press to stop being so outrageously pro-Israel and so anti-Lebanese, and to get Congress to focus on the fact that American weapons were being used to kill children. That's where I met Carrie, at a strategy meeting. We like to say that we met picketing in front of the Israeli embassy, which isn't exactly true, but almost! We did picket together after that first meeting."

Two years later Carrie and Alex were married. Since Alex's parents were stationed in Egypt at the time, the newlyweds spent a month there. A few months later Carrie's sister was diagnosed with breast cancer; she died within three years. "She was only thirty-seven, and it was very hard," Carrie said. "It took so much of my psychic and physical energy. A year later my father was diagnosed with cancer, too, and he died in 1990. That was very consuming and heart wrenching. Afterward Alex and I sat back and tried to regain our sense of 'us.'

"We had never used birth control. We were so consumed with the family that we didn't sit down every year and say, *Well, nothing's happened.* We didn't even stop to think. My father's death may have triggered something in our minds to start a family, to bring some joy back into the family. I thought, *Wouldn't it be wonderful if Daddy were still here when we have a child?* I was probably thirty-eight when we started thinking about adopting."

Alex remembered, "When Carrie's father died, we thought it would be very nice to have a spark of life, to reinvigorate the family. Carrie's Bruncle agreed, 'Why don't you at least adopt if you're not going to have children? You ought to do something life-affirming.'"

Carrie continued, "Alex and I decided to do the initial testing to see what was wrong. Neither of us is keen on the high-tech approach [to infertility], and there are so many children in the world. Having our own biological child wasn't important enough to us. For a period of three or four months I went to a fertility clinic. I did all the testing and had a laparoscopy." Carrie learned that one of her fallopian tubes was completely blocked and the other one partly blocked. She and Alex were told that, with in vitro fertilization, they could probably have a biological child, but they chose not to do it.

Alex explained, "A year prior to this we had seen friends go through an agonizing process to conceive, and we determined that was not something we had any desire to do."

Carrie elaborated, "Alex and I decided not to have our lives regulated by shots. We didn't want our sex life sterilized by the clock; I don't believe in medications. The point is we wanted to raise a child; it wasn't important to give birth to a child."

When Carrie and Alex decided to adopt, they didn't know how their families would respond. Carrie said, "My parents were always very gentle and non-intrusive. They never said, 'When are you going to have children?' But Alex's parents, who come from a family full of children where everyone is very fertile, said, 'Come on, when are you going to have children?' But they said it in a nice way. So everyone was thrilled."

Alex's brother knew people who had recently adopted from Chile. They gave Carrie an adoption agency's name and recommended a social worker there. "We wanted an infant," said Carrie, "because from what we had read, we felt in our hearts that it would be easier to bond. We told the agency Lebanon was the only country we were interested in. The agency had already done two or three Lebanese adoptions."

Alex elaborated, "We both felt foreign adoption was the way to go. It seemed that an adoption from a foreign country would be final, that it would have legal certainty; it would not be a kind of pioneering relationship in which the birth mother would become part of our family."

Carrie and Alex felt fortunate to have Vida, their social worker. Alex explained, "To us, Vida was more than a disinterested social worker; she became our friend and took a personal interest in us. She clicked instantly with Carrie, in part, I think, because they shared a European cultural background."

"We had a wonderful feeling from Vida," continued Carrie. "We enjoyed our sessions with her. The home study was fun. Alex enjoyed it. He told me, 'Nowadays it's very seldom that people ask you to talk about yourself and listen to you.' He's very introspective, and a quiet person. It was nice for him to talk about some of these things to someone other than me."

Alex remembered, "It was fun writing my autobiography, and I enjoyed reading Carrie's. It was almost flattering to think that someone other than Carrie and me would be interested in our lives. Opening up to Vida was easy."

But Alex had some reservations about adoption. "I was pretty wary," he said. "I had read too many stories about rip-offs, and I'm a naturally suspicious person. I felt we were placing ourselves at the mercy of strangers about a matter that was emotionally central to our lives, and it had the potential to be financially quite depleting. I was very concerned about money. How much? What are we paying for? What are we getting? I regret having approached the process with that attitude, but it was colored by what I had learned about adoption from just general reading, not from anybody I knew personally."

Carrie and Alex had hoped to go to Beirut and see the orphanage, but in 1992 Americans were discouraged from traveling to Lebanon.

"We thought it was totally absurd," said Carrie. "It should have been left up to us. The State Department gave me a whole list of things to do in case we chose to go to Beirut. We had to send certain documents to them and letters explaining why it was imperative that we pick the baby up in Beirut; then we had to have that confirmed by the agency and the orphanage in Beirut; and finally, all of that would be sent back to the State Department for approval. We could have flown to Rome and obtained Lebanese visas, but you don't want to do anything illegal when you're adopting, because you don't know what can happen. Vida said the babies were usually flown to Cyprus, and that would be the easiest way, rather than trying to go to Beirut ourselves."

Carrie and Alex felt some of the frustrations that other adoptive parents experience. They waited a long time for their fingerprints to be processed by the FBI (mandatory in international adoptions). Carrie explained: "The FBI had moved just at the point where our fingerprints were sent in. They had all their files in boxes! I called my congressman's office for help, and they were very good. Ironically, the moment I called them our fingerprints cleared, so they called me back and told me. There is a lot of empathy for people who are adopting."

Carrie and Alex started with the home study in July and finished in September. All the papers were filed in October. By February, when they still hadn't heard anything, they began to get anxious. Carrie called a Lebanese-American friend in Washington who traveled frequently to Lebanon and was well respected there. When he found out who their social worker at the Lebanese Children's Relief Fund was, he said, "Oh, I think I can help you. Yasmeen is my sister-in-law!"

Yasmeen was a social worker who volunteered in a Greek Antiochian Orthodox church in Washington that ran the Lebanese adoption program.

She identified babies for adoptive parents, worked with the lawyer associated with the orphanage, and was the channel to Lebanon. Yasmeen told Carrie that the outcome depended on the political situation. At one point the authorities had stopped adoptions, but currently there was a window of opportunity because feelings between the U.S. and Lebanon were favorable. Yasmeen told Carrie it would take a couple of months and asked if they wanted a boy or a girl. She told her they didn't care.

Carrie explained, "From that moment on, everything went beautifully. I had already talked to Yasmeen once or twice, and we had sent her a letter explaining why we wanted to adopt in Lebanon; at that time there was anti-Western and anti-American sentiment in Lebanon. But it turns out she was my good friend's sister-in-law! And that is what made the difference, because she knew that we were Middle East oriented and that we loved the culture and the people. In the Middle East everything is done via personal connections. I thought it was fate.

"By early March, Alex was getting restless and suggested that we consider another country. But I was adamant. I had such good feelings about Lebanon. I knew it would work out, and it didn't matter if it took a couple of months longer. I had painters come to the apartment so everything would be ready before the baby came.

"One morning Yasmeen called. 'We have a little boy. Are you interested? He's about three months old, and has been in the care of a family.' She explained that elderly nuns took care of toddlers at the orphanage, but infants were given to families. Jamie was with a family where there were three children and the wife was a nurse, so he had excellent care. She said he'd had all his tests and that he was a very healthy, happy little boy. She said he had brown hair and big brown eyes. 'He's a beautiful little baby and he loves people and he's loved. But the only thing is—I have to tell you—he's very spoiled! He wants to be held all the time.' I said that was just fine!

"Then she said there was one problem: the price had changed, and it would be increased by almost one-third. Alex was very nervous [about the money], and we almost had a fight. He asked if I thought it was blackmail, and I said no, that I trusted her. He wanted me to ask her questions about the baby's health, and it annoyed me because I knew the baby was fine. I wanted him to have the same implicit trust, but Alex is different. He's a lawyer, and his mind is analytical.

"That evening when Alex got home we called Yasmeen back and told her that we wanted the baby. She said she needed a check, which she would hold. She wouldn't send anything over to Lebanon until everything was certified. She was very good. She told us the orphanage would send his papers from Lebanon, and she'd forward the medical report and a little picture of him by overnight mail.

"The painters were still here when I got the package. I locked myself in the bathroom and just looked at the package. Then I opened it. There was this darling, tiny, sort of old-fashioned [photograph] with little serrated edges. It was taken up close, and his nose looked huge! I made photocopies of the picture, sent one to my mother, and gave one to Alex to carry in his pocket."

Alex remembered, "When we were told that it would cost more because the Lebanese attorney had upped the fee, all of my instincts were to be annoyed. We didn't get an explanation of what the money already given them was for, and this was on top of that. We didn't have any assurance that that would be the last of it; we could get there and have to pay more. I was getting very panicky.

"It was just a very nerve-wracking, uncertain time. I didn't know who Carrie was speaking to. Maybe it's because I was too detached from the process all along. By nature I'm a suspicious person, and I don't trust fate. There were no levers that I could grab hold of to assert control over the situation. Carrie was upset with me for being suspicious. But it resolved itself pretty quickly. I realized that we simply had to put our trust in people we did not know, had not met, and did not know anything about. We just had to go along with the process. As soon as I saw Jamie's picture I said, 'How quickly can it happen?'"

Carrie continued, "I was very excited, and I'm a calm person. We went out on the weekend and got a crib and changing table, because Yasmeen had said it could happen very quickly. She told us to get our plane tickets and a reservation at a hotel in Cyprus. I called British Airways and told them we needed tickets for an open period because we were adopting; the woman I spoke to was just wonderful. Ten days before we knew we could leave I was able to book a ticket with a date established.

"Yasmeen and I kept in touch almost every other day. Alex and I were planning to leave the weekend before Easter, and the baby would come to Cyprus on Monday or Tuesday. Yasmeen said she didn't know who would bring the baby. She explained, 'Sometimes the lawyer will come; otherwise she will entrust the baby to someone. The flight is only half an hour, but they don't fly every day.'"

Alex had a problem with the Immigration and Naturalization Service (INS). He remembered, "We had our nonrefundable airplane tickets and had taken all the money out of our savings; we needed a paper of some kind from the INS. In order to get that piece of paper we needed the adoption decree from Lebanon. We got that decree about a week before we were set to leave. We sent it to the appropriate person at the INS, and I called on the Monday before we were to leave to check on its status and to make sure we would get the paperwork by Friday. The person I spoke to said, 'Well, you're one of many. We'll do the best we can, but you're not at the top of the pile. I can't tell you how long it takes. These things take time.'

"That [attitude] was not satisfactory! I was determined to get this final piece of paper so that we could leave as scheduled. The person I spoke to over the phone wouldn't tell me where the office was, wouldn't give me any information. So I ended up looking in the Yellow Pages. I went to the INS on the subway and thought I'd better have some way of getting in there, and then I saw a flower stand and thought, *Flowers! That will do it!* When I went into the building and asked for the INS nobody knew where it was! So I walked up and down the corridors and eventually noticed a little door with a tiny sign that read INS. I looked in, and sure enough that was it. Inside I said, 'I'm here for so-and-so.' The receptionist saw the flowers. "Oh, I'll call her and she'll be right out." Out she came! I gave her the flowers and introduced myself. She took me aside and talked about my case. She was a very pleasant elderly woman, extremely gracious. She took care of me on the spot. I walked away with the paper."

Carrie and Alex flew out of Dulles Airport. "I love foreign travel," said Alex. "I've crossed the Atlantic dozens of times, and every time I do it it's a thrill. When we arrived they told us the baby would be a day late because Middle East Airlines wasn't flying on Mondays. I was determined not to let that sour the experience. I said fine. We were staying at the Nicosia Hilton. The Greek part of Cyprus is modern, bustling, and Western with very little historical or cultural interest left. We toured Nicosia for a day. The food is limited. Cyprus is short of two things, domesticated animals and foreign exchange. So there's very little meat. And the diet is neither Greek cuisine nor Turkish cuisine. It's a watered-down mixture of the two that essentially revolves around goat cheese! So they have twenty-five varieties of goat cheese on the menu, even for breakfast!

"We went to the U.S. embassy and talked to them about the adoption procedure. They had a good attitude; they were very friendly. They gave us a list of embassy-approved pediatricians. It was intimidating going into a U.S. embassy as a civilian. Having grown up as a foreign service brat, you think nothing of waltzing right in, and here was this imposing edifice with tremendous security. The waiting room was behind bulletproof glass, and various official notices were posted on the walls. Everyone there seemed to be a Cypriot trying to get a visa to go to the States. I didn't see any other couples adopting babies. I felt we were a rarity."

The baby was due to arrive at the airport at one o'clock on Tuesday. Alex narrated, "On the way to the airport to get the baby I was so excited! We drove thirty miles through the barren Cypriot countryside. I spoke to the driver because I was very interested in the political situation. I have a point of view about the Turkish-Greek dispute, particularly over Cyprus, and I was anxious to hear the local spin. [The driver] didn't express very much hope that there would be a solution.

"At the airport the staff from Middle East Airlines knew instantly that we were the couple they were supposed to be looking out for to pick up the baby from Beirut. They ushered us right through all the security checks to the back area of the airport where the people would come off the flight. We were sitting in front of the immigration officers. They engaged us in conversation; their English was good. In Cyprus and Lebanon anyone who has a secondary education speaks English."

Carrie added, "The Cypriot officials were very kind, but a little wary. They wanted to know why we were adopting." Alex continued, "I showed them the paperwork, and they were a little bit officious. They wanted to see the baby's American visa, and I didn't have it yet. I showed them his adoption papers, but I was nervous that they were troubled about the American visa. While I was trying to figure out a way of relieving their discomfort it occurred to me, *I have an airline ticket for the baby! That should make them feel better, because it will assure them that he is leaving with us.* That convinced them."

Carrie said, "We learned that the plane was going to be two hours late, so we sat there with the Cypriot officials and waited."

"When the airplane didn't land on time, I was like a father outside the delivery room!" said Alex. "We were waiting in a huge area and nobody was there except us on a little bench and the three officials. They were occupying themselves with their paperwork. All of a sudden there was a commotion. One of the officials said, 'The plane has arrived.'"

"We saw people coming off the plane," said Carrie. "The immigration men were really watching us at this point. It was cute! We saw a stunning stewardess, perfect in every way. I felt like Little Miss Hoboken next to her! Not only was she physically stunning, but she had Lebanese flair. She was perfectly dressed and coifed. She and the pilot walked together. He was a tiny man but also very chic. She was carrying a beautiful basket—big, brand new, pink and blue—under her arm, and he accompanied her. They came up to us and asked us our name. I was able to peek in at the baby, and I thought, *You don't look like your picture!* The stewardess gave the baby to Alex. The pilot said, 'You have a charming son. He captivated all of us. You have a very magical child.'"

Alex remembered, "A beautiful woman handed the baby basket to me. My first impression of the baby was, *What lips you have! Such voluptuous lips!* He was asleep and covered with swaddling clothes. I was afraid to look under the blankets, so I just stared at him. This all happened very, very quickly. I was in emotional shock."

Carrie added, "The stewardess took me aside to tell me about his formula and that she'd just fed him and changed him. Everything was brand-new. There were brand-new clothes in the basket—two outfits, diapers, two bottles—he came with everything! Alex was holding the baby and grinning. The Cypriot men were crying. Alex and I weren't crying; we were just too shocked! I thought I was going to throw up or faint! All of a sudden a plane lands and you have a baby! I don't even think I could recall what was going through my mind, because it was just shock! The stewardess said, 'I've given him his formula, but it looked a little thin, so I put some more in...' That's typically Lebanese. 'Well, they told me eight spoons, but I put in ten. With my baby I would give him more.'"

Alex said, "One of the immigration officers said, 'This is an important time; you should have a picture.' He used our camera and took a picture of just the three of us. It came out wonderfully!"

Carrie recalled, "As he left, the pilot looked at us and said, 'Take good care of this baby; he's very special. God will thank you later for what you have done.' I just want to weep now; it was very touching. Then the Cypriots stamped our papers, and we walked out and got into a taxi. We put the basket in the trunk, and Alex held Jamie over his shoulder. The baby was calm and placid. I hadn't even held him yet! Alex wouldn't let him go!"

Alex said, "In the cab I was holding Jamie. I put him on my shoulder and heard him breathing; he was so utterly dependent, so completely trusting. I think that's when I bonded with him, right there in the taxi. He was awake but quiet; he didn't cry. He did look like his picture after all. Clearly this was the right baby! I was a little concerned because he was congested. We thought he had a cold, and I was anxious to get him to the doctor. In the cab I became choked up. Tears came to my eyes. Carrie cried too."

Carrie recalled, "We went to the pediatrician's office right away. We'd chosen a British woman who was married to a Greek. The office was in her home. When we walked in she looked at Jamie—didn't really give him a thorough examination—and after about two minutes she said, 'Well, I think he's deaf. I don't think the child can hear, and he's very ill.' We turned white! I could kill this woman now. Jamie had just come off the plane; his ears were clogged from his cold. The doctor thumped his chest a little. She didn't take his temperature, nothing! At that point we were numb. I said, 'Well, I think the baby is fine. We know the people. They wouldn't have sent him if he was ill. He's been checked by doctors in Lebanon.'"

Alex said, "She was kind of a kooky doctor. When she told us the baby wasn't well I thought, *What could be wrong with this beautiful child?* She clapped and Jamie didn't respond. We expected the baby to be perfect in every way and she said, 'The baby's not responsive, he doesn't look well, and he doesn't hear.' When Carrie told her that Jamie had been checked by Lebanese doctors, she said, 'Well, actually, Lebanese babies have always been very hardy, and they're well taken care of, because the Lebanese adore children. I'll give you an antibiotic for him and stamp your medical certificate so you can go home and get him examined.'

"We went back to the hotel and called our lawyer in Beirut, who in turn called the woman who had cared for Jamie. The woman apparently burst into tears and said 'What do you mean? He listens to the radio and goes to sleep with the radio. He turns to me whenever I talk to him. He's fine. He just has a cold.'"

After the Lebanese lawyer assured them that the baby was well, Alex felt relieved. The new parents undressed their baby and looked at him for the first time. They put him on the bed and took pictures. They stared at him while he napped. That evening they took the baby to a restaurant with them. "He slept very well at the restaurant," said Alex. "He was asleep when we left, asleep in the restaurant, and asleep even in the taxi back to the hotel. Then he woke up! We paced and paced with him. It was wonderful but it was exhausting. We were jet-lagged. We had been running around like crazy, and we desperately needed sleep, so we took turns."

Carrie remembered, "We spent the first night clapping our hands and clicking our fingers in Jamie's ears! We'd say, 'Do you think he turned for this one?' It was a little scary, because he was breathing in a raspy way. He had a lot of congestion. I was awake most of the night. I kept getting up to look at him. The doctor had also given us these wonderful little capsules that they have in Europe. They're eucalyptus menthol, and you sprinkle drops on the sheet to help him breathe. The next morning he was a little better. Alex changed him; he was thirteen years old when his youngest brother had been born, so he knew how to change a baby. Then we went down to breakfast taking Jamie along in his little basket."

After breakfast Carrie and Alex took their son to the U.S. embassy for his American visa. While waiting in line, a vivacious woman engaged them in conversation and asked them all sorts of questions about the baby. She said, "Oh, what a sweet little baby. Where are his parents? What happened to his parents?" Carrie answered, "He was found at the orphanage—left as a foundling there."

Alex said, "I had told Carrie to be circumspect about any speculation about the baby's parents or any side information we might have from Yasmeen when talking with the embassy people. When we got to the window the same woman went around behind the window and introduced herself to us as the consular officer! She had just investigated us for the visa about the baby, his origins, whether his parents were alive, et cetera! That woman was doing her job. Her job is to let into the United States only babies who are legally within the definition of an orphan. These people use surreptitious investigation techniques. They don't want to encourage a black market."

Carrie remembered, "The woman said, 'I hope you don't mind, but I was already interviewing you.' We learned that another couple got into a fix because they didn't repeat the story that was on their baby's papers. His visa was held up for months!"

Carrie and Alex had three more days to spend in Cyprus before their flight home. They felt the baby was making progress, that the antibiotic was clearing him up. Carrie said, "The day we got him he didn't smile, but I think he smiled the next day. He was a serious-looking baby—very quiet but at ease with himself. You could tell by the picture that he was very self-assured. The look on his face the moment we got him was one of calmness."

Alex remembered, "In the first days we spent a lot of time in our hotel room. We put him on the bed to see what he would do! He was only three months old, but he rolled over from his stomach to his back three times! We took lots of pictures. We hung around the hotel and the swimming pool. The weather was beautiful, but we didn't take him into the water because of his cold. The hotel had a giant chess game, and Carrie and I played chess while I held the baby on my shoulder. We called our parents. They were delighted.

"As a boy I had vacationed in Cyprus with my family, and I wanted to show Carrie the places I remembered in northern Cyprus, so we decided to cross the border. This was an international border. It was like crossing into no-man's-land. There were a lot of shelled-out buildings. We went through a checkpoint and showed the officials every paper known to man. We had our American passports, Jamie's Lebanese passport, his adoption papers, et cetera. We were told that going over was easy, but coming back was hard. You can't spend the night on the Turkish side, and you can't let them stamp your passport, or they won't let you back in. But the Turkish part is historically interesting; it has the bazaars and is very Oriental. It was wonderful, so picturesque! I showed Carrie a monastery and a castle. The owner of a restaurant where we had lunch was happy to see us, very attentive to Jamie, and very congratulatory to his mother; so it was terrific!"

The family passed back over the border without incident, and the next day they flew home. Carrie said, "We flew from Cyprus to London and then to Washington. My mother and Bruncle were there with Alex's brother and his girlfriend. I had changed Jamie into a little outfit my mother had given him; he looked angelic and sweet. Everybody was so thrilled. My mother was beside herself! She held him right away. In the car, Jamie grabbed my mother's thumb and held on to it for the entire ride. He wouldn't let it go! The next day, Easter Sunday, everybody came to see the baby, which was touching. When I took Jamie upstairs to put him to bed my three male cousins followed me, watched me put Jamie in the crib, and stood over the crib saying, 'Isn't this great? Isn't this great?' They were so in love with Jamie and so mesmerized. He's the first baby in the family.

"I think being a parent is surprising. It feels very natural. You get the baby, and then all of a sudden you realize you've forgotten when you didn't have the baby. In the beginning you're so caught up in taking care of the baby and all of a sudden being a parent that the surprise is how immediately you bond with the child. You look at this little creature and you think, *Is this mine? Mine to care for all of my life?* What really surprised me, not as a parent but as a person, was how utterly delighted everyone around us was. It was so reinforcing. When we got to our apartment the neighbors ran up with a bottle of champagne and their camera. And Jamie's godmother, who lives across the street, ran over. Everyone was so pleased! It's been wonderful."

Alex added, "There are things to get used to—like a baby's crying for no apparent reason, and continuing to cry unless you comfort him. So physically, the stamina that was required was a bit of a surprise. But he is so unbelievably special—perfect in every way! We feel that we are the luckiest couple in the world."

"Vida came to see Jamie a couple of weeks after we got home," said Carrie, "and she thought he was sweet. She always joked with me, because I'm a neat person. She said, 'Well, Carrie, the house isn't going to look like this when I come next time!' I was honest with Vida. I told her there were nights when Alex said he couldn't stand to hear the baby crying. I could say things like that to her, but I didn't ask her for advice. I turned to my family for that.

"I think the follow-up visits are important for the social worker. Vida told me that occasionally social workers remove a child from a family. They look for warning signs. I admitted to Vida, 'There are times when I'm really tired, and I never knew I would have this much to do. You think there's going to be more of a balance, but it never turns out that way.' Vida said, 'Carrie, you'll find that when you go anyplace you'll be the last one to get dressed, because you'll dress the baby, Alex will dress himself, and then he'll walk out with the baby and you'll still be in your underwear!' It was great talking to Vita! I always felt very comfortable with her."

Alex said, "I thought it was kind of odd to have follow-up visits, still being tested after the baby was there. What were they going to do about it? We had papers indicating that Jamie had been adopted under Lebanese law, and it seemed absurd to be interviewing still. But Vida was comforting and very reassuring."

Carrie was surprised by some of the comments from people when they learned of their adoption. "My florist said, 'Why did you adopt from the Middle East? Why Lebanon? Isn't it sort of crazy over there?' I think Americans are very ill-informed. The Lebanese, the Beirutis, who consider themselves not Arabic but Phoenicians, are among the most sophisticated people I have met in my life. They have a *je ne sais quoi*, something about them that is really delightful. I think their tenacity enabled them to survive the war. They have an unbelievable spirit and I see that in Jamie. He is indomitable! It is very difficult to correct this child, because he is so sturdy within himself, even at the age of two. The Lebanese are tough but tender. They are strong souls but very emotional. They are very creative; they're just wonderful. They have a penchant for exaggeration, but they are charming. I think that all those characteristics thrown together helped them put up with the war, because they love their country with a passion. They might leave it, but they all want to go back. And many of them never left even through the worst months. I hope Jamie will be tremendously proud of his background.

"Once I told my mother's friend that Jamie is very strong-willed and sometimes has a temper that is amazing for such a tiny child; she asked me if I thought that came from his being Lebanese! 'I've heard they are very angry people,' she said. I just stared at her. Then I said, 'No, I don't think it has anything to do with his background; the Lebanese are wonderful people. It's just Jamie; Jamie is Jamie.' Things like that come out every now and again, and I know he will have to deal with it at some point; we have to prepare him for it."

Alex added, "One of the reasons that Lebanon was such a good place for us is that we both love Lebanon, Arabic culture, and Lebanese culture and history. We think Jamie has nothing to be ashamed of and everything to be proud of in his ethnic heritage. And because we know a lot [about Lebanon], we can teach him. I'm not afraid of Jamie's finding out about his ethnic heritage. On the contrary, I'm looking forward to taking him back to Lebanon.

"We want to adopt another child, sooner rather than later, although financially it's a big bite. But the decision is Carrie's, because we've got a traditional allocation of life responsibilities; we consider ourselves fortunate to be able to have that kind of lifestyle. Since Carrie is not working, it's really up to her when she feels she can take on the challenge of another child. Jamie has been a full-time occupation. He's entering the 'terrible twos' now. My perception is that he's becoming less dependent but not less labor intensive!

"I think I'd be more trusting next time. I wouldn't be suspicious about somebody trying to rip us off. It would be my inclination to ask for a girl next time, and I think Carrie might agree that we should balance out the family. There do seem to be differences in behavior between boys and girls. My feelings toward Jamie are every bit as strong [as they would be for a biological child], probably stronger, because he's adopted. Every time I look at Jamie I have a tremendous sense not only of love and pride but of accomplishment—that we've accomplished something wonderful!"

Carrie concluded, "We will tell Jamie that he was a chosen child. That's a term we picked up at his baptism. We had a little party at the Ritz-Carlton Hotel after we baptized Jamie, and a waiter kept bending over Jamie's carriage. My mother heard him say to Jamie, 'Aren't you wonderful. I'm a chosen child too!' Isn't that sweet? Then he came up to my mother and said, 'You know, I'm adopted too, and I think it's so wonderful!'

"My mother picked up on that and said, 'He called Jamie a chosen child.' I think it's a nice way of letting a child know this: 'You weren't unexpected, you were wanted, we chose to have you; that's why we went through all of this, and that's why we love you so dearly, because we made a conscious choice. We really wanted you. You were a chosen child. We went over there to pick you up. Life chose you for us, and you're very special because of that.'"